1977

To Harry & Margaret

With Love and Affection.

The Queen Charlotte Islands are just off the coast of B.C. and I travel over them in my work. They are beautiful. This Book is a history of their founding.
We Love You So Much and Look Forward to Seeing You Again Soon.
Have a Happy Christmas

Your "Adopted Children"
And "Grandchildren"

Al & Elaine
& Family

Taron – 10
Marina – 8
Jilan – 6
Dana – 4
Tylan – 2
Sunie – 1
Alana 8/15/79

Queen Charlotte Islands

Queen Charlotte Islands

A Narrative of
Discovery and Adventure
in the
North Pacific

by

FRANCIS POOLE, C.E.

Edited by
JOHN W. LYNDON

Introduction
SUSAN DAVIDSON

The Northwest Library / Volume 2

J. J. Douglas Ltd., Vancouver

ISBN 0-88894-012-2

*The publisher gratefully acknowledges the
co-operation and assistance of the Vancouver
Public Library in the preparation of this series.*

First published by Hurst and Blackett, Publishers,
London 1872.

J. J. Douglas Ltd.
3645 McKechnie Drive
West Vancouver, B.C.

Printed and bound in Canada.

Introduction

In 1862 the Haida Indians of the Queen Charlotte Islands lived essentially as they had lived for centuries before.

Their initial "discovery" by European explorers in the late 1700's, the subsequent short visits of trading expeditions and the resultant introduction of foreign goods only slightly influenced the traditional economy and social structure. New material wealth was simply and cleverly incorporated into existing systems of ownership, distribution and social ranking. No white man stayed long enough to understand the Haida ways, nor cared enough to try to impose changes.

Based on expeditions in 1862-63, the journals of Francis Poole contain some of the earliest written descriptions of the Queen Charlotte Islands and their aboriginal inhabitants. Dixon, in his *Voyage Round the World* (1789) records a few brief impressions during his short stop at the north end of Graham Island where he traded for sea otter pelts. Other traders and explorers make passing references to the island and the Haida, but Poole was the first white man to maintain a residence among the Canadian Haida. He stayed nearly two years just north of Jedway (site of recent iron mining operations), on 'Moresby Island.

Poole was a geologist first and foremost. He was intensely dedicated to locating copper and establishing suitable mining locations for future commercial operations. He cultivated friendships with the natives only as were necessary to facilitate his own ends. He deliberately remained aloof and forbade his men even to consider fraternization. He refused to become involved in inter-tribal differences, but was astutely aware of political developments and used them to his advantage when needed. Only in dire circumstances or where straightforward bargaining was possible did he ask for their help. He does admit a cautious compatibility with one Chief Klue, and even works out a way of communicating with him. But this advantage was not used to permit cultural investigations, nor to encourage close friendship, but merely to accommodate the discussions necessary between adjacent camps.

Poole was on the Islands before the ravages of smallpox decimated the population and caused immense social upheaval. The south end of Moresby Island was still inhabited by several independent villages. One of the first epidemics to attack the Haida came as a result of Poole's presence, and he felt intensely the responsibility of such acute suffering and fatality. Due to their near-annihilation in the following decades, the Queen Charlotte Haida eventually retreated to two villages: Massett, on the north end of Graham Island and Skidegate on the channel dividing Graham and Moresby Islands. In Skidegate today, the old people trace their respective lineages back to villages, still occupied in Poole's time — Cumshewa, Skedans, Tanu, and Ninstints. A foreshadowing of future problems is indicated by the tension between Chief Skidegatees and Chief Klue. Community decisions today are still complicated by the factions derived from traditional allegiances, dating to times past when there were several more autonomous units, each with its own dignity to uphold even at the expense of reconciliation.

Although there is no comprehensive documentation of Haida culture, there are many worthwhile ethnographic details which can be culled from Poole's records. No mention is made of any art work, except one unusual argillite carving in the form of a flute with frogs on it. One wonders where this piece is now, and why Poole makes no other reference to totem poles, house decorations, utensils, masks or other paraphernalia which excite other travellers of the day. Poole does not identify the internal clan divisions of Raven and Eagle which dominate Haida society. He refers only to their belief that they are descended from crows. This kind of reality is considered an acknowledgement which Darwin has yet to admit on behalf of homo sapiens in his evolutionary scheme.

Several other bits of valuable period information can be noted: a list of names of twenty-four chiefs entered on a certificate of character recommendation; the dimensions of a Haida big house given as fifty feet by fifty feet and excavated to a depth of ten feet, making the total height about forty feet; a gambling routine with sticks; a pole of scalps in the centre of Klue's house which interrupts Poole's night of rest there; and twice he mentions travelling in small domestic canoes, one only five feet long and the other nine feet. He is able to conclude even after such superficial dealings with the Haida that "the many feasts or festivals they keep during the course of a year...do not bear the least on religion, but are purely social gatherings." Years later religious and government agencies along the coast would attempt to abolish potlatches for reasons based entirely on their misunderstanding of the nature of these events.

The impressions Poole gives are very objective, tainted only slightly, and justifiably, by fear for his own survival. He is, after all, a foreigner, on alien land, at the mercy of the indigenous people who have already disposed of other Europeans for less provocation.

Poole makes other references of interest about the Queen Charlotte Islands. There is frequent mention of various flora and fauna observed, including summary lists of shellfish and birds in the second to last chapter. He discusses the possible presence of mountain goats, which I think has not been verified in later years. Other land animals include otter, marten, ermine and bear. Several animals now common on the Islands, such as deer which are abundant enough to allow open season, were introduced and multiplied rapidly due to the absence of natural predators. The Islands have been studied as a sanctuary of unusual species of wild life because of their distance from the mainland.

Poole predicts that the development of agriculture could be highly successful, having noted the prolificacy of native species and the ease with which potatoes are cultivated. But although there have been scattered home gardens there are no large scale operations today and fresh produce is very expensive because it is barged up from Vancouver.

In foreseeing a great future in the lumber industries Poole is more accurate. Logging is still one of the major economic resources.

Throughout the book Poole reveals himself as a man of strong moral character, courageous enough to enact his convictions. He is extremely negative about the activities of the Hudson's Bay Company, feeling that they purposely prevented the colonization of the West Coast in order to defend their trading monopoly with the Indians. The Company was, according to Poole, completely negligent in maintaining moral standards in their dealings with the Indians. No price was too small to offer for the invaluable furs. Fire-water, a very low grade whiskey, was provided without regard for the debauchery it precipitated, there being no concern to develop longstanding relations with the Indians. The goal was to load up the ship and rush the cargo back to England.

Another annoyance to Poole was the crude behaviour of American citizens. He has nothing but disdain for the rough ways of the Yankees and the lack of formal justice in remote places. He has occasion to wish for magisterial power to impose order on the rampant disorganization of his own isolated camp, but lacks the authority to control blatant insubordination. Nevertheless, he is completely fair to his mutinous crew, and leaves them supplies and full wages for time served, when he leaves for Victoria.

This volume is not a scientific report covering ethnography or geology. It is rather a travelogue such as was commonly written in the nineteenth and early twentieth centuries. The author includes a pot-pourri of his observations while travelling abroad in the New World.

Poole's journals then, were published as their editor indicates, to be "given to the English public...lest such an experience in the North Pacific should be wholly lost".

We are indeed fortunate that this narrative was published to record such early details of West Coast development. Such first hand documents always serve to complement and round out the frequently asceptic records of official historians. We are also fortunate that the book is now republished for to-day's readers to enjoy.

HARRIET HARBOUR, QUEEN CHARLOTTE ISLANDS.

QUEEN CHARLOTTE ISLANDS

A NARRATIVE OF

DISCOVERY AND ADVENTURE

IN

THE NORTH PACIFIC.

BY

FRANCIS POOLE, C.E.

EDITED BY

JOHN W. LYNDON,

AUTHOR OF "NINETY-THREE, OR THE STORY OF THE FRENCH REVOLUTION."

LOG-HOUSE, BURNABY ISLAND.

LONDON:

HURST AND BLACKETT, PUBLISHERS,

13, GREAT MARLBOROUGH STREET.

1872.

EDITOR'S PREFACE.

Two groups of Islands have been called after the Queen-Consort of King George the Third.

The first group is in the South Pacific Ocean. It was discovered in the year 1767, by Captain Carteret, R.N., but has since proved to be of comparatively little significance.

The second and larger group lies in the North Pacific Ocean (lat. 52° to 54° N., long. 132° to 134° W.), and will supply the chief subject-matter of the following pages.

Captain Cook, R.N., was the first white man who is known to have set foot upon those islands of the North Pacific. He landed in the year 1776 on their northernmost shore, and near a spot which now appears in the map as Cook's Inlet. The famous navigator minutely describes the incidents of this discovery, in the Admiralty edition of his *Voyage to the Pacific Ocean* (Vol. ii. pp. 416 et seq.), but conjectures that certain Russians had visited the place before him. He was doubtless aware also of land having been sighted, two years previously, in the same direction, by Captain Juan Perez, a navigator, whom the Spanish Government had sent out with a commission to search for the long-desired North-West Passage from the Atlantic to the Pacific. Captain Cook, however, could not tell whether the newly-discovered land was an island or merely part of the American continent. And, in view probably of the insufficient knowledge at his command, he forbore to name the country or to claim it, as otherwise he would have done, on behalf of the British Crown.

Eleven years afterwards, that is, in the year 1787, Captain Dixon ascertained Cook's discovery to consist of an extensive insular group; and, no civilized people disputing the right of the English nation to it, he took formal possession in the name of King George, and christened the acquisition Queen Charlotte Islands.

That the Islands form together a healthy, picturesque territory, rich in natural resources and well adapted to colonization, this volume will show.

Nevertheless, for the space of nearly a century, during which they have belonged to England, no serious attempt has been made to colonize them. Even the Admiralty survey is still wanting. There they lie, waste and fallow, yet marvellously productive, and awaiting nothing but Anglo-Saxon capital, enterprise, and skill to return manifold profit to those who will embark in the venture.

The only educated Englishman who has ever lived on Queen Charlotte Islands is Mr. Francis Poole, Civil and Mining Engineer. The best portion of two years he spent, either in actual residence in that outlying dependency, or in laborious work closely connected with it. Unfortunately, some years back, a severe illness, the evident result of former exertion and exposure, prostrated and much enfeebled him. This has prevented a detailed account of his discoveries and adventures, already communicated to a large circle of private friends, being sooner given to the English public.

At length, fearing lest such an experience in the North Pacific should be wholly lost, Mr. Poole placed his Diary and other manuscripts in my hands, for publication.

It is from these papers, written by him with pains-taking exactness in the very midst of his adventurous career, that I have faithfully, and I trust agreeably, prepared the narrative which follows.

J. W. L.

London, November, 1871.

CONTENTS.

CHAPTER I.

CHAPTER II.

CHAPTER III.

CHAPTER VI.

CHAPTER V.

CHAPTER VI.

CHAPTER VII.

CHAPTER VIII.

CHAPTER IX.

CHAPTER X.

CHAPTER XI.

CHAPTER XII.

CHAPTER XIII.

CHAPTER XIV.

CHAPTER XV.

CHAPTER XVI.

CHAPTER XVII.

CHAPTER XVIII.

CHAPTER XIX.

CHAPTER XX.

LIST OF ILLUSTRATIONS.

QUEEN CHARLOTTE ISLANDS.

CHAPTER I.

I HAD been engaged for some twenty months up and down Canada West, now the province of Ontario, in a successful course of "prospecting," and in other work bearing on mines, when I was induced to undertake a journey and voyage to the British possessions which lie along the western seaboard of the North American continent. Encouraging information having reached me, I wished to extend the sphere of my surveying and mining operations.

It was in the month of April, 1862, that I set out upon my long and toilsome journey, my starting-point being Kingston, on the northern shore of Lake Ontario.

In the summer and autumn it is customary to cross the Canadian lakes by steamboat. But, at that season, the ice still remained sufficiently in possession to render travelling by *ice-stage* a necessity of the journey, despite the danger resulting from the thinness of the top-ice on the upper lakes in April.

Shortly after midday of the 2nd, the guard or conductor cried—" All aboard for Cape Vincent!" with a sharp nasal twang, and, in a few minutes, the passengers had taken their seats inside the ice-stage, which was advertised to get to the American side of the lake in precise time to catch the " cars " due in New York the same evening.

The ice-stage is a square-built conveyance, in form resembling a colossal packing-box, only that the sides are composed of wind and waterproof curtains, instead of wood-work. It slides over the ice upon wooden runners shod with steel.

Our team consisted of two diminutive horses. These belonged to the Lower Canadian breed, and were wretched objects to look at; for all which, they really could do a deal of work, and tripped along before us with a lightsome and easy step.

Already the snow, though three feet deep, was giving signs of approaching dissolution under solar influence, whilst the sun itself began to shine out brilliantly, and the April air to feel mild and pleasant, as if prognosticating a lovely springtide.   Thereupon, our driver thought fit slightly to redeem his native surliness by cracking his whip in a cheery manner; and, as the Canadian shore receded, I tried to console myself for the many dear friends left behind by observing that the first prospects of my journey were at least not dispiriting.

Ere long, however, this source of consolation proved to be somewhat premature.   The driver was an American, and the conductor a Canadian; but both seemed to have sunk their nationalities in a conspiracy to make as much as possible out of their freight of trusting passengers.   Owing to the top-ice frequently breaking, the jolting soon became so severe and wearing that it was a positive relief when the conductor " invited " the male portion of his charge to come and assist in pushing the stage back towards the smooth ice.   Every now and then, too, we were enabled to heighten the pleasures of this employment by putting our feet right through to the lower ice, and having to hold on to the sides of the stage, till another safe footing could be obtained.

At length, after fourteen miles of such forced labour, we touched the limits of the ice-region, and were thence rowed in more comfort over the last mile

of our passage across to the American mainland—that is, if comfort can, by any stretch of
fancy, be said to associate itself with boots full of
water.

Surely so valuable a co-operation might, at any
rate, have met with its reward in an honest fulfilment
of their advertised contract on the part of the ice-stage
people. Our reward, as we neared the land, was to
see the " cars " moving off without us, an hotel-keeper
at Cape Vincent having bribed the stage-conductor
to defer our arrival with a view to the hospitalities
of his house, which he fondly trusted must needs
follow. The American landlord and the Canadian
conductor, however, had alike neglected to count the
cost of failure. For we forthwith proceeded to pass
our enforced stay in the one hotel of all which we
deemed the most unlikely to have cultivated the art
of bribery. Meantime, the superior claims of honesty
over " smartness " were being practically asserted on
the person of our late conductor. At home in
England, an appeal would have lain to the owners of
the public conveyance, or possibly to a court of law,
for damages through delays on the road. But the
transatlantic mode of redress is quite as instructive,
less expensive, and much quicker. When it appeared

certain that there was no going on that night, one of my fellow-passengers coolly walked up to the conductor, and, seizing him by the collar, in the twinkling of an eye put his head " in chancery," and served him out in the presence of an admiring public.

We started again next morning, under a genial sky, and were speedily flying, with all pressure on, behind two great " cow-catcher " railway engines of the country.

The part of the United States through which the New York road from Cape Vincent runs is flattish and unsightly, till Albany and the Hudson River are reached. But the English traveller, with his inborn taste for observation, never lacks subjects of interest in America.

Passing through the townlet of Brownville, I noticed some tall and handsome pine-trees. Now it is generally assumed in England that, where pine-trees are grown, the soil must of necessity be barren. From this opinion I altogether dissent, for I have seen the very best description of soil underlying large woods of pine, both in Canada and in Bedford-shire in England. This fact, it is true, does not tell so much on the North American continent, where generally the pine-tree roots run along the ground within a few inches of its surface, as it does in England, where the roots frequently penetrate fifteen feet into the earth. None the less it seems to me to furnish ample evidence in disproof of the assumption that, because pines prevail in the northernmost districts of the States, the soil there must necessarily be unproductive.

A singular property of British North American timber is its brittleness. Nothing is commoner in the Canadian bush than to see huge pieces of forest-wood blown down in all directions by squalls of wind. I well recollect one of those light squalls, so peculiar to Canada, overtaking me when riding once through the bush. In order to save my life I was obliged to urge on my horse at full speed: for I could hear and see the trees toppling over, here, there, and every-where around me.

As one travels south, the timber becomes more consistent. But Nature, not being a respecter of national boundaries, carries its Canadian singularities a long way into the States. In the forests beyond Brownville, quantities of trees, evidently not cut, but snapped and broken off, lay strewn about, right and left. Many of these were beeches of a very fine growth, and such as had apparently intended to develop themselves into stately forest trees. Those of their companions which had survived supplied a refreshing change to the eye, after the everlasting pines of Canada. In America, when a beech plantation flourishes, it is universally received as the surest indication of a fertile subsoil.

The country through which we passed was not so flat but that railway-cuttings were sometimes requisite. I observed a stratum of blue or shale limestone in the cuttings—proof of the near neighbourhood of coal, although, from aught I could ascertain, none had so far been discovered. I cannot doubt, either, the existence of iron in that particular district. Several of the railway-stations, or "dépôts," as the natives queerly call them, were built of deep red-coloured brick, showing iron to form a constituent part of the clay soil, which abounds here. Up to the present year (1871), the source of wealth latent in that iron-ore remains entirely untouched, the double cause being, doubtless, want of capital and workmen.

We now were steering eastward, and gradually getting into a milder climate. The snow had imperceptibly decreased from three feet to about four inches. But there was scarce anything to attract attention along the route, save the intense sameness arising from uncultivated lands, stunted woods, and miles upon miles of arid desolation. We would rush on for fifteen or twenty miles without more than an odd farmhouse or two varying the landscape, or without the trace of any living soul inhabiting the country, unless it could be discerned in the sign-boards which are stuck up where the farmers' roads intersect the railroad, and which warn wayfarers in the wilderness that, when they "hear the bell ring," they are to "look out for the locomotive." On every American engine there is a large bell, which the stoker takes care to ring whenever the "cars" come to a crossing or have to go through a town. If the engine should require wood or water, a loud steam-whistle is sounded, very unlike similar instruments in England, but which repeats the sounds *w-o-o-edd*, *w-a-tt-a*, as plainly as I here spell the words, and usually a mile before arriving at the station : so that the porters, or *employés* according to their Yankee designation, have good time to get ready.

We hurried thus through not a few straggling villages, all aspirants to the status of "cities." But none were of the slightest importance, until at last we sighted the " City of Rome."

In my capacity as a traveller from Europe, I naturally felt curious to see what sort of place *new* Rome could be. We just stopped to take water "on board." But, in that short time, I had time enough to note that the borrowed title was not such an absolute misnomer as I had expected. My American fellow-travellers said they were proud of this rising town, and with reason. When I saw " Rome " it had only seen ten years of life itself. Yet it already contained 12,000 inhabitants, and a considerable number of substantial, nay even imposing, buildings. It made quite a grand appearance from the station. And who can tell whether it may not be destined, in ages yet to come, to wield some undreamt-of power in the West? Neither ancient nor modern Rome has its destinies limited to a day.

Albany was the only town of consequence afterwards. Our "cars" did not enter it, as it lies on the opposite side of the Hudson River, which we had now reached. But, to judge by outside looks and by the manifest advantage of its position, it assuredly has a splendid future before it. Here we enjoyed the sensation, not known to travellers in Europe, of re-entering the haunts of civilization. A more delightful ride than that down the banks of the Hudson can hardly be desired. The scenery nowhere partakes of grandeur. What are called the Highlands of the Hudson are mere hillocks compared with the real mountain-ranges of America. They do not even approach the Rhineland for precipitate height and picturesqueness. Still, there is a breadth combined with a winding beauty proper to the Hudson, which is not to be found united on the same scale, in any river that I know of, throughout the European continent.

The views as we neared New York differed considerably from those of the Upper Hudson. It is a thousand pities that a bridge has not been constructed at some point about ten miles above the "Empire City." For there the far-famed Hudson opens up an expanse capable of holding vast fleets; and it cannot be doubted that a suitable bridge would materially add both to the interests and the beauty of the river.

An amusing incident happened "on board" the "cars," just previous to our arrival at New York.

The conductor, in the performance of his duty as ticket-collector, having applied to a passenger fresh from the Emerald Isle to give up his ticket, the following conversation ensued:—

Conductor. "Your ticket, sir."

Patrick. "Ah, dhin, what d'ye want it for?"

Conductor. "I want to see it."

Patrick. "Do ye, now? And, faith, and ye won't."

Conductor. "In that case, you must pay your fare over again."

Patrick. "Would ye raly like to see it, now?"

Conductor. "I must have either the ticket or the money."

Patrick. "Bedad, and ye wont have the ticket— divil a bit of it."

Here Patrick pays the fare.

Conductor. "Why couldn't you have said at once, that you had no ticket?"

Patrick (winking at the passengers). "Arrah, be aisy, conductor. Maybe, ye'd like to see it *now?*"

Here the Emeralder pulls the ticket out of his stocking, and, showing it to the conductor, slips it quickly again into its hiding-place, with the self-satisfied air of a man who has got the best of the argument.

It was a matter of lively speculation in the "cars" as to how long Patrick would be likely to reside in the great go-ahead country before he underwent the process of having his wits sharpened.

Darkness had fully set in when we were deposited at the railway "dépôt," in Thirty-seventh Street, New York.

As to give a just appreciation of the "Empire City" would take more materials than a transitory visit could have afforded me, I shall here simply pass through it, so to speak, on the way to my outward-bound vessel.

CHAPTER II.

BOUND FOR "ASPINWALL"—AMERICAN COASTING—THE GULF STREAM—SAN SALVADOR—MARIGUANA—THE "QUEEN OF THE ANTILLES"—JAMAICA—THE "WINDWARD PASSAGE"—ACROSS THE CARIBBEAN SEA—PHOSPHORESCENT WATERS.

JUST at that period hosts of gold-hunters were rushing out of the United States to Cariboo, British Columbia. I chanced into their very midst.

It was not without considerable difficulty, therefore, that I succeeded in obtaining a berth, by paying a high price for it, on board the *Northern Light*—a ship of fifteen hundred tons burden, bound from New York to Colon, or Aspinwall, as the Yankees affect to call it.

Under British laws such a vessel would not have been allowed to carry more than eight hundred souls in all. I made one, however, of 1694 passengers, besides the crew and the usual quantum of "stowaways." A more motley collection of human beings, and of absolute nondescripts, mortal eyes never beheld.

That April afternoon was bright, with a warm southerly wind, as I got my traps finally conveyed to the vessel, and before dusk we had steamed along under the heights of Staten Island, through the Narrows, by Sandy Hook, and out into the broad Atlantic. The sun dipped down gloriously behind Long Island, and there seemed every prognostic of a pleasurable if not a rapid passage.

Three o'clock the next morning discovered us off the Delaware coast, with the mainsail flapping in a gentle breeze. The beautiful sunset over-night had been followed by a moonlight equally beautiful, and so shiningly clear that I was enabled to read and note my diary while sitting on deck.

We were soon, however, to experience the varieties of American coasting; for, as the day dawned, large numbers of porpoises began to tumble about near the ship's sides, whilst flights of sea-gulls added a still surer presage of the coming storm. In a short time "white horses" were cresting the waves, the vessel took to pitching and rolling, the cordage rattled, the planks creaked, and we saw we were in for a regular gale. Suddenly the thermometer fell to near freezing-point. I lay in my berth, not sick—I wish I had been—but in that perfectly wretched state of existence which would as lief accept death as life, for some measure of release from the punishment. If there be any consolation in knowing that others are suffering contemporaneously with oneself, I had it in abundance. From my accommodation-berth, five feet long by one and a half wide, I could hear and feel that scores of the crowded passengers were as prone on their backs as I was, the men cursing and the women screaming, and both lamenting in piteous terms their folly in venturing upon the treacherous ocean.

"Where are we?" I asked of the Captain, as I descried him passing my cabin door.

"Off Cape Hatteras," was the curt reply.

"Do you think there's any danger, Capt'n?" half-shrieked a middle-aged dame, in the next cabin to me.

"Danger, mum? Not the slightest. Just a capful of wind."

"That's the worst of them navy men," I heard the middle-aged dame's husband remark, as soon as our Captain had disappeared up the gangway. "When the waves is a-runnin' mountains, they says it's 'rayther fresh,' and when it's a-blowin' of great guns, they tells us it's 'jist smartish sea-going,' they does. Where's the comfort o' that?"

There seemed a good deal of truth in my next

neighbour's homely criticism, supposing that the Captain's duty does include comforting his passengers. The practical difficulty would probably lie in the Steamship Company having to provide a duplicate of the Captain and his ship's officers.

Within twenty-four hours the storm had abated, and determining now to try my " sea-legs," the first object I caught sight of on gaining the deck was an immense shoal of sea-weed, which, the boatswain informed me, was proof positive that we had entered the Gulf Stream. Here, too, I saw for the first time some of the cetacean mammals of the deep, together with flying fish in vast quantities, sporting a few feet off our ship's bows.

On the fifth day, we sighted San Salvador, or Cat Island, the name by which the first land seen by Columbus (Oct. 8, 1492) has since been desecrated. Our course was S.S.W., with a strong easterly wind and a long ground-swell; and, on the following morning, we passed Mariguana Island, two miles on the starboard bow, the ship now steering W.S.W., in order to make what is known as the Windward Passage, or the road leading from the Atlantic Ocean, between the islands of Cuba and San Domingo, into the Caribbean Sea.

The Island of Mariguana has a type of its own, and quite different characteristics from the West Indian islands in general. As a whole it is as flat as it is possible to imagine land to be. The northern parts, however, are covered with thick and rich-looking woods, whilst the southern, for many miles inland, present the appearance of a wild, uninhabited common—very much, in fact, what the pristine navigators of these seas must have originally found it. The Bar, which lies out almost two miles seaward, offers an insuperable obstacle to Mariguana ever subserving the interests of commerce to any great extent. While hove-to and waiting our pilot, I had an opportunity of observing the bay. From the deck of our vessel it certainly did look very pretty, with its still, pale-green waters, contrasting with the deep-blue sea outside the Bar, and its pipeclay-coloured shore banks, which strike down abruptly and are topped with luxuriant verdure. Numerous flocks of sea-hens were enjoying themselves over the placid surface of this ocean-lake, and demonstrating by their evident tameness that the Mariguanians are no sportsmen. The shores of all the island, I heard, have a deep deposit of white sand. The shore itself, not the sand, emits a sulphureous smell. Once or twice I thought a whiff of it reached out to the ship. Those who know the pleasures of volcanic eruptions will scarce be thankful if fate should cast them upon Mariguana. The place just looks as though, some day or other, it might go down bodily into the depths of the ocean.

Far otherwise is the aspect of Cuba, which island was hailed, not long after, by our look-out man from the main-top.

Columbus landed in Cuba, at the end of the same month that he took possession of San Salvador. It is 800 miles long, and 125 broad, and lies on the verge of the Bahamas coral-beds. The Spaniards have surnamed it "The Queen of the Antilles," and well does Cuba deserve the title. As we steamed fast towards it, full in view lay this richest jewel in the crown of Spain, its mountain-peaks towering majestically to the sky, and its rich vegetation stretching out of sight to the furthermost horizon. On the left were the lofty peaks of San Domingo, splendidly flanked on the left again by the island of Porto Rico, and on the right by that of Jamaica, as, before making the Windward Passage, we could dimly perceive them in the remote distance. In all nature it were hard to conceive a scene more redolent of delights. The Antilles, looked at from without, well realize the mediæval fable of the " Enchanted Islands."

What a strange and rapid vicissitude! Hardly five days ago we had been watching sportive whales and enduring a cruel cold, and now we were launched into a climate so fearfully hot that an awning of blanketing was obliged to be rigged on the hurricane-deck before any one could attempt to sit there. Fortunately the water had become smooth as a pond, so that our lately bedridden passengers could crawl up from their berths, and, packing themselves together in a dense crowd, inhale a few breaths of fresh air, and feast their eyes on the magnificent diorama revolving before them.

In this region, the voyager from the North gazes wonderstruck upon a firmament hitherto unknown to him. As night comes on, he cannot fail to remark that the moon gives out a radiance much stronger and more lucid than in higher latitudes. Even when there is " no moon," the planet Venus and the Milky Way are so extraordinarily brilliant as, in a measure, to supply the want of the light which is reflected on our own planet through the medium of the moon. Then, the disclosure of entirely novel constellations, the grouping together of stars sublime in their magnitude, the nebulæ scattered broadcast over the prodigious space above, combine to invest with new-born interest the first view of a nocturnal sky in the tropics. The great Humboldt describes himself as having been deeply affected when he beheld it.

As we pressed onward, past Jamaica, and across the Caribbean Sea, I noticed that the water was peculiarly phosphorescent at night. Before starting on my journey I had been prepared for this phenomenon, and had heard scientific men attribute it to the animal life which, they said, causes it in the Pacific. A subterranean communication, it is asserted, exists under the Isthmus of Panamà, between the Pacific and the Atlantic Oceans; and, the Pacific being confidently believed to have a higher water-mark than the Atlantic, whatever phenomena are produced in the one will be reproduced in the other. I too believe both in the subterranean passage and in the superior altitude of the Pacific; but I explain the phosphoric appearances in either ocean very differently. A species of asphalte (chapote) is found to bubble up from the bottom of some fresh-water lakes in Mexico, and to wash back upon their borders. It has a pungent smell, similar to that of asphaltic bitumen, and possesses many of its qualities. Now it is a salient fact that a phosphorous night-light, akin to that seen in parts of the Atlantic and Pacific, also sparkles out of those Mexican lakes. But the ebullition, effluvium, and phosphorus which belong to them have been geologically traced to a volcanic origin. Wherefore, assuming the axiom that like effects proceed from like causes, one surely cannot err in accounting for the phosphorescence of the Mexican Gulf and Caribbean Sea on the hypothesis of semi-extinct volcanoes lying sunken underneath their waters. I am strengthened in this opinion by a test which I had a subsequent opportunity of applying to the falseness of an assumption commonly allowed in support of the contrary opinion. It is assumed that the phosphorescent light confines itself to the water-surface. Having tenacious doubts on this point as well, I hired a canoe, months afterwards, when on the Pacific coast between Vancouver Island and Russian America, and, taking a crew of Indians, I made them row me, one mild but very dark night, about half a mile out from the shore. Fastening the canoe to some kelp—kelp is often 80 or 90 feet long in the Pacific—I first got my Indians to splash or stir up the water with their broad paddles. The immediate result was that I could see plainly to read a newspaper. I then attached five fathoms of cord to a large piece of iron shaped like a spoon, and, on sinking the spoon, I saw with the utmost clearness the track of light it left as it went down the five fathoms. I had already convinced myself that sea-phosphorus is not the product of animal life: but now I returned to land satisfied that the deep sea—most probably to the very bottom—contains phosphorus no less than the surface does, thus adding strong corroborative testimony to my theory of volcanic agency being the cause of this salt-water phosphorescence.*

But, amid all these disquisitions on natural history and the science of the globe, how fared it on board the *Northern Light,* which introduced us to them?

If I say of our ship that she was seaworthy, I shall have praised her sufficiently. The Captain proved to be crassly ignorant, careless, and coarse. What

---

* Trustworthy information has been received in England this year (1871) that the Government of the United States of North America are making preparations on a large scale, under the direction of their Superintendent of Coast Surveys, for a complete investigation of the deep-sea bottom of the Gulf Stream.

provisions we had were of the roughest kind, such as would hardly have been tolerated in the forecastle of a Newcastle coal-brig. If the vessel had been properly freighted, the accommodation would perchance have sufficed; but, with a double complement of passengers, it was execrable. In England there is a preventive remedy against all these evils. In Yankeedom neither law nor moral sense provides the seafaring traveller with the means of redress, prospective or retrospective.

A ship-load of that sort, coming straight from the United States, naturally furnished studies of character and habit in every variety. A few seemed to be travelling, like myself, in search of health and knowledge, or in pursuit of some professional avocation. The great majority, however, braved the perils of the deep, and suffered the hardships of the passage, solely with the hope of amassing wealth in the gold-fields of California or British Columbia. At least four hundred of my shipmates were Canadians; and very interesting it was to mark the difference between their behaviour and that of the American passengers. These appeared to be utterly bereft of the kindly feelings and social tendencies which help to make life endurable. There was hardly a day, or an hour in the day, that they did not contrive to get up some dispute or other about the veriest trifles: whereas the Canadians made themselves agreeable throughout, retaining withal a respectful language and demeanour towards every person on board, after the manner of men who know how to consider other people's rights, not less than their own.

The 20th was Easter Sunday.

When day broke, we perceived that we were rapidly approaching the far-famed Isthmus which slenderly links together the two continents of North and South America; and by eight o'clock that morning the *Northern Light* was safely moored alongside the jetty at Aspinwall, having made the passage from New York in eight days and $19\frac{3}{4}$ hours, exactly—that is, a distance of 2338 sea-miles, at the average speed of somewhat over eleven knots an hour.

CHAPTER III.

THE appellation by which the world at large will ultimately recognise the northern port on the Isthmus of Panamà is still a matter of uncertainty and contention. Speculators from the United States have dubbed it Aspinwall, after one Mr. W. H. Aspinwall, a New York merchant, who was the chief originator of the Panamà railroad, and therefore, to some degree, of this seaport town. But the natives, and indeed all South Americans, insist on the place retaining its ancient name of Colon, the Spanish form of Columbus. It must be confessed the natives have both taste and right on their side. That a locality should be handed down to posterity in connexion with the greatest maritime discoverer that ever lived is an honour which even a Yankee trader of the nineteenth century could scarcely hope to cap. As to right, what should we English think if a party of Frenchmen were to take possession of some harbour on our coasts, and pretend to substitute Lafitte or Clicquot for some time-honoured name prominent in our history? The trading interest of the North American States will probably succeed in imposing its nomenclature upon Panamà. If right were to prevail, it would not be so.

On board ship, we talked of our destination as Aspinwall. But, once landed, I feel I ought to refer to it as Colon.

It is situated on the island of Manzanilla, in Limon or Navy Bay. There had been a village there originally, when, in 1850, a larger settlement was begun, for the purpose of surveying the Isthmus, with a view to a railway. Since then Colon has grown into a town of real importance, and at present contains some 200 houses, in which about 2000 inhabitants permanently reside. Its trade depends exclusively on the railroad, nearly the whole of the male population being either labourers or officials employed by the Company. A small fleet of steamers— engaged for the most part in the Chilian, Peruvian, and Californian trades—may generally be seen riding at anchor in the bay. But the bay itself, though deep enough to float the largest vessels almost close up to the shore, lies so exposed that no ship is perfectly secure in it. The construction of a break-water has been long intended, and will no doubt eventually be accomplished. Until the promoters of the railroad arrived in Panamà, the country, as far as the eye could reach from the bay, was one forest of mangrove, mahogany, and manzanilla—a medicinal plant from which the island derives its name. But now, the low level of the waste land, the marshy character of the uncovered ground, the decayed vegetation, the deposit of birds, the refuse of fish, the heat of the atmosphere, and the superabundant rainfall, have all united in creating a dangerous and clinging miasmatic fever, justly dreaded by un-acclimatized strangers.

The line from Colon to Panamà City cost, it is said, the life of one man for every foot of its construction. Two miles outside Colon is the burial-place of that forlorn-hope of railway navvies. They came in crowds, enticed by the wages (100 dollars a month, that is, 20*l.*); but very few lived the month out. In short, the wide world does not con-tain a spot, Sierra Leone perhaps excepted, more undesirable as a residence than Colon and its neighbourhood. However, for those who are simply passing through, the malignant fevers have now almost ceased. And fortunate it is thus, because a voyage to the Pacific Ocean comprises nothing so interesting as the railway journey across the Isthmus of Panamà.

The housing at Colon may be dismissed with the remark that it consists principally of wood-built shanties, having zinc roofs and brick floors. They are hotels, warehouses, railway offices, or labourers' cots.

That which struck me most, on landing, was the vitality of the vegetable and animal creation. Nature, as seen on the Isthmus, cannot be fitly portrayed. She appeared to have decked herself out with extravagant luxuriance, to bid us wayfarers from the bleak North a festive welcome. There is an inexpressible loveliness in the deep-green pendants of the palm and cocoa-nut trees, as the eye, unused to a southern clime, first lights upon them.

Pine-apples sold at twopence each, and prodigies they were too. A plentiful supply of delicious dates, bananas, oranges, and all sorts of fruits and vegetables proper to the tropics, met one at every turn, and at fabulously low prices.

Turkey-buzzards seemed to be hopping and flying about as common as crows in England; and the monkey-tribe had evidently become domesticated, for a representative monkey sat squatting at the entrance to each store, inn, or private house, just as cats and dogs do with us.

But the truly surprising and amusing characteristic was the *insect fauna* kingdom. Not to mention Brobdingnag beetles, taking their "constitutional" down the main street in broad day, I was shown a Norfolk-Howard, which had only been born three weeks before, and had yet attained to the dimensions of a young turtle. A little black boy was playing with it on the footpath, much in the same way that little white boys play with rabbits. He had got a string tied to the hind leg of his Norfolk-Howard, and I stood by while he urged on his ungainly playfellow with a stick.

The distance from Colon to Panamà City is forty-seven miles. In the afternoon of the day of our arrival we all left together by a tremendously long train.

It was here, more than anywhere, that the marvel of the contrast between a temperate and a torrid zone really revealed itself. As our train rolled slowly along, we took in reaches of the surrounding country.

No sign of habitation, or even of soil, was visible in either lowland or highland. Mountain rose up magnificently behind mountain, every one clothed to its summit with flowers, fruits, and foliaceous life. I saw clusters of dazzling white lilies, bowers of the broad-leafed plantain, thickets of tall geraniums, groves of palms and rival fern-trees, stacks of verdant sugar-canes, and, above them again, enormous trunks of the sycamore and the mango, interwoven with Virginian creepers and a still virgin brushwood. All these stretched out, like the marshalled forces of some giant army, for miles and miles athwart the landscape. Gazing from my carriage-seat over this panorama of wondrous floriage and foliage, basking in a daily recurrent sun-sheen, I could not avoid the thought that possibly Panamà-land had once been part of Eden.

Nearer to Panamà, the mountain-ranges decreasing in size, we caught a cursory view of the great Picacho, which rears its 7200 feet far off to the westward. Reaching almost up to Mount Picacho is the famous Sierra de Quarequa. It was from its crest that, on September the 29th, 1513, Nuñez de Balboa sighted the Western Ocean. Irrespective of the glory attaching to such a discovery, the rapture with which he and his followers, first of all Europeans, are said to have surveyed that glistening sea and the grove-covered islets studding it, can easily be credited by any one who has looked upon the Bay of Panamà. There are few scenes, viewed at a distance, more suggestive of an earthly paradise, according to the old-fashioned notion of it. Happy were it if a closer inspection carried out the illusion.

By the banks of a meandering stream, and in among beautiful groups of hillocks, green as only Panamà grass can make them, our train kept sauntering on until, after a journey of about two hours and a half, it finally landed us safely at Panamà City. The town occupies a promontory which juts out some good way into the sea. As a place of transit it has now become all-important. I would fain have stayed there awhile; but necessity compelled me to defer my examination of it till my return.

A short half-hour more, and two tenders might have been seen steaming away to the offing, with the whole of us cargo of passengers from the *Northern Light* on board, and another hundred, who had come straight from England by the Southampton steamer, superadded. All told, we counted nearly eighteen hundred. The Californian packet, which was awaiting our arrival, had hardly room enough to accommodate a third of that number comfortably.

Her name was the *Golden Age*, an American-built four-decker, and, if she had not been so shockingly overcrowded, on the whole as goodly a ship, both inside and out, as one could wish to sail in.

At ten o'clock the same evening she weighed anchor, and bore away for Point Mala, the south-western headland in the Bay of Panamà, and thence, after two points further in a south-westerly course, due north-west for her voyage to San Francisco.

That was on the Sunday. By noon on the following Tuesday we had made a run of 366 miles, having steamed between the mainland and Quibo Island, and hugged the shores of Costa Rica, till we could discern with our glasses the broad entrance to the river Estrella.

The water of the ocean looked as smooth and limpid as though we were merely crossing a lakelet in Canada. And when we sat down to our meals in the large saloon, without any more disturbance from the elements than we should have had in an hotel on *terra firma*, I could not help recalling the three months of uninterrupted calm weather experienced by Magelhaens, when he first doubled Cape Horn, and which induced him to christen these seas the Pacific Ocean.

At this stage of our Californian voyage, the food they gave us in the *Golden Age* was infinitely superior to that provided in the *Northern Light.* We had delicious coffee, fresh butter, juicy beef, and biscuits of the very best American flour. But what pleased me most was the dish of huge Californian potatoes which always garnished the dinner-table. In shape and measurement the smallest of these potatoes resembled a large-sized cocoa-nut ; and to get through half a one was quite as much as any of the diners could satisfactorily accomplish.

By degrees we veered off from the coastway, and as the ocean maintained an unruffled surface, the monotony came to be temporarily relieved by an incident extremely characteristic of the lands of the Far West.

A berth forward having been found less its blanket, the missing article was discovered, after a persistent search, in the possession of one of the steerage passengers. Whereupon his messmates determined to clinch the matter by taking the law into their own hands. Some were for stringing him up summarily to the yard-arm, others proposed to crop his hair and brand him P.P. (*i e.* Provincial Penitentiary), whilst a third party thought a good ducking under the pump would be the right thing. But milder counsels at length prevailed. So, stripping the delinquent of his coat, they pinned a card behind him, with the word *Thief* in bold letters on it, and then marched him in that unenviable attire up and down the deck for a couple of hours.

When we turned in that night, we were opposite Cape Blanco, keeping well in the open, and still in a dead calm. But before the next morning a strong land-breeze sprang up, and by ten o'clock, though we had run 339 miles, we found ourselves in the midst of a hurricane, the sea raging terrifically, our ship pitching and rolling in a fearful manner, and all hands lying out on the yards to double-reef the sails, or securing the mainmast with extra bracings to keep it from going by the board.

This exceedingly unpacific state of the Pacific Ocean continued with little diversity for several days, during which I, and about a dozen other passengers, were the only persons amongst our eighteen hundred who could stand the deck. Of all the ills that flesh is heir to, none can compare with sea-sickness. But its horrors are enhanced tenfold when you feel that every dip of the ship into the deep, and every assault of the sickness itself, is simply part of the process by which you are being torn from your native land, and from the home where you have left your dearest friends.

In this part of the Pacific it takes no time, so to speak, to get up a storm. The reaction, on the contrary, is extraordinarily slow. Hence, though that gale duly subsided, we did not again enjoy the same smooth waters as at first.

To enumerate all our points and distances would be tedious. Suffice then to say that we ploughed on our way bravely enough, oftener standing out to sea, yet occasionally running right under the coast, and twice putting into harbour.

For beauty and sublimity nothing in Europe can equal the scenery on the western coast of Mexico. As seen from ship-board, it appeared to consist, for hundreds of miles, first, of countless hillocks, clothed with a verdure of rich and varied shades, and, further inland, of high mountain-ranges, which likewise looked one mass of green to their topmost crowns. The singular slant of the lower hill-country points, in the clearest way possible, to this portion of the globe having been transformed—presumably at some remote period, history being silent about it—by a volcanic eruption which operated across no considerable width, but along a surprisingly disproportionate length of territory. The unquestionable fact of snch a convulsion seems all the more curious because, now and again, the higher mountains infringe upon the elongated continuity of the lower, pushing spurs down to the seaboard, and even precipitate promontories out into the sea. Viewed together, those Mexican coast-scenes make up a description of landscape such as would repay many of our first-class artists the trouble of a voyage, provided always that they escaped the deadly coast-fever. However, with so much beneficence in nature, it was sad to think we were viewing it from the point where " distance lends enchantment to the view." For not only do those grand mountain-ranges abound in gloomy caverns and repulsive ravines, filled with everything most horrifying in the brute creation; but, as we were trustworthily informed, the passes which lead over them are, and probably will long be, the abode of merciless banditti, who have subjected Western Mexico to a reign of terror, and have rendered existence there an insupportable burden.

One morning we ran into the harbour of Acapulco, our object being to deliver a hundred tons of freight, and to ship as much more in export stores. This town, if viewed through European spectacles, is a conglomeration of poverty and untold misery. Yet the people had a satisfied look, reminding one forcibly, as they lounged in front of their houses or under the trees on the plaza, of the lazzaroni vegetating on the Chiaja at Naples. If the rest of their provisions are as cheap as what they brought off to the *Golden Age*, they must certainly have enough to eat, without any great labour. Oranges were selling at a halfpenny, bananas at a shilling for a bunch of fifty, cocoa-nuts at a penny, and six large cakes of molasses at a shilling. We had green parrots offered to us at two shillings each. The harbour is sufficiently deep to float large-sized men-of-war. We saw here the flag-ship of Vice-Admiral Sir Thomas Maitland, and saluted it as we left. Three other English ships of war, and a French one, were also at Acapulco: an unpleasant station, I fancy.

Another morning we again diverged from our course, to enter Manzanilla Bay, for the purpose of shipping a cargo of silver from the mines of Colima. There was the same familiar reach of country: but it impressed one as uncultivated, almost waste in fact, and only too fit a background to the tumble-down port of Salagna at the bottom of the bay.

The heat of the sun had been dreadful. But now, each turn of our screw withdrawing us gradually from its worst effects, I soon began to recover. A tropical sun, while it lasts, is a wicked master. I can best describe the sensation it causes as resembling the pain that would be produced if any one were to seize a handful of your hair, and use his utmost efforts to pull it all out by the roots. European travellers to the South invariably fall into the error of wearing light and airy head-gear. But, in a hot climate, there is no defence like a thick, stout cap. The same for the feet. The action of a tropical sun is absolutely perpendicular, not leaving any room for shadows. Whenever it exerts its power, and nowhere more so than when bearing down upon the deck of a ship, thick soles to one's shoes are essential.

After Manzanilla we kept to windward of the coast, never sighting land for a week, even once: till, on Sunday the 4th of May, we steered in again towards the shore, and before evening saw the tall, snow-clad mountains of Upper California, which overhang the lovely Bay of Monterey.

At daybreak next day the firing of two small

guns from our bows imparted the welcome intelligence to the wayworn passengers that we had reached the entrance to the land-locked harbour of San Francisco, and that we should land at that city in time for breakfast.

The last act of us English on board the *Golden Age* was to sign a protest to the Captain against the provisions we had been served with. Our two days' feasting had turned out "a mockery, a delusion, and a snare." During the rest of the voyage nothing could have been coarser, dirtier, or more wholly repellent than our saloon-table—not even that of the *Northern Light*. But, of course, our protest went for waste paper.

The passage from Panamà to San Francisco occupied exactly thirteen days and eighteen hours, deducting twelve hours for delays at Acapulco and Manzanilla; thus making 3500 miles at the average rate of ten and three-quarter knots an hour. A fair speed, considering the gale.

CHAPTER IV.

THAT part of California which, in the form of a peninsula, runs down the western coast of North America, was originally discovered by the Spaniards; but they did not at first colonize it, and they hardly named it. For quite a century afterwards it was known to Englishmen as New Albion, Sir Francis Drake having so named it when, in 1579, he touched there during one of his buccaneering expeditions. As soon, however, as the Spanish Government began to make settlements on the peninsula, they restored its old Indian name of California.

The discovery of Upper California dates much later. Indeed, it was only in the year 1770 that the first ship sailed into the Bay of San Francisco. The pioneers of this great commercial mart of the nineteenth century were certain Franciscan friars, who, in 1776, founded a mission station on the spot, with a view to civilizing the savages of the interior. It is from them that the name of San Francisco has been derived.

In a purely trade point of view the City of San Francisco is splendidly placed. It lies at the north-east corner of a strip of land which serves to divide and protect a deep and roomy bay from the Pacific Ocean. But as we rounded the headland and approached the town, it was depressing and almost appalling to see the completeness of the desolation encircling it on every side. There are high hills, some twenty miles off; and between the hills and the town not ten arable acres exist, or could be made to exist, and no trees whatsoever. Since the time I am writing about, the Pacific Railroad has been brought to San Francisco. Even now, however, only one road leads out of the city, none other being likely to be wanted for many a long year to come : and the traveller by that road literally does not reach a single place of shelter from the burning rays of the sun, to say nothing of a pleasant landscape, until he has traversed the sandy plain for twelve miles.

Up to 1834 the missionary friars had retained

complete control, secular as well as religious, of the settlement in this bay. In that year the Mexican Government secularized all the missions of California; and thenceforward they rapidly decayed. Although the first houses of a new colony were erected in 1835, it advanced so slowly that a census taken in 1847 only showed a population of 459 persons. But in 1848 the first Californian gold was discovered, and two years afterwards there were more than 30,000 people living in San Francisco, under the government of the United States, which had annexed the colony. No such rapidity of growth had ever been witnessed in any town in the world. In 1860 the population had increased to 56,805; and since then the increase has steadily gone on, at the rate of about 10,000 a year.

I had been conning these facts over in my berth long before we made the Bay of San Francisco; and they had quite prepared me to see in California order and disorder, grandeur and squalidness, and all the heterogeneous elements which constitute society in the abstract, jumbled up into a concrete of most extraordinary admixture. And I was by no means disappointed.

Hardly had I arrived at my hotel when two

respectably-dressed men, engaged in hot dispute, rushed out of it. The case was the interminable one of North against South. Taking it for no more than an usual American " difficulty," I turned to enter the hotel; but chancing to look again, I saw that the Northerner was about to add violence to his slanderous and abusive language. Already he had drawn a revolver from his pocket. The Southerner, however, was a match for him. Quick as an eagle, he drew his own revolver, and shot the rowdy through the heart, in presence of all the people. Arrest, it is true, followed—or rather, the killer gave himself up; but he was soon released, the Southerners being still predominant in California. This may have been an improvement on the state of affairs which existed in the earlier days of San Francisco, when crime, under the forms of incendiarism, robbery, and murder, reached such an alarming height that the towns-people became persuaded of the total inefficiency or corruption of their law-courts, and, forming a vigilance-committee, seized the prisoners in the gaols and hanged them in the open street; but that homicide should continue to be committed, in broad day and in the public highway, with impunity, and even with approval, seemed to me to demonstrate beyond a doubt how little the San Franciscans could yet pretend to civilization.

As a contrast to street-ruffianism we were regaled, the same evening, with a really striking sight in Portsmouth Square. It happened to be the anniversary of the formation of the first fire-brigade, and the firemen celebrated their day by a procession about the town. Incendiarism and the fragile build of many of the older houses in San Francisco, and indeed all over the United States, have combined to make the fire-brigade in that part of the globe an institution of far greater importance than in any other country. The immense number of engines did not surprise me, therefore. But their handsome brass and plated mountings, their tasty decoration with flags and flowers, the glittering uniforms of the men, and the general arrangements of the procession, formed so odd a counterpart to the unpunished crime of the morning, that seeing such a display could alone have made me believe in what it suggested. So long as a people preserve to an appreciable degree the instinct of order, even though it show itself in nothing more important than a procession, real prosperity may always be prognosticated for them.

Many of the passengers by the *Golden Age*, who had left England and America with the intention of emigrating to British Columbia, unexpectedly dropped into good situations at San Francisco, their wages averaging four to six dollars a day, besides board and lodging. I myself received two offers immediately on landing, one at 100 and the other at 170 dollars a month, the latter equal to 510*l*. a year, and both places excellent in their way. But I declined them, in anticipation of a better opening further on.

Having only a few days for San Francisco, I bethought me to make the most of my time by inspecting the city from every point of view, inside and out. In my opinion one should always begin with the outside of cities. It gives shape to preconceived ideas, and begets a plan of inspection better than much unguided wandering within.

The finest view of San Francisco, or Frisco, as the citizens love to call their city, is obtainable from Telegraph Hill, an eminence in the north-eastern corner of it. From the top of this hill, in a north-westerly direction, is to be seen the famous Golden Gate, or sea-entrance to the Californian *El Dorado*, against the rock-bound portals of which the white waves are for ever dashing, and into which the ocean breeze sweeps daily with its chilling but purifying mists. Turning round to the south-east, I could discern, nearly forty miles away, the conical peak of Monte Diablo, 4000 feet high, and looking like some giant sentinel who for untold ages had stood guard over these waters, whilst their broad surface re-echoed no human sound save the paddle-splash of some Indian in his frail canoe. Due south, and as beneath my feet, lay the city, which it is easy to see will at no very distant date become the great capital of the United States in the Pacific.

The settled portion of the town appeared to cover an area of about ten miles. From my position on the hill I observed that what had been told me concerning the denseness of the buildings was not exaggerated. The original streets lie together in a sort of amphitheatre formed by three hills, Telegraph Hill being one. These streets are built in rectangular blocks, and with but a narrow roadway. Of late years they have been used solely as the business quarter. Beyond these the streets become much wider, with houses standing back in gardens at considerable intervals, or in terraces having rows of trees in front. The quays make an admirable appearance. The position they occupy was originally a chaos of loose sands and mud-hills, furrowed by the refuse-water of centuries. In 1854, a series of gigantic operations, such as are only known in America, entirely reclaimed the chaos, so that, while the largest vessels can now ride in safety alongside the quays or piers, the heaviest waggons are able to convey with facility all kinds of merchandise down to the very ship-board. · Excepting New York, there is no finer array of wharves on the American continent. The quays of San Francisco are, in point of openness and accessibility, even superior to those of New York. By-and-by, when both have consolidated their present woodwork into stone, they perhaps may begin to rival Liverpool, with its six miles of splendid masonry. The shipping in the bay was numerous, and included craft of every tonnage, from schooners of thirty tons to a fifty-gun English frigate, with its pennant streaming from the main, and "the flag that braved a thousand years" flying from the mizen-yard. By the aid of my glass I could make out a red-coated marine pacing the flush-deck aft. Amid so much to admire in the future capital of the West, it was grateful to reflect that, as yet, our Empire of the Seas showed no inclination to decay.

On descending from my survey-post, I walked through twelve bran-new squares. Most of them were, so far, either covered with brushwood or completely in the rough. Only one, Portsmouth Square, gave me the impression of being civilized. It is tastefully laid out in grass plots, marble fountains, and the beginnings of shady walks. The City Hall, an ugly gazabo of a building, flanks one side of it, and private houses run along the three other sides.

The most remarkable public resort, after this square, is Montgomery Street. I will only say that it irresistibly reminded me of Broadway in New York, or rather of what Broadway probably looked like before its trees were removed. The housing in the squares and principal streets is of a yellowish sandstone, nearly identical in look and substance with the stone used for building purposes throughout our own Northamptonshire. But a very large number of the original houses still remain, some having brick frontages, the majority, however, being wooden constructions, and, in not a few instances, the merest shed-work. Montgomery Street, and one or two others, are tolerably well paved; but the general system is plank-work, as in Canada and in so many cities of the United States; only that at San Francisco planks have been adopted for the roadway as well as the footpath. In the absence of granite or lime-stone, planking is doubtless the handiest method of road-making, particularly where virgin-forests are still within reach; but every one can see that in a city existing by traffic it is not a system to last long. If the San Franciscans should find it too expensive to imitate the New Yorkers, who imported Aberdeen granite to pave their Broadway, they will probably before many years substitute asphalte or some cognate composition for their present road-planking. Though as a matter of course tramways were in opera-tion, they seemed less in favour here than in any American city I had seen, whilst omnibuses and other hackney conveyances were proportionately more numerous.

The finest building in the town is, without doubt, the Custom-house. It stands upon ground over which the waters of the bay formerly flowed. Its foundation is pile-work, the piles having been driven thirty feet down, through soft clay, in order to get at a hard and solid bottom. A substantial and really imposing edifice having been afterwards erected upon this, the establishment of the Custom-house is justly considered as a feat of engineering skill. The entire structure, I was told, cost 800,000 dollars, or 160,000*l.*, which I can well believe.

The " American " Theatre (so called in contra-distinction to the " Chinese " Theatre) is, externally, as handsome a public edifice as the United States can boast. The interior appeared to me almost an exact copy of the Music Hall in New York. I went one evening to see the performances. These were the *Colleen Bawn* and the *Silent Woman*. The coarse and undisguised immorality of the latter piece so utterly disgusted me that I left the theatre abruptly. The house was a full one, and quite half composed of respectably-dressed females; but not another soul in it stirred. Where the passions are thus played with indiscriminately, it is no wonder they should often take the direction of murder, that the most hideous crimes should be easily condoned, and that the general tone of morality should have descended to the very depths, as I was given to understand is the sad case at San Francisco.

No visitor to Frisco omits to see its " China-town." But there is really much less to see in it than one is led to expect. In 1866 it was calculated there were about 100,000 Chinese in all California, of whom some 10,000 lived at San Francisco. Their quarter consists of from fifteen to twenty narrow streets, all of wood, and wallowing in a most iniquitous state of filth. It presented the usual Oriental features, with which every eye is familiar—open bazárs, striped awnings, and an unassorted collection of nondescript goods. For all that, there was an evident spirit of thrift and activity amongst those Chinese emigrants, separating them widely from genuine Orientalism as we imagine it. In passing through the thronged streets I did not come upon one idle man. The inhabitants were described to me as sober, orderly, and peaceful, and as excelling all other classes in these respects. And yet they have invariably belonged to the lowest stratum of society in their native country, whilst the very faces of the greater number, particularly of the women, betrayed an ingrained demoralization shocking to behold. As my information precisely coincided with what I saw, this is a proof that vice may permeate whole communities without any of the concomitant manifestations of it to which we are accustomed in Europe.

Thus I took a four days' glance at the city of San Francisco.

My conception of it, on leaving, was that years will

elapse before its throes of premature civilization are altogether over, but that its present flourishing condition is none the less as certain a fact as its future mercantile mastery in the Pacific Ocean is an assured consequence.

CHAPTER V.

BOUND FOR VANCOUVER ISLAND—DISCOMFORT OF THE VOYAGE—FIRST SIGHT OF VANCOUVER—HARBOURS OF VANCOUVER—ESQUIMALT—VICTORIA— THREE MONTHS IN THE CASCADE AND BLUE MOUNTAINS—COPPER ON QUEEN CHARLOTTE ISLANDS—FORMATION OF THE QUEEN CHARLOTTE MINING COMPANY—CHIEF KITGUEN OR KLUE.

IT was a Thursday afternoon, May the 8th, when again I committed myself to the pathless ocean, this time in a small steam-vessel called the *Pacific*. About three hundred passengers would have made a respectable freight for her. Nobody seemed to know how many we had on board; but I guessed twelve hundred to be near the mark.

I shall give this part of my narrative in the words of my Diary:—

" *Friday, May* 9*th*.—Awoke this morning in a miserable state. Two English gentlemen and my-self had slept on deck all night, having contrived to rig some canvas to protect us from the driving rain. We might certainly have got wetter without it."

" *Saturday, May* 10*th*. — Steamer making little

progress. Nothing but rain, rain, rain. Wind very high, a real nor'-wester, with thick fogs, which render the voyage extremely dull and uninteresting, not to mention the awful misery of such a crowded and unprovided ship. An English friend of mine, who has also come out from Canada, begins to curse his fate in leaving that land of comfort for the prospect of gold in the mines of British Columbia. There are a good many more who share his opinion. For my part I feel perfectly sure that the hardships at the mines cannot equal those we are subject to on board this steamer. Horses, mules, sheep, pigs, oxen, huddled together. All hours of the day and night, hundreds of the passengers, in various stages of sea-sickness, may be seen clinging to the rigging, with the hope of imbibing a mouthful of air. Food is almost an illusion; and oftentimes I would sooner go without a meal, such as it is, than risk losing some hole or corner where the crush is less, and where one has a better chance of escaping the hoofs of the Mexican mules—a kick from whom might soon enough send one 'down among the dead men.' It is reported that several passengers were lost overboard, in both the *Northern Light* and the *Golden Age*, without being missed till the end of each voyage. I can well credit it: for it appears to me a hundred people might tumble over the sides during the night, and their surviving comrades not be any the wiser, or the Captain and crew be at the least pains to save the lost ones. Close astern of the figure-head is the place I usually aim at. The wind blows fiercely there. However, one does not encounter so much dirt forward as aft. It is consequently healthier, though, like every other available spot, choke-full of passengers."

"*Sunday, May* 11*th*, 10 P.M. — A wet dreary night before us, and still nowhere to lay my head. This comes of travelling by Yankee ships. Thank heaven, I shall soon be again under the good Union Jack of Old England, where the rights of the humblest passengers are respected, to say nothing of those who pay large sums as their fare. Commend me to British vessels for sterling loyalty to whatever arrangements they make."

"*Monday, May* 12*th*. — Cramped and sore from having ventured to take a stretch on the wet deck when tired out with standing. Tried to dry and warm myself against the steamer's funnel. Strong easterly gale now blowing, heavy sea running, ship straining fearfully, as with double-reefed topsails she rises out of it, and lunges over to windward, and again pitches headlong into the ugly sea-trough.

" 6 A.M.—Was quite half an hour in reaching the heel of the ship's bowsprit, the throng of people and cattle on deck being so great. Horizon clearing at last on the weather-bow. Gives us a sight of Cape Hancock, at the mouth of the Columbia river. This river divides the State of Oregon from that of Washington. There is a bar which lies about two miles westward of the mouth of the river, and pre- vents large vessels from entering. This is a fortunate circumstance for British Columbia, as it necessitates the United States' traders seeking a harbour within the limits of our territory.

" 4 P.M.—Weather clear. A beautiful sky in the west promises a fine day for to-morrow. Rapidly nearing the Strait of San Juan de Fuca."

To the best of my recollection, I had just finished making the last of the above entries in my Diary, and had fought a way to the forecastle, with the hope of catching the first glimpse of British soil, when one of my fellow-passengers, an Englishman I believe, suddenly cried " Vancouver Island!" Thrice welcome sound it was, indeed. For there, well in front of us, like some transformation scene emerging from the great repertory of nature, lay the craggy shore and high land of Vancouver. At first it appeared as the veriest outline in the dim distance. But the rough sea of the morning had been gradually calming, and we made such rapid headway that within half an hour the coast began to stand out in bold form, and to reflect gloriously the rays of the declining sun.

It seems necessary to journey long away from the sheltering ægis of British institutions in order fully to know the joy of again hailing the land where the privilege of being plundered and otherwise injured by one's neighbour, whenever he listeth, is at least limited.

Soon we were alive from stem to stern: ducks and hens clucking, cattle lowing, sheep bleating, mules restive, and every human passenger intent on gathering his or her belongings together—all certain indications that the end of our four days' misery was not far off. Before sunset, in fact, the *Pacific* steam-vessel had weathered Cape Flattery, and was going ahead in delightfully smooth water up the Strait of San Juan, which constitutes the line of demarcation between British and American territory. The pace was too rapid, however, to allow us to see, on either shore, more than a moving panorama of steep red-coloured cliffs, those on the American side running back into a range of high and rugged peaks, grandiloquently styled the Olympian Range by its owners.

I may here say a word, parenthetically, about anchorage. It is a common mistake of writers who casually mention British Columbia to talk of Vancouver Island as possessing *numerous* safe and commodious harbours. They confound a part with the whole. Many excellent harbours certainly do exist on the mainland, although but few of them are as yet in general use. Owing to the powerful tides and currents, and to the contrary winds so prevalent on the coast, those harbours are and must remain practically closed, unless to steamers of high pressure. I knew a clipper-schooner which took two weeks to do the Inside Passage, a distance of only three hundred miles. Besides, I can speak from personal experience, having sailed several times up and down the Passage in sloops, as well as once in a schooner, and paddled it on another occasion in a canoe manned by Indians. And I testify that, notwithstanding the pleasant and generally safe character of the Passage, steam is what alone can ever turn the harbours of the mainland to practical account in the interests of commerce.

The first of the mainland harbours is that known as the North Bentinck Arm, which I shall afterwards notice. The second is New Westminster. Of both these it is especially true that they never can serve as anything more than ports of entry for steamers. At New Westminster, the current of the Fraser river is marvellously strong. No sailing-vessel has a chance against it. Even high-pressure steam-vessels find it an absolute impossibility to make the harbour without putting on an unlimited quantum of extra pounds to the inch. In Vancouver Island proper, however, there *are* three fine harbours. The first of these is Esquimalt, situated three miles west from Victoria, the capital of British Columbia, and its seat of Government. The formation of Esquimalt harbour is an irregular circle, some two miles in width by three in length. It averages about seven fathoms of water. In facility of ingress and egress it surpasses all other ports in British Columbia. Excepting a few patches of rich loamy soil, the ground round about this harbour is very rocky; but on that account perhaps it adapts itself all the more readily to the purpose of a landing-place for the heavy wares likely to be wanted in a prospective commercial country. Hence not less by reason of its extraordinarily good anchorage than because combining close proximity to the capital with the easiest access to the ocean-highway, Esquimalt Harbour appears the great natural port of entry to Vancouver Island, and indeed, for many a year yet, to the whole of British Columbia. It lies exactly nine miles from the Race Rocks, in the Straits of San Juan de Fuca. On the western point at entrance, a white tower-lighthouse, called the Fisgard Light, from an English frigate of that name employed in this service on the coast, has been constructed. The lighthouse stands low, but is nevertheless so admirably placed as to be visible at every point of approach towards the harbour. Ships of any size can ride here at anchor, in all security. Esquimalt is chiefly used as a naval station, the Admiral's flag-ship being usually anchored inside: but, the large steamers belonging to the Pacific Steam Navigation Company, which ply between Vancouver Island and San Francisco, putting into Portland on the Columbia river, also use it as their terminus.

Nootka Sound is the second of the Vancouver harbours. The Admiralty reports well of it; but when the place has been colonized and its harbour submitted to probation, it will be safer to criticize the official report. The third is Victoria itself. When I last saw it there was a bar or spit running right across the entrance, a short way to the leeward of Ogden and Maclaughlin Points. The bar has since been thoroughly dredged; and now Victoria Harbour affords sufficient anchorage for a few larger vessels, and for a considerable number of smaller craft. Despite which a grave error is unanimously admitted to have been committed in choosing the site of Victoria for the capital. The reason alleged was the quantity of good land in its immediate vicinity. But port advantages rank among the primary requisites in a new country, and with such a port as Esquimalt close at hand, lying quite near enough to the good land, how its superior claims could have been overlooked appears inconceivable. The truth is, therefore, that, although British Columbia does possess many harbours, only three of them are likely to serve as commercial ports, one, however, Esquimalt, having pre-eminent capabilities.

Upon the lovely spring morning of May 13th, then, and at the beginning of an equally lovely summer, we all landed—English, Canadians, Americans, in a heap and a jumble—on the wharf in that harbour of Esquimalt.

A sudden influx of 1400 people would have taxed the supplies in an ordinary civilized town. Consequently, the capital of British Columbia, which at that date counted only about 6000 fixed residents, with a floating population of miners and stray Indians, was hardly the place to find accommodation for an invading army like us. How the majority fared, I know not. But fortunate were those who had brought any kind of housing with them. As for me, I was able, in partnership with some of my English travelling-companions, to pitch a tent for the time, on a slight eminence off the *Squymalt* road (the Yankee corruption of the euphonistic *Esquimalt*), commanding a view of Victoria. Fancy arriving in England after a four days' journey from Southern Europe, and being condemned to go a-gipsying on Hampstead Heath—glad too of the chance. I do aver we felt uncommonly Bohemian. We formed a sort of camp—at least those did who had tentage. Numbers, however, found themselves completely without shelter, and sad it was to see them wandering for many days, in couples, or by families, about the crude Victorian streets. Eventually, though very gradually, they all disappeared, being absorbed, in virtue of some occult process of nature, into the body colonial, mostly over to the mainland, which subtends the Island of Vancouver.

I shall here skip some three months, or account for them in general only.

My professional acquirements enabled me, sooner than many of my fellow-emigrants, to obtain an engagement. What an emigrant looks to, on landing, is to be employed in any manner. For although he may have to endure great hardship from the unwonted nature of the employment offered him, he knows that if he will but keep steadily at it he is certain to get on. Sometimes, no doubt, he acts with unwise precipitancy; but the stimulus to active exertion is none the less, even after a disappointment at starting. It is so disposed, perhaps providentially. A feeling of this kind led me, in the first instance, to join a prospecting enterprise on the mainland. My Canadian experience had inured me to venturesome operations in the open air, from which I rashly inferred that I could stand their equivalent in British Columbia. But for all my eagerness to earn a status in the colony, could I have foreseen one tithe of the privations before me I should have shrunk back appalled.

Being wishful to take my reader on to Queen Charlotte Islands, which is the chief object of this narrative, I shall sum up what I underwent during the three months after my arrival by saying that the exploring expedition I joined included in its operations forcing our way across the Blue and Cascade Mountains, here climbing up half-perpendicular hill-sides, there springing from rock to rock, then down again by precipitous tracks, where one false step would have flung me into an unfathomable abyss, at one time up to the middle in soft alkali mud, at another breasting swift mountain-torrents, scrambling over roots and fallen trees, or battling with the densest brushwood. More than once it occurred to our party to find ourselves benighted amidst a superabundant vegetation, reminding me of Panamà, with a temperature of 98° in the shade, and with myriads of the customary hot climate accessories in the shape of mosquitoes, sand-flies, black-flies, and a species of ant as large as the common English fly, besetting us in every direction, each little fellow having obviously embarked his energies in a concentrated effort to excel our other persecutors in the quantity of blood he could extract from us victims; whereas the next day about noon we might have been seen, had anybody watched our progress, in the midst of the snow, shivering on a mountain-top,

16,000 feet above the sea-level, and therefore higher than Mont Blanc or the Jungfrau; but again, the very same evening perhaps, down once more into the hot plain or valley. If to such reckless pulls on one's constitution it be added that for five or six days we were in hourly dread of attack from hostile savages whose country we were prospecting, that our food consisted principally of the bark of trees, and that, though we left a sorrowful trail of blood behind us, nay, the body even of one of our companions, we had no trail to guide our path save our pocket-compasses, some idea may be formed of the pluck which was necessary to carry us through with the expedition, and some palliation be accepted for the hopeless failure in which it resulted. Never did means prove more inadequate to the end. But it served to start me in British Columbia. It was under these circumstances that for the second time I arrived at Victoria, on this occasion without a penny in my pocket, and without a friend or relative nearer than 6000 miles.

However, after a fortnight's rest and good living I began to recover the use of my feet, and to feel that my constitution was not altogether destroyed. As soon as I had strength sufficient to get about, I stated publicly my conviction that, from observations and calculations I had made on the mainland, almost opposite Queen Charlotte Islands, there was copper to be found in the group of islands which lie out from the coast to the north of Vancouver. This opinion happened to receive a singular confirmation from the fact of a native of those islands having, some months previous, brought down a sample of copper-ore to Victoria under the impression that it was gold.

In a marvellously short time the nucleus of a Company was got together and entitled the Queen Charlotte Mining Company, which so inspired me with hope and confidence that I offered to go up and sink the requisite shafts. As mining engineers are not a commodity which is landed every day in British Columbia, the directors were only too happy to accept my offer.

Before closing the bargain I thought an interview with the Governor, Sir James Douglas, would be both proper and profitable. The long service of Sir James Douglas to the Hudson's Bay Company, his intimate acquaintance with the various tribes of natives, and his knowledge of the requirements for developing the resources of this the most important colony of England in the Pacific, rendered him at that epoch eminently qualified to fulfil the duties of Governor of our North-West American possessions. I have no object in bepraising him other than a desire to record my humble sense of his eminent merits. But such I know to be the verdict of all unbiassed men who had the advantage of living under his wise and able administration. In my case he regretted that he could not take upon himself the responsibility of giving me the more substantial protection of a gunboat and a detachment of marines. The hostility attributed to the natives of Queen Charlotte Islands the Governor declared to be well founded. The risk and expense would be too great, he said, for the Government to incur in a private undertaking; but he ended some valuable advice by recommending me strongly to supply myself with plenty of arms and ammunition. It did not look very encouraging. I was bent upon making the venture, however. As it chanced, Kitguen, who claimed the head chieftainship of the islands, was then at Victoria; so I took him before the Governor, to whom he promised that his tribe should not molest us, and that he would bring his influence or power to bear in our behalf should any other tribe seem disposed to contest our landing or interfere with our explorations. In fact, we took the bull by the horns, and with capital effect. The Governor spoke to Kitguen in his own language, which he interpreted as an honour and deference intended to be shown to his chiefdom. Of this impression he gave unmistakeable evidence when he afterwards returned to his tribe, they and the other tribes consequently regarding him in the light of a chief who had attained to an influential position with the chief of the white men.

Fully alive, therefore, to the daring character of the attempt, I took up my appointment from the Queen Charlotte Mining Company.

In another day or two we had chartered the *Rebecca* schooner of twenty tons, and proceeded forthwith to load her with provisions and implements necessary for rough mine work. Kitguen being anxious to go back to his island-home, I gave him a free passage, and, having likewise shipped some men as helpers in my operations, I was to be seen, one summer eve, standing on the beach of Victoria, surrounded by newspaper reporters and a number of the leading men of the town, who had come down to wish me success and a pleasant voyage.

I have always considered it a real pity that Vancouver possessed, in those days, but a small number of men of spirit. Had there been as many in it then as there were subsequently, I have no hesitation in saying that British Columbia would ere this have got far ahead of any State in North America, not excepting California. That is the opinion of everybody that knew the colony when the mercantile and emigration world was giving its splendid chances the go-by.

> " There is a tide in the affairs of men,
> Which, taken at the flood, leads on to fortune:
> Omitted, all the voyage of their life
> Is bound in shallows and in miseries."

As of men so of countries; though I heartily hope that many more tides in the affairs of British Columbia will lead on to fortune.

Backed only by a handful of individuals, like all originators in Vancouver at the time, I had simply to do my best to make the concern worthy of the enterprise and energy of those who had embarked in it.

CHAPTER VI.

BY sundown on the evening of August the 4th I had got everything on board. Captain Macalmond having then cast away his shore lines, we hauled off from the jetty, and with the aid of the ebbing tide the pretty little clipper-schooner *Rebecca* glided gently out of Victoria harbour.

Her ultimate destination was the Stickeen River gold-mines; but we had partially chartered her to deliver myself, my men, and my freight, on her way up there, on Queen Charlotte Islands.

Opposite Ogden Point we anchored for an hour, to trim ship and await the captain's wife.

At 10 P.M. we cleared the harbour, and proceeded to take the Inside Passage towards the Gulf of Georgia. The weather being calm and foggy, however, and as from my recent experience I already knew the difficulties of that route, I strongly advised the Captain to make for the Outside Passage—a plan he at once agreed to adopt, greatly to my satisfaction.

There has always been much dispute as to which of the two routes is the safest and best to the Head of Vancouver. As aforesaid, I have gone the Inside Passage more than once, and I shall again refer to my knowledge of it; but it may also help to show the relative advantages of those rival highways if I here quote from my Diary the precise time it took to accomplish an average passage Outside, together with some of the circumstances attending it.

After our vessel's course had been reversed and the Captain had headed her W.S.W., we turned into our respective bunks to sleep off the excitement of departure.

"*August 5th.*—Up at sunrise this morning, finding sleep impossible, what with the schooner's tossing in the ground-swell of the strait, and the closeness of the atmosphere below. Only too glad to inhale the sea-breeze, although the morning smacks damp and misty, as I hear is frequently the case beneath the shadow of Mount Baker. This mountain forms a useful landmark for mariners on the coast. It is the highest of the Olympian range, the frowning precipices of which converge into its westernmost point, in the natural boundary between British Columbia and the United States. The scenery all around, when illumined by sunlight, must be grand in the extreme. As I now see it over the top of a sea-fog, it looks rude, desolate, and un-inviting.

"Good English breakfast, thanks to the British Constitution. But the passengers leave the Captain and me to enjoy it, the landsman's inveterate foe—sea-sickness—having taken full possession of them. As for me, I begin to consider myself an exempt. In fact I am never blessed with so glorious an appe-tite as when ploughing the deep or otherwise under-going invigoration from the sea-air.

"In this country the winds are perceptibly affected by the sun. At midnight last night it blew quite a small gale: but as soon as the sun appeared on the eastern horizon the wind suddenly dropped, and the sea became as calm as a mill-pond. Precisely the opposite would have taken place had it been calm in the night. We should now be in a gale. These sudden changes with the sun are the rule out here.

"The live-stock on board the *Rebecca* consists of the Captain and wife, the mate, steward, one A.B. seaman, myself, and eight mining-workmen, with two Hydah chiefs and four of their women; all of us, Captain and wife excepted, being stowed away in the hold amongst two tiers of bunks, kept separate from the general cargo only by a slight boarding. The overpowering atmosphere of this hold, which rancid oil, burning grease, and the fishy stench characteristic of Indians renders still more oppressive, induces me to court the deck as long as possible.

"I have just been joined here by Kitguen, who, albeit the very pink of uncleanness, proves to be an intelligent biped and a sociable Indian. If his chieftainship would but wash himself once a week and cover his skeleton shanks with unmentionables, he would make a rather respectable-looking member of society. I did give him a pair of pants, and he wore them while at Victoria; but no sooner had we distanced the capital than he quickly threw them off, and on my inquiring the cause he replied, "*Wake closh*," which being interpreted means "*No good*." He does not appear to possess much physical strength, neither is he handsome. His cheeks are sunken, and his cheek-bones are more prominent than a Celt's; he has a dull and inexpressive eye; his hair, thick as brush-wood, reeks with fish-oil and tumbles down the back of his neck; but his face is absolutely beardless. Smooth faces, it seems, are fashionable with his tribe, every man of whom systematically eradicates the hairs of the face, and carries a tweezer about for that express purpose. It was some time before I knew the cause of Kitguen's evident partiality towards me. At last I discovered that it arose from my being 'cleaner than most whites he had seen'— in other words, because I did not wear a beard. The passion for wearing beards is, I need scarce say, as prevalent amongst our countrymen in British Columbia as in England. Yet I noticed at Victoria that many eschewed the custom altogether, and not without reason, I think. Beardlessness has two undoubted advantages in this colony: first, it disposes the natives to make friends with you; secondly, and by no means least in importance, it leaves a more open field for the slaughter of the mosquitoes when they attack you in the visage—indeed, they are hardly get-at-able when they fill your beard. I judge Kitguen to be about thirty-five years of age, although the habit of painting from childhood upwards, and the life of frightful exposure led by the Indians,

have combined to give him the appearance of fully
fifty years. He stoops somewhat, and is rather bow-
legged—defects common to the seaboard tribes of
Indians, and doubtless arising from overmuch sitting,
tailor-fashion, in their cranky canoes. It rather sur-
prises me to see no tattooing on any part of him;
but he has a very amusing ring of silver through his
nose, and in each of his big splay ears are several
ornamental holes, large enough to let my little finger
through up to the first joint."

Kitguen was a man, take him for all in all, whom I
found to be a very fair specimen of a Queen Charlotte
Indian, which is the reason why I describe him here
at more length perhaps than might otherwise seem
justifiable. We became great friends. I tried to
teach him a little English, which he reciprocated by
initiating me into the mysteries of the Hydah tongue,
as well as by many friendly services. The other chief
belonged to the Skiddan tribe. He was of a more
quiet and unambitious disposition.

"*August 5th*, 6 P.M.—We have just passed out of
the Straits of San Juan de Fuca, and are entering
the open Pacific, the evening lowering calmly, clearly,
and delightfully. At this moment we have crossed
the bows of a large barque, within sixty yards of

her. She is called the *Gold-Hunter*, and is bound for San Francisco, one Hoey commanding her. Captain Macalmond, who is both owner and commander of the 'saucy' *Rebecca*, as the British Columbians have surnamed our schooner, has good reason to feel proud of his little vessel, which he declares outsails all other ships, of whatever tonnage, on the coast.

" The schooner's course is right under Vancouver Island, of which we have a close yet comprehensive view from where I am writing this on the deck. At the present season of the year the island does not appear to its best advantage, the ground being evidently parched, and the pastures scorched to nothing, from sheer want of rain. But a little later the Autumn will set in, and then we shall have what is known in North America as the *Indian summer*. Still, the foliage of the forest-trees and shrubs presents a wondrous aspect to any eye unaccustomed to it. In that, British Columbia only excels in degree what may be met with in kind all through Canada, and indeed all over the northernmost parts of the North American continent. I have seen leaves of every imaginable tint draping the shore of the great St. Lawrence, the golden hue of the water, as the sun rises or sets, vastly augmenting the splendour of the effect. Occasionally too the leaves of one tree would display a mass of the brightest scarlet, whilst its next neighbour would soften off into lake-colour, or show an infinitude of variegated tinges on its different branches. When this happens it is a sure sign that a severe winter is approaching: but the beauteousness of the present often lures one to forget the harshness of the future. The thought of the lovely forest-life to be seen at every step in Canada, during quite seven months of the year, never recurs to me but I think likewise of the silly ignorance exhibited by the French "statesman," who, when his countrymen were obliged to yield up Canada to us, described it as merely "a few acres of snow." As I gaze across to Vancouver, it appears to surpass even my old Canadian visions. The background is high, and looks intensely rocky. We are now sailing so close in-shore, however, that with my glass I can make out perfectly well a rich alluvial soil of a deep black colour, filling up the long valleys between, and seeming only to await the ploughshare of the husbandman in order to make it abundantly productive. The tree-leafage runs down in luxuriance to the very water's edge, presenting a marvellous variety, from dyes of malachite green or topaz yellow to the most delicate shades of pink."

" *August 7th.*—It was past eleven o'clock last night when we turned into our bunks, tired at last with gazing, by the silvery moonlight, upon the wonders of creation.

" In the *Rebecca* we are not restricted to time, as on board regular packet-ships. We have no 'eight bells, and all lights out.' The Captain does all he can to see to our comfort, and leaves us to our own devices. But, on the other hand, we are a contented lot of passengers. All of us lend a hand at the helm, or make and shorten sail, as each man knows how, and just as though one were in a private yacht.

" This morning sailing along still closer, if possible, under the land.

" The prospect, lit up by the blaze of the ascending sun, strikes me as truly magnificent.

" And yet this island has remained in obscurity for upwards of half a century since its full discovery by Captain Vancouver of the English Royal Navy. It is 270 miles in length, with an average breadth of fifty miles, and a superficies of 14,000 square miles—or in other words, it measures about a quarter the area of England and Wales. In my opinion the fault of the emigrating world's having been so long kept in ignorance of this grand outlet for our surplus population lies mainly at the door of the Hudson's Bay Company, to whose custody our Government foolishly relegated it, after England and Spain had settled their dispute about its possession. That Company, now happily defunct, found the trade with the Indian tribes too lucrative not to make it a stringent interest to hide the natural resources of Vancouver Island from the 'outer barbarians.' No doubt some few strangers did contrive to exist there, previous to 1859, when the Company's charter expired: but the monopoly of the latter was too great, and every branch of colonial trade too much affected by it, to leave the slightest chance of success to the individual speculator. Dating from 1859, however, the colony has experienced a slow but steady and increasing prosperity.

"4 P.M.—Vast shoals of whales were playing near us in the forenoon, one as near as forty yards across our bows, his length some seventy-five feet, measured by the eye.

"This afternoon we have had another kind of visitation, in the shape of four canoes crammed with Indians. The majority of these were females, but painted so black as completely to hide the expression of their features. The men, who sported a costume the reverse of 'full dress,' had unprepossessing and stupid countenances. They wanted to sell us fish; but we had got provisions enough on board without it.

"9 P.M.—When the sun went down in the west this evening, there was the slight movement on the water so often seen in these parts.

"I have just come from viewing the island to great advantage. The declining sun added immensely to its otherwise extraordinary beauty. But the change is amazingly rapid. A variety of the liveliest colours tinge the tops of the gigantic pines and cedars with which Vancouver abounds, and which are divided from the golden waters by a line of sombre-hued and jagged rocks thrown up into all manner of shapes. While the eye is endeavouring to take in the splendour of this feat of nature, from the far south-east to the far north-west, suddenly down dips the sun into the ocean's bosom, and the gorgeous landscape is almost instantaneously enveloped in midnight gloom.

"I write now by a lamp. The cause of this sudden darkness is the absence of all twilight."*

---

* The complete want of twilight on the North Pacific coast is remarkable. Science explains why day immediately succeeds to night in the Tropics;

"*August* 8*th.*—We are off Berkley Sound this morning with a strong north-easterly head-wind. It smacks of a land-breeze. So we alter our course a few points, which will take us out of sight of land until we sight the island we are sailing for.

"I am almost the only passenger not sea-sick again. It is rather singular that the Indians should be troubled with sea-sickness, since they are so continually on the water, and in much rougher weather than we have to-day. I hear, however, that no Indians are ever sea-sick in their own canoes, even in the midst of the fiercest storms. There must be something in the construction or movement of our vessels which does not agree with their stomachs or brains.

"I was forced to turn out of my bunk betimes just now, owing to the frightful effluvium below. Moreover, I had found sleeping utterly impracticable on account of the four Klootchmen (Indian women), who chattered and quarrelled unceasingly all the night through, spitting at one another like cats. As I have often seen Chinese do the same, this reminds me that

---

but how it comes that the same phenomenon should occur in a country in almost the same latitude as England, is a problem which still remains for scientific solution.

many peculiarities are common to both races. The
Indian mode of dancing bears a strange resemblance
to that in use among the Chinese. The straw or
dried-grass hats peculiar to Chinamen are also
made by the Hydah Indians, although with a stouter
material. From these and numerous kindred
similarities, I see reason for acquiescing in the
opinion that they sprang originally from the same
stock."

I may here add that, while on board the *Rebecca*,
I took pains to persuade the Klootchmen to relin-
quish the frightful and repulsive habit they have of
disfiguring their faces. The two elder women did
not appreciate my good intentions; but they were to
be excused, as the coats of paint certainly served to
hide their decay and wrinkles. I succeeded with the
two younger, who forthwith consented to wash themselves several times a day. It agreeably surprised
me to find that one of them, the daughter of a chief
named Skid-a-ga-tees, was really interesting, and the
other quite a beauty. And as I did not care to conceal my admiration, of course the newly-discovered
beauty and I became great friends: and so indeed
we ever continued, as long as I remained on Queen
Charlotte Islands. Once she had the courage to bid

defiance to all her tribe, and even to her own father, a chief, in order to save my life, when I was alone and unarmed in the presence of a dozen Indians, dancing round me with drawn knives and thirsting for my blood.

"*August 9th* —Strong wind all the forenoon off the land. Found ample employment in cleaning my revolvers, with a view to using them, if so compelled, against the Indians. However friendly Indians may appear, they are never wholly to be trusted. I was careful therefore to let my travelling-companions see that I had a portable arsenal not at all to be despised.

"At noon, the wind shifting round to the port side, the Captain gave orders to 'put on the bonnet.' The *bonnet* is an additional piece of canvas tacked on to a sail, in moderate weather, to hold more wind. It is rather bold of our Captain putting it on just here, as the sky looks threatening, and as by this time we must have entered Queen Charlotte Sound, and are probably already in the broad reach of sea which separates Vancouver from Queen Charlotte Islands, and where the winds are never to be depended upon. Still, a real storm is of rare occurrence during the summer months in these seas.

Our Captain tells me he intends to make a dash across while the weather holds up, in hopes of catching sight of the islands before dark, and thus run us in direct to our destination. Sailing a point or two out of the course has often resulted in the vessel passing the islands. The Captain says that actually happened to him once before. He did not know the least where he was till he had the good luck to fall in with a whaler, some 300 miles in another direction, south-west of Queen Charlotte. In our case, had we known of any kind of harbour near the Head of Vancouver, we should have doubtless run in there for shelter, and so have made sure of a whole day to scud across. When these northern shores become colonized, this running-across difficulty, which must then occur daily, will assuredly be obviated by the erection of two lighthouses, one on Scott's Island at the Head of Vancouver, the other on Cape St. James, the most southerly point of Queen Charlotte.

" Our steersman gives such little satisfaction to the Captain, that the latter, having ' cunned' the schooner nearly all the day, has at last been obliged to take the wheel himself. To *cun* a vessel is the nautical phrase for directing the man at the helm how to steer. It is a common thing in all new countries

to see men assuming a responsible position without
a trace of the qualifications necessary to enable them
to fulfil its duties. This is very noticeable in the
United States, and, so far, not less so in British
Columbia. When our colony has been better popu-
lated and organized, such incongruities will no doubt
duly disappear under the influence of English civilization. At present, nothing is commoner out here than
for a man to be a tailor or a gold-miner one year,
and the next to find himself a merchant, a banker,
the captain of a coaster, or even a chief magistrate
in some of the back settlements. It was no wonder,
therefore, that the *Rebecca* should have been temporarily consigned to the guidance of a professed
steersman whose appearance and acquirements
seemed to point rather to tailoring than to
steering.

" 5 P.M.—Going on deck after tea-time, I was met
in the face with a novel kind of shower-bath. It consisted of a sort of sprinkling of sea-water, which swept
in a perfect tempest from the surface of the waves
and fled like a vapour before the wind. The British
Columbians call it the *spoondrift*, and I am not
aware that it exists, at least not with the same inten-
sity and continuity, in any other part of the globe."

"*August* 10*th.*—We were not able to sight land before sunset last night. We consequently kept on our course in the dark, trusting that early dawn would not fail to give us the first inkling of our long looked for destination.

" This morning I turned out with the *dog-watch*, that is, at 4 A.M. The wind had fallen during the night, however, and there was not a sign of land to be seen.

" We sailed perseveringly on over a deliciously smooth sea, everybody keeping a sharp look-out, when towards eight o'clock I was the first to observe two little shadows about the size of a hat, which seemed to be suspended above the water. As we coursed onward, they gradually assumed a more substantial form, appearing to touch the water. We all believed it to be land; but, after a prolonged straining of our united eyes, we felt satisfied that it really was Cape St. James, the most south-easterly point of Queen Charlotte Islands. Having indulged a moment in the pleasant prospect of our voyage speedily terminating, all the passengers crowded down the hatchway to breakfast. Upon our regaining the deck, in half an hour's time, the veritable Cape St. James had come distinctly into view.

"10 A.M. — All is now still and serene. The glorious expanse of sea, over which our little vessel wends its solitary way, tends to induce tranquillity of mind and to invite to serious thought.

" Astern of us lies spread out the vast Pacific Ocean, completely alive with whales and porpoises. The whales are quietly ploughing the surface, and every now and then spouting streams of water high up into the air, whilst the porpoises, in a widely extended *corps d'armée*, toss their ungainly carcases hither and thither athwart the placid main, and yet, led by some leader more swift than his fellows, seem somehow to be all making their way seaward. Who dare foretell how soon these frequenters of this half-known ocean-path will be driven from the field of their sports, and their inheritance be taken possession of by the fleets of civilization?

" Our schooner's bearings being now altered from W.S.W. seaway point, with $1\frac{3}{4}$ variation point, to N.W. $\frac{3}{4}$ W., we see right ahead of us the island, or rather the islands, which since a few years after their discovery, towards the close of the last century, have gone by the name of King George the Third's Queen Consort.

" My first observation shows me that the lay of

the land is unexpectedly low.* Its greatest elevation, as I hear from the Captain, does not exceed eight hundred feet above the sea-level. The mountain tops, or, to speak more correctly, the hill-tops, are sharp and peaky, thus manifesting at once their volcanic origin. Here and there the hills open out, revealing a series of matchless harbours, from which large flats shelve off well into the interior. The flats are covered with forests of stupendous timber, chiefly pine and cedar.

"I have just looked hard from my seat on deck at these reaches, which begin almost from the water's edge, and seem endless; and my strong idea is that the soil itself must be of the very richest kind to produce such stately and perfect timber. I take it that, in the background among the ridges, there are lying near the surface extensive treasures of minerals, only wanting a few blasts of gunpowder to divulge them to the light of day.

" As far as the eye can reach either way, the land is a picture of loveliness. The very atmosphere seems laden with the perfume of its vegetation. The

---

* There is a good description, with an excellent illustration of Cape St. James, in Captain Dixon's *Voyage to the North-West Coast of America* (p. 214), published in the last century.

outer-shore lines look black and shapeless; but they are backed by a gigantesque fringe of wood-country. Such is the closeness of the heavy timber that, at this distance, no great variety of colour presents itself to view; but again, if this country lacks brilliancy in its foliage, the massive green of the trees amply compensates for it. Were an uninformed stranger, who had never travelled in southern latitudes, put down suddenly on Queen Charlotte Islands, his first idea would be to fancy himself transported to some tropical clime. In order fully to carry out the illusion, nothing but the indigenous vegetation of the south need be added to the luxuriance which I see filling up the landscape at every point. Various natural provisions combine to afford grateful shelter to all this forest-land. The principal of these causes is the arctic current which sweeps down along the coast the whole year round, the chilled sea-water being modified in its turn by warm westerly breezes. Hence the temperature is nearly always mild, and never high. Neither, as our Captain asserts, do the islands harbour green flies or any of the destructive *insect fauna* which impede luxuriant growth in Europe, and deteriorate the pleasures which we derive from the rich vegetation of the south. For this reason it requires little perspicuity to foresee a day when the fair land we are now approaching will be able to boast of such an open-air fruitage and florage as would do honour to any nobleman's hot-house in England.

" Upon whose shoulders rests the blame, then, that valuable islands like these should have remained totally uncolonized, and to all intents and purposes almost unknown, for well nigh a century since Captain Dixon first took possession of them in the name of the king of England?

" It is not necessary to speculate on part at least of the answer, when we know that for fifteen years a combination of traders, known as the Hudson's Bay Company, kept undivided control over them."

CHAPTER VII.

LATE in the afternoon of August the 11th we let go our anchor off Skincuttle, a very pretty little island, comprising some forty acres of superficial area.

Thus we did the passage from Victoria, Vancouver, in exactly six days, nineteen and a half hours. Had we kept to the Inside Passage, it would, I feel assured, have taken us the best part of a month to reach Queen Charlotte.

Skincuttle lies in latitude 52° 18′ 0″ N., longitude 131° 07′ 0″ W.—that is to say, in a line nearly north-west from the southernmost point of Cape St. James.

At low water this islet is seen to be joined to several others of a similar character, which, when not submerged, form a connected strip of land stretching out towards the Sound.

Although these islets lie together in an open position, and are unprotected against storms from any part of the compass, none of them bear evidence of having suffered much, if at all. In other countries where trees have to struggle to maturity in the midst of storms and adverse winds, as for example on our Cumberland and Westmoreland seaboard, they seldom attain to great altitude, and are not to be mentioned in respect of real straightness. But here, on this outlandish sea-girt holm, every tree is marvellously high, besides being thick in proportion, and as straight as an arrow to the very top. One of my first amusements was to go and take the measurement of a fine cedar. I found it to measure, at a spot I could touch with my arm, four feet ten inches in diameter, which gave fifteen feet four inches in circumference. Its height was two hundred and fifty feet—not exactly that, perhaps, but very nearly so, as I measured by a means which, though wanting in elegance, is simple and effective, and has been generally adopted amongst experienced bushmen and lumberers throughout North America. This plan is to walk away from the tree till you can sight its topmast branch when looking backwards between your legs. You have then got the tree's height in the distance between the spot where you stand and the base of the tree itself. The accuracy of this process in " natural trigonometry " is astonishing; for after a little practice it can be relied upon within a foot or so. The largest trees on Skincuttle, and indeed on the main of Queen Charlotte Islands, are the cedars; but the pines are more perfect and more numerous. They shoot up, ramrod-like, without one single branch, or without a knot even, to mar their bolt-uprightness, if I may be allowed to coin the word, till near their highest point, when they push out some famous tufts and bunches, which give them the appearance of overgrown umbrellas.

The following brief extract from my Diary describes the look-round, soon after landing, of the first Englishman who ever went to reside on Queen Charlotte Islands :—

" I note a ridge extending into the sea for a distance of several hundred yards on the east side of this islet (Skincuttle). At high tide the ridge is almost covered with water; and parallel with it on the west side another ridge runs out, plentifully supplied with timber. The soundings between either ridge and the land are thirty feet deep, and there is capital holding ground. These waters form little lagoons, in fact, and seem to offer admirable shelter to boats and schooners. If it were not for the presence of the Indians, I could easily imagine myself on one of our home islands, in the embouchure of the river Clyde. However, as I look landward again, I am soon undeceived. And yet the grand views which surround me on all sides help to cheer my spirits, and to make me temporarily forget that I have come six thousand miles away from my native land, and that our party is separated by a broad sound from the nearest civilized beings. Sitting down to make this entry in my Diary on a rising ground above the little harbour, I can take into one reach a variety of exquisite landscape. Cedars huge and venerable, pines stalwart, yet everlastingly young, crowd together upon almost every available space of ground. Away on the shore of another islet opposite, a cluster of pine-trees is conspicuous among the rest. A sheet of water can be partly seen through them; while at their left rises a high hill, upon which I observe a darkish object. It will serve me excellently as a landmark by-and-by. Through my glass it appears to be an extinct volcano; for it is hollowed out like a decayed tooth, and its immediate vicinity is devoid of timber."

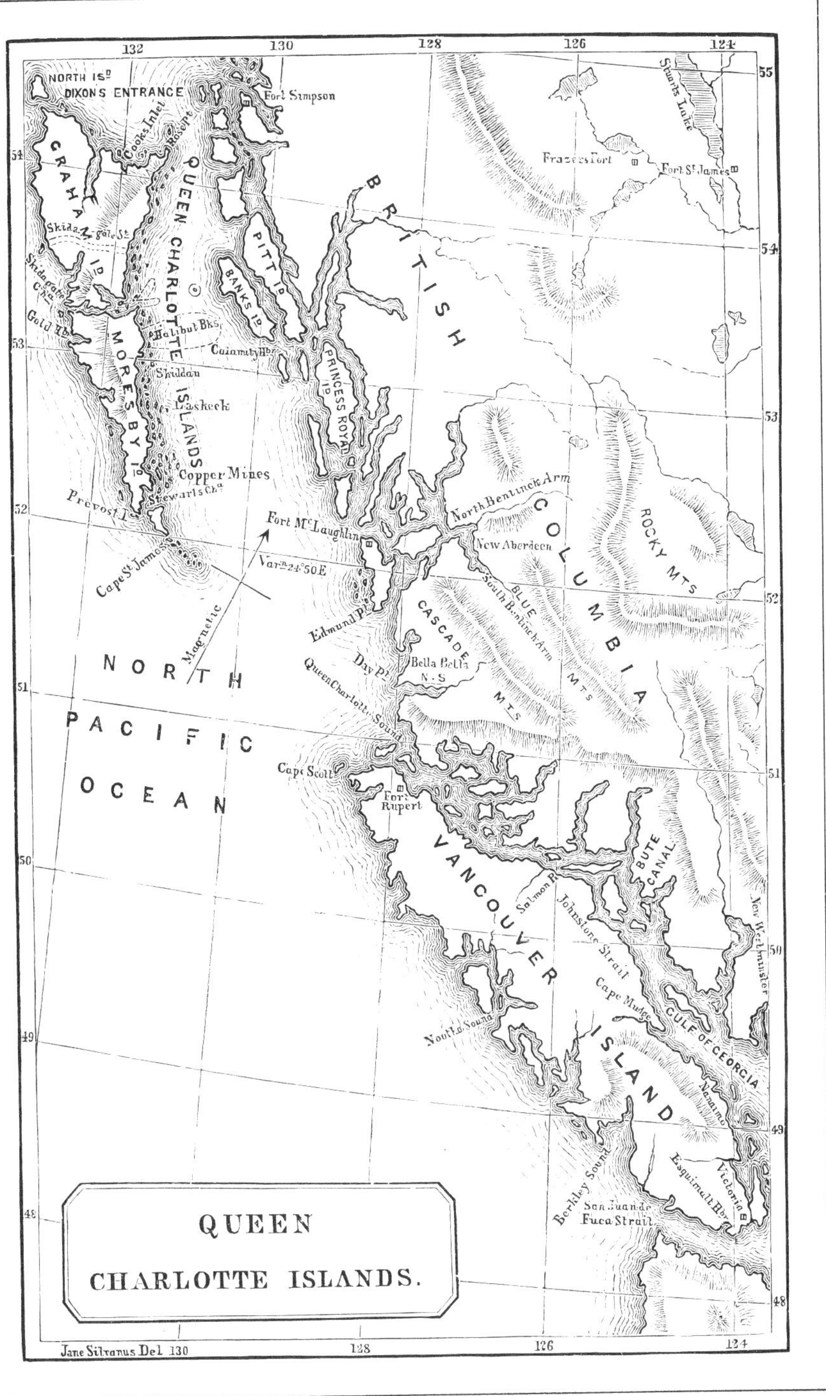

NORTH IS.
DIXON'S ENTRANCE
Fort Simpson
Stuarts Lake
Frazers Fort
Fort St James
GRAHA
Cooks Inlet
Rose Spit
QUEEN CHARLOTTE
BRITISH
Skida gate St
PITT ID
BANKS ID
Skida gate Cha
Gold Hbr
Halibut Bks
Calamity Hbr
MORESBY ID
ISLANDS
Shiddan
Laskeek
PRINCESS ROYAL ID
COLUMBIA
ROCKY MTS
Copper Mines
Stewarts Cha
North Bentinck Arm
Prevost I
Fort McLaughlin
New Aberdeen
Var. 24° 50 E
South Bentinck Arm
Cape St James
BLUE
Magnetic
Edmund Pt
CASCADE
MTS
Day Pt
Bella Bella
N S
MTS
NORTH
Queen Charlotte Sound
PACIFIC
Cape Scott
OCEAN
Fort Rupert
VANCOUVER
Salmon R.
BUTE CANAL
Johnstone Strait
New Westminster
Cape Mudge
GULF OF GEORGIA
ISLAND
Nanaimo
Nootka Sound
Berkley Sound
San Juan de
Fuca Strait
Esquimalt Hbr
Victoria
QUEEN
CHARLOTTE ISLANDS.
Jane Silvanus Del 130

The group known as Queen Charlotte Islands*
consists of two large islands, called Graham and
Moresby, measuring together with two others smaller,
called North and Prevost Islands, 180 English miles,
by 60 miles at its greatest width. There are numberless islets besides, lying about the coast in various
directions, but principally around Moresby Island.

Amongst these Skincuttle holds a prominent position; and it was here that, upon due inquiry, I
determined to fix my head-quarters.

The day after we arrived, the *Rebecca*, having first
discharged our portion of her cargo, set sail again for
the Stickeen River gold mines, with a fair but stiffish
breeze. The whole morning the rain came down in
torrents, at which I mightily exulted, knowing that
the Indians would be sure to connect my arrival with
whatever natural phenomena it happened to coincide
in point of time. Their spring and summer had been
so extraordinarily dry as almost to amount to a
drought. This, then, being their first rainfall for
many months, the honour and benefit of it was im-

---

* All the principal islands, points, straits, rivers, and inlets on the North
Pacific coast which have not retained their Indian nomenclature, are called
after the different English navigators who discovered or explored them, or
after the private friends of those explorers, or after the celebrities of the
day in England, or after the date of discovery.

puted to me. Without precisely pleading guilty to the soft impeachment, I thought it would have been folly to attempt to enlighten them at that stage of the intercourse. Their happy augury as to the landing of the English mining-party on Skincuttle was therefore thankfully accepted.

Afterwards I learnt, partly too by my own experience, that a prolonged dearth of rain is by no means uncommon in these islands, which seems the more singular if the prodigious quantity of timber they contain be considered.

The departure of the little schooner brought home to my men, though more particularly to myself, that we were now destined to settle on a comparatively desert island. Bar the solitude, and our life was to be a mild edition of Robinson Crusoe's. But as none of the men were in any degree desirable companions for me, I soon perceived that, in a great measure, I should have to endure the solitude also.

My first care and duty was to decide on a site to encamp. This, however, I could not do until I had ascertained where the copper ore lay, supposing such to exist in any available quantities on Skincuttle. Consequently, as soon as the rain would let me, I proceeded north from the little harbour, or rather canoe-entrance, and had scarcely gone a hundred yards, when, by the help of a quick eye and my geological hammer, I hit upon evidences of a fine underlying lode. I got the men up at once, and gave directions for the construction of the necessary huts, and for adequate preparations towards the sinking of a shaft.

Meanwhile, those of the Indians whose homes were in this neighbourhood made off to their friends, to distribute the diversified stock of presents or purchases, from a button to a revolver, which they had brought with them. Judging by the demented condition of not a few among the natives, on that first evening of ours, whisky, I should say, figured copiously in the distributions.

My agreement with the Queen Charlotte Mining Company was that the miners we employed should be paid at the rate of fifty to sixty dollars a month— that is, in round numbers, twelve pounds, besides their board. Such a rate sounds high, but the field was new and experimental; while the gold-diggings at Cariboo created too constant and attractive a demand in the Victorian market not to make labourers independent.

It is certain that anybody who does not mind the

risk, labour, and exposure of the Cariboo district, under the grim shadow of the Rocky Mountains, can speedily amass a fortune there, provided he has capital—say, at least 100*l*. to start with. If he should try it on less than that, he is equally certain to return with nothing, or, in plain English, ruined. With 100*l*. a farm might be bought, or an interest secured in one of the successful gold-claims which are always in the market. I know no place in the world, however, where more wit is required, or, better, where a larger amount of small cunning is the *sine quá non* for getting on in life, than Cariboo. If your seller should be a Yankee, it will run hard with him if he does not have the best of the bargain. The Yankee axiom in the sales at Cariboo is that, the higher the sum wanted for the gold-claim, the greater the proof of its value. I have known Cariboo claims offered, ay and sold too, for as much as 100,000 dollars, when they were not worth five dollars, or would not pay the cost of developing. On the other hand, I once had a claim there myself, for which I asked 3000 dollars, a fair price in the English sense of the term; but the claim was summarily condemned, because of my low valuation of it; whereas, if I had been unprincipled enough to put it up at 20,000, it would have assuredly found a ready purchaser. In other words, Cariboo is one immense gambling-table, upon which any man may chance to win a competence in a day, but yet to which labour, at enormous wages, comes necessarily in aid.

With such a rivalry at our elbow, therefore, it will cause no surprise that we were well content to be able to retain eight able-bodied men, despite the price they asked.

While the men worked away, I went off in a canoe, accompanied only by my gun, my hammer, and one assistant, to explore some of the islets which lie between Skincuttle and Cape St James. The very first we landed on was a mere ledge of rocks, and so wholly destitute of vegetation that I had little difficulty in prosecuting my search. And soon, in fact, I discovered a rich spur of variegated copper running E.S.E., with other cupriferous in-dications up and down the islet's surface. The variegated copper lay in a vein of beautiful stalactitic spar, averaging two feet in width, by thirty feet in length, on the out-crop. I named the ledge Rock Island. Thence we paddled across to what seemed the mainland, but what proved to be surrounded by water. This I named Burnaby Island. All these islets have extremely rocky and precipitate shores, though of course in miniature. Groping along Burnaby's rock-bound shore, I was fortunate in making further discoveries of copper. I then gathered my specimens into the canoe, and, leaving them in charge of my assistant, I scrambled into the bush with my gun, but could not light upon any game. It was late when I returned, without any result, except a strong conviction that St. Patrick must have paid an occult visit to these regions, for no toad, reptile, or creeping thing of any sort could I perceive.

Not long afterwards I noted down some experiences of the brute creation on Queen Charlotte Islands, in my Diary, as follows:—

" The only dangerous animals or birds here are the bears and the eagles. The black bear family (*ursus americanus*) is the most numerous, though the eagle tribe bids fair to compete with it. Both bears and eagles, however, studiously avoid man. I have passed many a pleasant afternoon watching the eagles at their game of fish-catching. Their practice is to perch themselves on a high tree close to the sea-shore, and invariably on the verge of some promontory. From these elevated positions they come down 'in one fell swoop' upon the unsuspecting fish, devouring them then and there if they are hungry, but otherwise carrying them 'away to the mountain's brow' as food for their young. Sometimes the sea-gull will try the same manœuvre, though of course on a very limited scale. Upon that, the ever-watchful eagle, uttering a ferocious shriek, darts instantly after him in pursuit. But even before the eagle can reach him, the terrified gull has dropped his little fish, which his pursuer catches again before it touches the water. There are here two species of eagles, the common grey and the bald or white-headed. The latter, known to science as the *haliaëtus leucocephalus*, may be seen in every part of these Islands, and is the one of all the genus which has made itself the most famous, or rather infamous, by leading a life of robbery. It was this propensity which made Franklin enter his strong protest against adopting the white-headed eagle as the type of the nationality of the United States, urging, as his reason for objecting, that it was 'a bird of bad moral character, who did not get his living honestly.' "

I often listened to animals crying wildly, particularly at night, on the tops of the hills. To my ear the cry resembled that of the mountain goat (*aplocerus montanus*), so plentiful on the mainland of British Columbia. It was never possible to me to get near enough to see. But I consider it probable that they are mountain goats, as Point Rose, the north-easternmost promontory of Graham Island, is so near some other islands lying close in upon the American continent as to afford an easy refuge to the goats, in case of their being pursued by their relentless enemies the wolves.

CHAPTER VIII.

ABOUT a week after my arrival at Skincuttle, leaving
three of the men to construct a shed or covering
over the copper-shaft, and three others to go on sinking the shaft itself, I proceeded up the east coast in
a canoe I had bought from the Indians, taking with
me my two remaining men, who, with the Chiefs
Klue and Skid-a-ga-tees, and two sons of the latter,
made seven persons in all.

We landed on an islet, and, while my men looked
to the provisions and cooking, I took a careful survey
and searched for minerals, finding several veins of
iron pyrites, traces of coal in the form of lignite,
and lastly, though not least, an extensively defined
vein of silver, as I thought, on the strength of which
I ventured to name our landing-place Silver Island.
There was no means of testing this on the spot.

Seriously believing it to be silver, however, I had as much taken down to the canoe as it could safely carry, and, after a frugal picnic in high spirits on the rocks, ordered a speedy paddle back to Skincuttle. Imagine my disgust, on applying a test, to discover that, though a rare vein, it was only a vein of metallic arsenide.

This sudden return to head-quarters so completely disarranged my previous plans, that I now decided upon a lengthy expedition instead of a short one.

I gave orders for storing the canoe with a month's provisions; and meantime I thought to try whether Rock Island was as barren of sport as of grass. To my surprise I beat up a large flock in no time, and blazing right into them, killed thirty-four brace in one single shot. These were large birds, and of the species known on Vancouver as Wilson's snipe (*gallinago Wilsonii*). It was pleasant to feel I could enjoy a day's sport, any time, at a moment's notice, whenever the fancy took me.

By this time I had become good friends with several of the Indian chiefs, a friendly word spoken in my behalf by Kitguen, or Klue,* having smoothed

---

* I must here explain that Kitguen, my first and fast friend among the Queen Charlotte Islanders, and Chief Klue, are one and the same

the way very considerably.   It is a mistake to suppose that frankness and plain-spokenness have not their due effect on savages, as well as on ordinary mortals. The savage, no doubt, generally entertains a lurking suspicion of your motives; but if he does afterwards turn upon you—unless of course a greed for gain should prompt his treachery—it will always prove to be that he considers you are not acting up to your professions.

One bright morning, therefore, we started in my canoe for Chief Klue's settlement, at a place which the Indians called Laskeek, on the eastern coast.   I took two others of my men with me.   The chief was accompanied by two of his Siwash or petty chiefs, who rejoiced respectively in the style and title of Shilly-gutts and Laugh-goon-us.

A fair wind gracing our expedition we crowded on every stitch of canvas we could muster, and all of us paddling lustily together, the canoe reached Laskeek Harbour in about twelve hours.   Now mine had been the only canoe down at Skincuttle, and, I need scarce add, the electric telegraph is still an

___

person. Kitguen was his former name, and is still his familiar name; but on succeeding to the Head Chieftainship of Laskeek, his own section of the Hydah tribe, by the death of his elder brother in a fight, he assumed for public use the title his brother had held before him.

institution of the future for Queen Charlotte Islands. And yet, although my visit to Klue's settlement had not been arranged till the previous day, by some incomprehensible means peculiarly Indian, accurate news of my intention to come had preceded us to Laskeek. In consequence, there was a general turn-out, even to the papoose in arms, to see me land.

The sun not having set as yet, I was enabled to take a comprehensive survey of my expectant hosts, as far as concerned their external presentment. There was not a clean face to be seen amongst them, nor a decent pair of hands. The faces and hands of men, women, and children, were so thickly beslimed and befouled with the blackest of black paint, that no one feature could be discerned in its natural form. Hardly did I recognise human beings in the creatures who crowded around me on the strand. Klue promised, however, that they should all be washed the next morning, which was certainly considerate of him, as, by putting on a beautiful black polish, the poor things had intended to pay me the highest mark of respect. It is their full-dress uniform, in fact.

The harbour of Laskeek is situated in lat. 52° 50′ N., long. 131° 28′ W.

The morning after my arrival, the Klue chiefs, high

and petty, taking advantage of my presence at Las-keek, held an extra-parliamentary session. They had heard that an English gunboat or two might shortly be expected from Esquimalt, and they requested me to give them—the chiefs assembled in Council—a reference or protection note. I presented my new allies with the following certificate, first making a copy of it for the amusement of friends in England:—

" This is to certify that the undermentioned Chiefs are good men, and well disposed towards the whites. At least *they say so ;* and you must take their word for what it is worth. I encamped amongst them last night while prospecting for minerals in this section, and found them honest during my short visit.

" F. POOLE,

" Engineer to the Queen Charlotte Mining Company.

" Chiefs.

Gundless.	Skish-gills.	Hotten.
Tong-law.	Stash.	King-a-Kona.
Ich-gum.	Sklash-Hagan.	Hy-ass.
Link-is-tus.	Ki-ush.	Hous-te.
Skutch-a.	Naw-way.	Got-quance.
Ga-lla.	Kiss-a-gura (Sen.)	Kad-da-ga-cow.
Skid-a-ga-tees.	Lamma.	Co-a-delly.
Sah-qua.	Kiss-a-gura (Jun.)	Skilte-killong."

In the afternoon of the same day, Klue invited me to go with him to the home of the Skiddan Indians, a tribe with whom he was on friendly terms, and who also dwelt on the sea-shore, but further up the coast. Klue's people are a branch or section of the Hydah tribe, all the various chiefs of which seemed to consider themselves as a sort of vassals to the great chief of the Skiddan tribe. How this reconciled itself with Klue's claim to the Head Chieftainship of the whole islands, I never could quite make out.

As I afterwards took down my adventures and impressions during this by-expedition with Klue, I shall here transcribe them literally:—

"The high and mighty chief Skiddan sat in state, that is, at Skiddan Harbour, somewhat to the northward of Laskeek. He did not rise when I entered, but continued sitting on a rough kind of platform, with his legs crossed like a tailor's. I was invited to stand on his right, however, whilst my cook, who did duty as my aide-de-camp and private secretary, had a place assigned him to the left. The whole of the tribe then squatted down, also cross-legged, on some low benches or logs.

"Skiddan himself delivered a grand speech, the

general purport of which I gathered to be an advice and solemn injunction to his people to afford me every protection and assistance. They listened attentively, now and then interrupting Skiddan's harangue with a queer uplifting of arms and murmurs of approbation, or with a sudden outburst of complimentary grunts directed at me. As soon as the chief had ended, I took up the thread of the proceedings, by assuring, the tribe through Klue, of my 'sentiments of the highest consideration,' meaning under the circumstances not much more than a Frenchman means when he sticks those absurd words at the bottom of a letter.

"The first part of the ceremony being over, I offered a pipeful of tobacco to each of the petty chiefs.

" This is a present which they always expect from a stranger. But greatly as the gift of tobacco pleases an Indian, it does not approximate in his eyes to the value of 'a testimonial,' or 'a paper,' as they term it. Fortunate it is that this way to their good graces comes cheap; for they set quite as great a value on an old invoice or a receipt as upon a genuine certificate. So long as the paper contains writing, it matters nothing what the writing is. I have already had abundant proof of it. For on several occasions Indians have brought me bundles of waste paper, in the firm belief that they were, every one, so many bonâ-fide references. They had received these as testimonials of good behaviour, or more probably begged them from some merchant or other at Victoria. Of course it was not only lawful but well to leave those Indians in the delusion that their 'papers' were *hyass-closh*, that is, very good. I saw no reason for undeceiving even the great Skiddan. Give the Indians a small piece of tobacco, or a few fishing-hooks, and they are not merely satisfied, but they will make large returns in fish or game, and sometimes in really valuable fur-skins. After all, the true valuation of these things is relative, according to the want and mind of the purchaser. Lately I bought two fine skins of the black bear for twenty-five cents, or one shilling apiece. In Europe they would certainly fetch 12*l.* each. They are a drug in the home-market of the North Pacific Indian.

" Having, upon urgent request, distributed a few bits of paper, the Skiddan made me a formal present of a minz or mink skin, together with a couple of uncommon duck-footed birds, whilst from one of the Indian women I received a very singular kind of crab (*echinocerus cibarius*), which I believe is only found on the coasts of the North Pacific, and rarely even there.

"The building in which I was thus glorified consisted of very large frame-house. Its shape was nearly a square, its dimensions being some fifty feet by fifty, quite ten feet of which were dug out of the earth, so as to make the real height from the ground forty feet. It had been substantially constructed, and it readily accommodated the seven hundred Indians who met me under that roof.

"However, my glorification did not in the least deceive me. That a White should have been so received there, was solely referable to the report of the gunboats coming up. Skiddan has the character of being the most selfish and bloodthirsty savage on the coast. He has always been treated better than any of the other chiefs by the English government, and yet he is ever giving us trouble.

"The sun was fast sinking as at last we pushed off in Klue's canoe. On looking over our effects, I was glad to find that only a few tin spoons had been stolen. But I was still more pleased to think that every stroke of our paddles took us further from

Skiddan's harbour; for my friends at Victoria had well warned me never to trust my skin to him after dark.

"At 10 P.M. we paddled into Cum-she-was Harbour, a place about fifteen miles more to the north, and there we encamped for the night. The next morning the Cum-she-was Indians held a meeting of their tribe. They received me in a "great house" not unlike that of the Skiddans, and with a ceremonial which almost exactly repeated the scene of the day before, including however a dash more of sincerity. What astonished me was to see the whole of the walls inside their building hung with linen, fine, white, and clean. This formed a very unexpected feature in my reception. I should have been sorely puzzled to account for it, had not Klue whispered to me that, many years ago, a large trading vessel of some sort put into Cum-she-was, the crew of which were murdered and its stores pillaged. The linen was part of the pillage—not a doubt about it.

"I saw nothing of interest to detain me among the Cum-she-was; and considering that I had gone far enough north for this one trip, I turned the canoe's head towards Laskeek, just calling on our way at Skiddan Harbour, and scattering there a few more presents, in the shape of pins, needles, and shirt-buttons.

" We did not get back to Laskeek till 11 P.M., and, as it was too late to pitch my tent according to custom, I accepted Klue's invitation to sleep at his patrimonial mansion.

" I have some reason to remember my first night under the roof of Chief Klue.

" His house was a largish one, built in the usual Indian way, of wood laid horizontally in light logs, and slightly elevated above the ground upon a platform. Despite the sheen of the moon, I looked in vain for the entrance, and was beginning to think there must be some Indian dodge in its concealment, with a view probably to providing against sudden attacks, when a Klootchman young lady came tripping along to my assistance. Approaching a big hole, three feet in circumference, and three feet from the platform's base in the front of the house, she, very unceremoniously, thrust first one leg through, evidently without touching the bottom on the other side, secondly her head and arms, and finally, by means of a dexterous jerk, dragged the rest of her body after her. This was the door, then, through which the inmates, both male and female, had to scramble whenever they felt disposed to retire to the domestic hearth. The manœuvres required to accomplish the feat in question were assuredly anything but graceful, especially for a lady: and yet the ladies performed it in the most satisfactory manner, without ever doubling up in a heap on the floor inside. Perforce, I tried the same method myself, and, though unsuccessful at the first attempt, I did succeed at the second, greatly to the delight of the pretty Klootchman, who turned out to be Klue's daughter-in-law, and my chambermaid for that night.

" Inside the house these was little to be seen, either by day or by night, owing chiefly to the smouldering fire, which, having no outlet, filled the one large room with its smoke. There were no windows, the Indians despising such a convenience. The only rays of light, from sun or moon, came through the big hole in the wall, *alias* the door. But on my getting in, being conducted to the central fire, I found cedar-bark mats spread over the hard ground, and upon these we all lay down together, with our feet firewards, and with our heads outwards, like the spokes of a wheel. No little nerve was requisite, I must acknowledge, to make up one's mind to sleep in such an atmosphere; but, as they would have been terribly offended had I refused, I made a virtue of necessity, and took to it kindly.

" Other horrors besides the atmosphere now awaited me, for I was assigned the place of honour in the family-couch, namely, under the same blanketing with the chief and his daughter, a very interesting young girl, and to lie between them.

" Having been paddling away all day, as hard as any Indian, I naturally felt anxious to restore my strength with sound refreshing sleep. Some indefinable sensation, however, seemed to be keeping me awake. I tossed about nearly all night, not much to the comfort of my bedfellows, I should fancy. As the small hours of the morning advanced, I found my head inconveniently knocking against an upright pole. Surely a most extraordinary position for a pole, since it undoubtedly served no architectural or ornamental purpose. By degrees this pole gained complete possession of my thoughts, and the more I went on thinking, the more persuaded did I become that it had something hideous connected with it. An impulse then seized me to get up and examine it; but, as that would have looked like a betrayal of fear—a consummation always to be avoided in the presence of savages—I lay still. Presently, an accidental kick from one of the Indians caused the fire to flare. The flare lasted only two or three seconds, yet quite long enough to reveal to my horrified senses at least a hundred scalps fastened round the top of the pole, right above me. Fancy my feelings! Despite Klue's professed friendship, and the place of honour I was occupying in the family couch, I instinctively put my hand to my own poll, and was not without a throb of thankfulness to find it so far safe. Need it be added that I made my escape as soon as I could prudently do so?

" The excuse I gave for such early rising was my anxiety to get the benefit of a sea-bath, in which I and my two men forthwith indulged, our clothes being meanwhile hung up to air on a tree, to the infinite diversion of a crowd of spectators.

" But nothing appeared to tickle the fancy of the Indians so much as our swimming. It supplied the crowd with a perfect fund of amusement, and was, I believe, wholly new to them. I have never seen any of the North Pacific Indians swim, unless previously taught by me. In this they differ from all other coloured races, who are mostly good swimmers. And yet the Queen Charlotte Indians of every tribe live continually on the water."

Having prospected Laskeek Harbour, without obtaining anything out of it to repay me for the trouble, I returned in another day or two to Skincuttle, Klue and my other companions coming back also.

CHAPTER IX.

COPPER—NEW SHAFT—ATTACK BY INDIANS—RUSHING IN AMONGST THEM—
THE BONE OF CONTENTION—CHIEF SKID-A-GA-TEES—THE "KECKWALLY
TYHEE"—SKID-A-GA-TEES DRAWS OFF—THE CUM-SHE-WAS—A CRISIS—
REMOVAL TO BURNABY ISLAND—THE RAFT.

I NOW spent a considerable time in superintending
the working of our copper-shaft at Skincuttle, and in
erecting a comfortable log-house to serve as our habitation.

About the middle of October I had my first taste
of annoyance from the Indians.

One day I stood leaning against the walls of our
wild home, trying to converse with Klue in his own
language, when somebody near us raised a cry of
surprise. Instantly numberless eyes were directed
towards the offing of our little bay, and, on looking
myself, I observed several canoes full of strange
Indians, who soon after landed. What on earth did
they want? I said to Klue, who answered at once,
that, whatever the new-comers might pretend, they

were his mortal enemies, and that their real object certainly was to find out whether we explorers could not be plundered.

Sure enough, though they began by affecting an anxiety to trade with us, it was evident, from their not having brought down any article of traffic, that they had very different intentions. If I had once allowed them to commence trading, they would have expected to enter the log-house for that purpose. I therefore firmly resisted their specious overtures, and, in spite of repeated entreaties from them during the afternoon, continued obdurate to every blandishment, simply ordering my men to look well to our fire-arms.

The following morning our suspicions were confirmed by the arrival of additional canoes-full. Upon which Klue, thinking it was getting too hot for us, suddenly vanished off in one of those odd flights so common in Indian life, but so incomprehensible, as regards the method of it, to civilized minds.

Our invaders quickly divined that he had gone to collect reinforcements amongst his tribe. At the same time strong signs showed themselves of an approaching change in the weather, very dangerous to the safety of the canoe-flotilla. Impelled by either of these causes, or perhaps by both, the hostile Indians unconsciously agreed with Falstaff that " the better part of valour is discretion;" for hardly had Klue disappeared ere they likewise took their departure.

The drama was not half over, however. I extract from my Diary the record I made of the next scene, thus :—

" I set my men, and two of Klue's Indians, who had just come (the day after the invasion) to work at chopping wood, in order to lay in a stock for the winter. While they were so employed, I stepped into my canoe and paddled over towards Prevost Island.

" I intended to take a south-westerly course, in the direction of Cape St. James, and then return by N.N.W. to Skincuttle Island. I started early in the forenoon: but the distance being greater than anticipated, it was late in the afternoon before my one companion and myself reached the point proposed. Some miles to the south-west of Skincuttle I discovered a magnificent harbour, which I named Harriet Harbour, but had no time then to enter and prospect it.

AN INDIAN RAID.

" As we steered homeward along the other islets, what was my dismay to see our own little harbour absolutely crammed full of canoes? Each canoe had in it a large crew of Indians, bedaubed from head to foot with war-paint, and otherwise martially arrayed: whilst the clearance round our log-house was crowded with a herd of their fellow-savages, yelling and dancing lustily.

" My companion and I lifted our paddles an instant, to contemplate the rather appalling sight; and not perceiving any of my other men about, I came to the conclusion that they had been every one murdered, and that the Indians were now awaiting our advent to serve us in the same manner. They had possession of the islet as clear as noonday. The impossibility of our escape seemed equally certain. I consequently resolved to put a bold front on the matter, and venture into the midst of them.

" Saying a few inspiriting words to the man with me, and especially cautioning him not to betray the least sign of fear, I headed direct for the landing, and, dipping our paddles deep into the water, in another moment we were ashore, and in amongst our enemies, who had swarmed down to the beach for the purpose of intimidation. Finding I was not to be browbeaten, and seeing my revolvers ready in my hands, they made no resistance, while I dashed through them right to the log-house. It was completely in their possession, but, thank goodness, all my men were safe. I had arrived just in the nick of time to prevent a massacre. This measure, no doubt, they had decided on carrying out; but knowing full well that, before they could accomplish it, many of them would 'bite the dust,' they evidently lacked the courage to begin.

" The fact was, unseen eyes had watched me out to sea, whence the cowardly villains, concluding that my outing would last as long as the previous one, had judged the time to be favourable for a renewed descent upon Skincuttle. My unexpected return caused the hostilities to be suspended, and straight-way a great *wah-wah* (talkee) took place between the leading Indians and myself.

" A bone of contention, not wholly unreasonable, lay at the bottom of all this trouble. Shortly after our first landing in August, the brother-in-law of Ninstence, chief of a tribe inhabiting the southern-most portions of Moresby Island, had declared himself the proprietor of the land we were then settling on, and, to keep friendly with the savage, we had paid him down fifty 'two-and-a-half point'* blankets.

"His chieftain-relative, however, having violently appropriated the blankets to his own use, the rest of the head-chiefs all over Queen Charlotte Islands, especially Skiddan and Skid-a-ga-tees, were seized with a fit of jealousy. 'Why should Ninstence have fifty bran-new blankets, and his brother chiefs have none?' was the practical form which the question now assumed. There seemed to be only two ways of solving it. They might attack Ninstence, but then he was strong, whilst even a victory over him would not necessarily give each of the rival chiefs any very notable share in the fifty blankets. Or, we whites might be distrained for another fifty. This latter plan commending itself to the statesman-like views of Chief Skid-a-ga-tees, the treacherous wretch, whom I had taken with me in my coast expedition, and whom I had included in my good-conduct certificate, determined to make a raid upon us. His tribe being the most numerous, combative, and powerful of all the tribes in the

---

* The staple trade of the Hudson's Bay Company with the North Pacific Indians was in blanketing. The size and quality of each blanket used to be marked on it by means of short lines or "points" and "half-points," the meaning of which the Indians had learnt perfectly to understand.

islands, there could be little difficulty in executing the plan, he thought. So the other Indians of the day before having failed in their trading stratagem, down had come Skid-a-ga-tees with his whole body of warriors, during my absence, and had impudently demanded fifty more blankets. In fact we, as the supposed weaker party, although entirely unoffending, were to suffer for the intertribal jealousies of the chiefs. A truly Indian mode of settling the difficulty, and yet one not altogether without its counterpart amongst natives professedly civilized. My people very wisely and courageously refused to deliver up the blankets, whereupon Skid-a-ga-tees, who was not accustomed to be thwarted, tried to bully them, and threatened to burn down our log-house, carry off all our stores, and slaughter my companions to the last man.

" I have little doubt he would have done it, but for my turning up in time to assert my authority and use my influence.

" The abject submission of an Indian to his own chief is notorious and proverbial. It may not, however, be so well known that they extend the same respect to those whom they see placed in analogous positions amongst foreigners, especially if these are English. As I, then, am the acknowledged chief of our little party, the Queen Charlotte Indians usually treat me with marked deference, always referring to my chieftainship for justice in any quarrel which may arise between my workmen and themselves—that is, so long as we do not give them any grievous cause of offence; for in such a case I myself should be the first attacked.

" In this particular instance I imagine that, if the men had been massacred, I should have been seized and detained in confinement as a prisoner of war.

" From the first a great deal too much familiarity has unfortunately prevailed at Skincuttle. Seeing how I make friends with the chiefs, my men think they cannot do better than be ' hail-fellow-well-met' with the other natives. It is hard persuading them that I have judicious reasons, which their private position does not suggest. The circumstances are just of the kind to nullify argument, and to invite temptation, notwithstanding the many warnings we have had. For example, the Indians have hung about our log-house so perpetually and continuously, that of late it has often been close on daybreak before we could get rid of them, without wounding their touchy natures. It was soon coming to such a pass that we might as well have set up a regular joint-stock establishment, if one of my men, an eccentric Californian, had not conceived the brilliant idea of mixing red pepper with newly-ground coffee, and dropping the mixture on to the red-hot stove. The effect was instantaneous. They thought it must be the *Keckwally Tyhee* (Chief of the Deep) coming up out of the fire. I caused this to be repeated for several nights at eight o'clock sharp, and it was highly amusing to see them watch the clock till the hand pointed nearly to the hour, and then make a rush together out of the door, which we quietly locked inside, and afterwards scrambled up in peace to our sleeping bunks. My men, however, required a more forcible lesson than being merely bored. I fancy they have now received it.

" Skid-a-ga-tees's raid met with no more success than the strategic tactics of his predecessors. I assured him that I should willingly have made him a present of some blankets if he had asked me for them civilly, but that the claim he asserted was pre-posterous. I had honestly paid the proprietor of the soil, and should pay nobody else. The *wah-wah* ended, therefore, in my resolutely declining to have anything to do with him till he desisted from his threats and drew off his warriors. I forthwith ordered the Indians out of our log-house, and motioning them to keep beyond the clearance-ground, if they did not want to be shot, I retired to prepare for defence in the event of things still coming to the worst.

"Of course Skid-a-ga-tees was unconvincible. We had a restless night consequently, taking it turn-about to walk round the house, lest the Indians should attempt to set fire to it. In one of my turns as watchman, I spied a Cape St. James Indian in the very act of drawing his revolver, with his pair of gleaming eyes fixed upon me. I had previously suspected the fellow, having observed him skulking for some time among the trees. On my complaining to his chief, who happened to be near at hand on the island, I had been coolly told that he was a little 'foolish.' Wise or foolish, he had killed a white down at Victoria. As, then, such a man could not be left at large armed, I just went and put a stopper on his villany by taking his revolver from him, and punching him well in the ribs.

"Thus our position was one of no small danger. But we had counted on these emergencies in coming; and, after all, they were not really greater than what commonly fall to the lot of the pioneers of civilization.

" The next day we found that Skid-a-ga-tees, though he would not leave, had drawn off most of his fighting men. This was to some extent a triumph. In the afternoon, while calculating our chances, we had the pleasure to see two huge canoes, choke-full of Indians of the Cum-she-was tribe, paddle swiftly into the bay. Union Jacks were flying at the bows of each canoe, in order to intimate to us the approach of our friends. The Cum-she-was had heard that the Skid-a-ga-tees had come down to massacre us. So they made all haste to our assistance. And right welcome it proved.

" The new arrivals were decked out in tip-top war style: that is to say, both males and females — a goodly number of the latter being in the company to do the screeching business—had their bodies painted a shiny black, and their hair thoroughly greased and well sprinkled over with the fine breast-feathers of the goose.

" However, no attack on the Skid-a-ga-tees was intended. The Cum-she-was, seeing how matters stood with us, simply wished to demonstrate what they could and would do in case of need. So they landed, and treated me to a war serenade, females as well as males dancing frantically to wild music. I made them a few presents, after which they paddled off again, round Burnaby Head to Silver Island, to meet their chief, for a distribution of the blankets and tobacco which had been recently sent him from one of the old Hudson's Bay Forts, in barter for furs.

" Naturally enough this interchange of compliments did not by any means please our enemies, the Skid-a-ga-tees; and the following day, some of their warriors having returned, they were about to give us unmistakeable proof of their vexation, when suddenly Cum-she-was himself, accompanied by a host of his people, came paddling like mad round the headland. Fierce were the looks of Skid-a-ga-tees when he beheld me feasting Cum-she-was and his pretty papoose (daughter) upon biscuits, slap-jacks (pancakes), and sweet molasses. 'This is coming it rather strong,' seemed to be his reflection, if not in these identical terms, at least in their Indian synonyms. It was our crisis with Skid-a-ga-tees. Finding the bullying and robbery speculation not to answer, or possibly remembering that, but for his treacherous misconduct, he too would have been included in the feast, he very prudently took time to consider his position, the consequence being a gradual relapse on both sides into our former amicable relations.

"But I must digress a moment to cull from my Diary another incident, which also well-nigh brought all my explorations to a premature end.

"Fortified by the presence of the Cum-she-was, I resumed work as before. Crossing over to Burnaby Island, I began to trace up the course of the main copper-lode, and to my surprise found it outcropping extensively and well defined. Upon the strength of this, and likewise for the sake of convenience and economy, the 'lay' of the land rendering Burnaby Island much more approachable than Skincuttle, I resolved to choose Burnaby as the site of our main shaft, chief works, and head residence. The men, then, having been transferred from one islet to the other, were soon engaged in building a new and larger log-house, workshops, and adjuncts. But the transfer of our provisions, implements, and the rest, had still to be effected. This job, with merely what help my cook, a little Frenchman, could afford me, I took entirely on myself. So, paddling together across to Skincuttle, we first of all collected timber sufficient to construct a raft, upon which we then piled up everything belonging to us. Attaching the raft by a rope to our canoe, we essayed to recross the strait. Now I know from experience that rafting in the rapids of the river St. Lawrence, though often attended with danger to the raft, is rarely dangerous to the raftsman, who, in the event of his raft going to pieces, will generally jump on to a single spar and land himself safe on either shore. It becomes a totally different affair, however, in a strait closely communicating with the ocean, whither a strong current threatens every instant to carry you out, whilst only one shore protects you, and broken islets on the other serve but to intensify the strength of the current. Such was the fix in which the cook and myself found ourselves. Never shall I forget that fearful day's work. First I tried a series of indeterminate noises, hoping to be heard above the wind on Burnaby Island. Then, I am sorry to say, I waxed wroth and swore. Our situation not improving, I shouted through my hands with all my might. But again, as truth obliges me to record, I indulged worse than ever in oaths and curses, adding a slight dash of blasphemy. All was vain and vexatious. Meanwhile, both the paddling and the steering devolved upon me alone, the French-man showing hardly any strength, and less snese.

In the middle of the whole thing, what should we see on Burnaby but our companions gathered together in an agony of despair, down by the water side? And well might they be agonized, for they had no canoe to aid us, and on the raft was every atom of our provisions. Away we went, drifting with the current. One solitary chance remained, namely, to try by a supreme effort to gain Rock Island, the ledge of rocks already mentioned, lying nearly midway between Skincuttle and Burnaby, and covered over at high tide. Fortunately, it was now low tide. Wherefore, summoning our last energies to the task, we paddled towards the ledge, nervously and deftly, till, after a prolonged struggle, I was enabled to scramble on to the rocks, and to hold the raft, whilst my Frenchman got into our light canoe and made the best of his way to Burnaby, in order to bring off some men to my relief. It so chanced that all the Indians on Burnaby Island had gone in the morning on a predatory excursion; otherwise our companions would have borrowed one of their canoes, and have fetched us sooner. Under the circumstances, thankful indeed were we to reach our destination at length, though it had cost us seven hours of terrible mental anguish, and of the severest bodily exertion that I ever went through in my life, or that probably any other human being ever encountered either."

This, however, completed our transfer to a locality which promised to be much more effective as a basis of operations, and also a more permanent home.

CHAPTER X.

I THINK it was the very day after our sea adventure,
that the daughter of Skid-a-ga-tees and my friend on
board the *Rebecca*, walked up to where we were all
working at the new log-house, and reported that
her papa had built his *ranche* (house) within a mile
of ours, and had now come to reside there.

A pleasant neighbour, in good sooth.

The pride of the Skid-a-ga-tees tribe was too great
to endure self-humiliation. But the present announcement signified that their chief wished to make friends.
" He would have sent men to help in the building,"
said the dusky young lady, magniloquently, " if it
had not been for a promontory which so effectually
separated our encampment from his as to have kept
him, till just then, in a state of utter ignorance as
to our transmigration to Burnaby Island."

At this my Californian workman developed an extraordinary capacity for winking, the French cookie tittered and giggled himself into convulsions, whilst a sarcastic Englishman of our party suggested that the murderous old chief might turn out to be sweetly innocent after all. To me the story certainly sounded "very like a whale:" but I nevertheless considered the more prudent course would be to keep my own counsel from the wily Miss Skid-a-ga-tees. "It was the chief's intention," she officially declared, "to pay me a visit the same evening;" and meantime, in token of friendliness, she "begged leave to caution us against a bear which had been seen sniffing about the island."

Immediately I took my Enfield rifle, and sallied forth in search of the animal. I remember it occurred to me that there was positively little choice between the society of human savages and the proximity of wild beasts. If anything, the latter are preferable: for a bear at least does not pretend to be your friend whilst in reality your foe.

As I could not come upon this individual wild beast, I concluded that his bearship had reconsidered his project of hunting without a licence, and had probably taken himself off to one of the surrounding islets. But noticing a superannuated bear-track, I followed it up and discovered an Indian trap for bears, of such ingenious contrivance that I stopped and sketched it. In another respect, too, my bear-chase was not time wasted, inasmuch as it led me to stumble upon a new vein of copper, which I carefully marked and mapped out. My rifle being still loaded, I emptied it on the way back, and brought down a splendid specimen of the native crow (*corvus caurinus*), called *klail-kula-kulla* by the Indians. The Queen Charlotte Indians hold views, on the subject of their aboriginal ancestry, decidedly in advance of the Darwinian theory; for their descent from the crows is quite gravely affirmed and steadfastly maintained. Hence they never will kill one, and are always annoyed, not to say angry, should we whites, driven to desperation by the crow-nests on every side of us, attempt to destroy them. This idea likewise accounts for the coats of black paint with which young and old in all those tribes constantly besmear themselves. The crow-like colour affectionately reminds the Indians of their reputed forefathers, and thus preserves the national tradition. Mr. Darwin and his disciples are scarcely so consistent or devotional.

I found my men collected round the log-house door, in a state of excitement. Skid-a-ga-tees, having duly arrived to pay me the promised visit of reconciliation, had seated himself very independently on one of the lower bunks. Our cook had been foolish enough to resent this as a liberty, and had told my visitor somewhat sharply to stand aside. Upon which the latter, instead of obeying, had mounted on to the bunk and begun an indignant *wah-wah.* The cook had then lost his temper, pulled the chief down, and like a madman kicked him in the chest. But the chief had struck back at his antagonist so cleverly with a long knife, that, but for a prompt parry from the Californian, the blow must have proved fatal to the Frenchman. However, the wrath of old Skid-a-ga-tees had now been fairly aroused. And yet to have contended against those overwhelming odds would have exposed him to certain defeat. He had therefore darted out of the house and away to his camp, in order to raise his whole tribe and avenge the insult.

Such was the agreeable prospect which greeted me on my return from my abortive bear-hunt. I saw at a glance, that we had not a moment to lose. Our sole hope lay in his accepting the apology which, as his clear right, I at once resolved to make him. But the procedure was not so easy, considering my total ignorance of his peculiar dialect. When then I went over alone to his camp, I hardly dare to think what might have befallen me if Miss Skid-a-ga-tees had not compassionately undertaken to interpret.

As I expected, the old chief was in a towering passion, and, the instant he caught sight of me entering his log-house, he brandished the same long knife in my face, and urged his fellows to go down to our camp and slaughter us, one and all. So the daughter told me. I waited in patience until he had calmed sufficiently to listen to my explanation. But " why could I not interfere, now at least?" he argued. I replied that, even " if my man had killed him, I was powerless to punish the criminal myself, such matters, according to the laws of the whites, being dealt with only at Victoria." Hearing that, he laughed contemptuously, and said he could not understand it. No doubt it did seem unaccountable to him that I, although a chief amongst my men, should not possess the power of life and death over them. But ultimately, on my pledging my word to send the cook back to Victoria in the first provision-vessel that came to us, and have him there adequately punished, he vouchsafed to be mollified.

I then offered a propitiatory sacrifice in the likeness of a plug of tobacco, whereupon the redoubtable Skid-a-ga-tees and I once more vowed eternal friendship; and in testimony thereof he sent me down next day a large halibut weighing over a hundred pounds.

My narrative has now reached a point when summarizing becomes a necessity. We were on the verge of Winter. But two Winters on Queen Charlotte Islands being before me, I shall only say of this one, that the Indians ceased for the present to molest us, and that, having partly received from Victoria and partly laid in ourselves a fair stock of provisions, we kept to work with a will at the copper-shaft which we had sunk near our log-house on Burnaby Island.

If it had not been for the hardworking spirit of my men, winter-time would have hung with awful heaviness upon our hands. Occasionally we varied the week's labour by means of a day's shooting, or, when the snow covered the ground, by an attempt at a bear-hunt, but never, in either case, with any noteworthy success. We had no greater alleviation than to sit together, after the burden of the day was over, round the log-house fire, whilst one man cleaned our guns and revolvers, another sharpened our tools, a third washed our clothes, a fourth set our little pantry to rights, and each took his turn in spinning yarns of his adventures and hair-breadth escapes.

One man, who had before been my travelling-companion through Canada, was a host in himself, as regards this kind of story-telling. Many an hour of a darksome evening did he thus beguile for us. Some of his stories equalled those of the immortal Baron Münchhausen. With a view of showing how we pioneers contrived to get through the long Winter hours, when we could do no outdoor work, I shall here give a sample or two of tales he used to tell around our blazing camp-fire:—

"When I was working at getting out timber, near Hudson's Bay," he began, one evening, "I thought, having an idle day, that I would go to a small lake about two miles distant, and have a shot at some ducks. I took my rifle and a few bullets, for I never use small shot, and down I crept as quietly as a mouse, till I got within fifty yards of the bank. Seeing several hundred ducks on the opposite side, I raised my rifle to my shoulder, but found I could not shape the range enough in line to knock

off the heads of more than five or six. I therefore
'concluded' to try a favourite plan of mine, which
would enable me to bag perhaps half the whole
number. So back I went to the shanty, to leave my
rifle, and to fetch my bag-net. In a few moments I
had fastened the net round my waist, and was swimming across the lake to where the ducks were. Coming
sufficiently near, I dived; but, instead of rising again
to the surface, I dodged about a bit under water. Presently, what should I see, just overhead, but a pair
of yellow legs? I pulled the legs down and stowed
their owner comfortably away in my net. Finding I
was in the right place, I swam about here and there,
in the same manner, till I had filled the net with the
owners of at least a dozen pair of yellow legs.
Then I thought I would make for the surface. But,
unfortunately, on my getting to the top of the water,
the net turned out to be only half full, which gave
the ducks plenty of room to spread their wings and
fly up into the air. This I had not calculated on;
and when I had got a mile air-high, it struck me
very forcibly that I was rather out of my latitude.
So I drew my jack-knife across the net, and away
flew the ducks, whilst I tumbled into the lake again,
though somewhat more swiftly than I had mounted

up. Such indeed was the velocity with which I now descended, that I went slap down to the bottom of the lake, a mile deep in that particular spot, and sank to my chin in a bed of tough clay, where I stuck hard and fast, in spite of most desperate efforts to regain my liberty."

"Snakes and alligators!" burst in our Californian, " I guess that's not trew, or yer wouldn't be here to tell the tale."

" Let me finish," rejoined my imperturbable Canadian friend. " The fact was," he continued, " that, not relishing my position, I at last went back to the shanty, brought down a shovel, and dug myself out."

Roars of laughter followed, after which he of California said the Canadian's story " flogged creation, that it did." There could be little doubt about it.

On another occasion, we were treated to this :—

" I was once 'trapping' in the Red River Settlement," said my Canadian, " when it occurred to me that I might as well improve the occasion by trapping eels also, and upon a patent principle of my own invention. I had a square box made, which I divided into two compartments. These I caused to communicate one with the other by metal tubes, each a size smaller than the average eel, the tubes, too, having sharpened edges. The box was open at one end, and of such a measurement that it exactly fitted into one of those 'shuts' which carry off the surplus waters where the lakes are dammed up. Well, this is the way it acted. The eels would come through the 'shuts,' and into the first compartment, and, perceiving the tube-holes, would dart through them into the second, leaving their skins behind. Large quantities of valuable eel-skins were thus placed at my disposal every week. But when the season was over, I left my box still there; and returning next year, I found the first compartment full of beautiful skins, and the second full of eels, which had passed through the tubes, but each eel with a new skin. It was a profitable investment, was my patent box, I do assure you."

"Darn my skroikes!" exclaimed our Californian, thumping the bench with his fist, whilst a gurgle of approval passed round the convivial circle. Not being conversant with the Californian language, I am unable to explain in what the process of *darning one's skroikes* precisely consists. But it may be taken to denote some high degree of eulogium, for immediately two other Americans vociferated for an extra glass of grog to toast the Canadian, in which sentiment I heartily concurred.

I revert to my Diary:—

"*March* 18*th*, 1863.—A few mosquitoes have put in an appearance. Hence we know to a certainty that summer is nigh. These islands are freer than most woody countries from the mosquito-plague, the reason being the comparative absence of swampy soil. Swamps, combined with heat, not only nourish mosquitoes, but develop them daily into life from decomposed vegetation."

"20*th*.—This morning I paid a visit to old Skid-a-ga-tees. By great care I have managed to keep friends with him all the Winter through. The principal object of my visit to-day was to see a sick Indian, who lay dangerously ill with an ulcerated throat. I gave the man doses of ice, to use as a gargle, and made him stick to it for six hours. Before I left last night, he was as well as ever."

"28*th*.—I have just returned from an excursion, a comfortless though not altogether a useless one, and my first this year.

"In defiance of a high sea, I ventured out in my canoe to try to finish the prospecting, which I had commenced last fall (Autumn), in Sockalee

Harbour, at the mouth of the Burnaby Straits, almost due north of our camp. I took with me two expert Indians. But this canoe is small, only five feet by four inches—in fact, no larger than an ancient British coracle. I had in view to discover some cross-veins of copper, if possible. Such however was the state of the sea that we soon drifted off to westward, and were glad enough to be able to make for the nearest shore. It was on the other side of our Western Headland, and although the beautiful little harbour or cove where we now landed, lay within two miles of us, I had never been into it before. I spied a blue jay flying about near the beach, and, as this was the first bird of the species I had seen on Queen Charlotte Islands, I named the place Blue Jay Harbour. Evidently it would have been impossible, in such a sea, to weather the headland towards home. I therefore made up my mind to encamp under a huge cedar-tree; but having forgotten to bring matches, I sent an Indian into the bush to procure the requisite tinder (dead rotten wood), by means of which we quickly kindled a brisk fire, roasted our potatoes, and toasted some dried fish we had with us.

"It will ever remind me of this benign climate,

to think how, on a night in March, even while stormy winds raged, I was not merely induced to take my night's rest in the open air, as I did beneath the outspread branches of that cedar, but was able next morning to rise from sleep, as unharmed and refreshed as if I had been in bed.

"And yet the depredations of the storm were wonderful to look at. During the night hundreds of trees had been blown down, and now were strewn high and dry along the beach.

"To a solitary civilized being, the storms in these northern latitudes always have a peculiar grandeur. A solitude seems to reign here, and even at Victoria, which goes home to the heart of the stranger from Europe, and fills him with desolation. Not that a pioneer's life is dull, for there are subjects in plenty to engage his attention ; but that every now and again a feeling of loneliness creeps over him, such as no pen or tongue can portray. It makes him mark and cling to the glories of nature with tenfold ardour. But hence, too, he views with tenfold sensitiveness the sight of those glories battling furiously together.

"After breakfast we set off in the direction of a high mountain, situated in the interior of the island, intending, if possible, to ascend to the summit, and secure one of the many hundreds of eagles' nests which I could plainly discern through my field-glass. Though the distance to the base of the mountain was only about three miles, so dense a bush separated us from it, that we found it absolutely impracticable to proceed more than two. Indeed, the last half-mile I performed alone, my Indians having given it up as "unco uncanny," to borrow a phrase from yonside the Tweed. They aver that I penetrated into the interior further than any Indian has ever gone. This does not surprise me, considering their natural dislike to exertion of any kind. They plead in excuse that the game is too scarce, and the under-bush too obstructive and dangerous, to offer them sufficient inducement. As I was forced to go back myself, I must admit their plea to be a reasonable one.

"About noon, the sea having calmed a little, we resumed our voyage of discovery in the tiny canoe. In an hour or so we put into another pretty harbour, where I made out a vein of crystallized limestone, the only pure limestone I had seen in this geological section. The vein was four feet wide, and traceable for a distance of 150 feet, from W.N.W. to E.S.E.

Paddling then around the land, I found it was an island, not much less than twelve miles in circumference. I bestowed the name of "Malcolm" upon it, in honour of a friend in Canada. Observing smoke to proceed from an adjacent island, we paddled over to it, a distance of some four miles. Time failed me to examine the interior, even if the chaos and tangle had allowed me; but by the smoke and the strong smell of sulphur prevailing, I judged that Volcanic Island would not be a misnomer to give it.

"During the last two days we three explorers have consumed quite sixty pounds weight of flour, besides other provisions. These Indians think nothing of devouring their ten pounds each at a meal, particularly if the flour be made up in the form of pancakes. Catering for Indians comes expensive."

I may here note that the commissariat difficulty referred to in my Diary was shortly after obviated by another smart notion, for which we were again indebted to the genius of our Californian. Amongst the stores we had a large cask of tallow, such as is used in rolling cartridges, or in greasing tools. I took a quantity of this with me, when I next went out to explore, and fried the pancakes in it instead of in butter. Of course I took care to cook the first pancake without tallow, slipping in a piece of butter on the sly for myself. The Indians gobbled up their tallowed pancakes with infinite gusto. But ever after one pancake apiece amply sufficed to them. And rare fun it was to see their amazement and vexation at not being able to accommodate more than that at a time, in spite of their undiminished appetites.

After this brief exploration the copper-works on Burnaby Island kept me too closely occupied to allow of another absence for some while to come. All went on much as usual till the latter end of August, when our camp and that of our ally Skid-a-ga-tees were thrown into commotion by the report of an invasion to be expected from a neighbouring tribe, booty being their undisguised motive. Though we quickly put ourselves into a state of defence, it is hard to say what might have been the result but for the most opportune arrival of the little schooner *Rebecca*, the mere sight of which ludicrously changed our would-be foes into pretended friends.

The *Rebecca* was on her way back from the Stickeen River in Russian America, and had on board an old Canadian friend of mine, a Mr. Car-michael, who also was returning from the gold-mines in those parts, having lost all his money, and likewise his health, not to mention a narrow escape with his life from hostile Indians.   As the nephew of Mr. Hogan, proprietor of the famed St. Lawrence Hall Hotel, in Montreal, my friend had gone out influentially recommended, fully stocked, and well in funds. Few men, therefore, could be better qualified to pass an opinion on the prospect afforded by the Stickeen River.   It is here enough to recount that he had left the gold-mines with the determination of never going back to them.

Fearing that, as soon as the *Rebecca* departed, I should again have trouble from the Indians, I ostentatiously despatched a letter to the Governor of British Columbia, requesting the presence of a gun-boat.   The mere fact of this request served to protect us for the nonce.

CHAPTER XI.

NEARLY a month elapsed before I received any answer to my request. Meantime, our pugnacious neighbours, emboldened by the delay, sent a small "army of observation" over to Burnaby Island to watch us, and, if occasion offered, to threaten us.

Very early in the morning of September 19th, I noticed a great stir in their camp; and ere long those who had been plotting our total destruction came up to the log-house, laden with skins, furs, and fish, and loudly proclaiming their amicable sentiments towards the white man.

Nothing in the Indian character used to astonish me so much as its shallowness. The Indians are wonderfully acute in reading other people's actions; and hence one would expect them to be less clumsy in dissimulation. Here they were, however, palpably false and hostile to the backbone, and yet thinking to make me believe in their professions of friendship and truthfulness by means of a few transparent overtures. But does not a like trait characterize the savages one meets with now and then at home?

I could not restrain a laugh at the blatant imposture, especially as, happening to look through my glass across to the enemy's camp, I saw they were actually breaking up and beginning to move. Upon which the members of the deputation laughed too. All this assured me that some external cause must be operating in our behalf.

My men and I were still balancing probabilities, when suddenly the sound of heavy guns in the far distance solved every doubt; and at the same moment a friendly Siwash (one of the Skid-a-ga-tees tribe) came running over the promontory to announce that a " smoke-vessel " was in sight. Our double-faced enemies had been observing it from early dawn.

Without loss of time I mounted to an eminence above our camp, and there, plain enough in the offing, was an English man-of-war. I immediately put off to her in a canoe. She proved to be

H.M.'s gunboat *Hecate*, and by nine o'clock A.M. I had the satisfaction of piloting the welcome gunboat into a safe anchorage opposite our mines, and not more than a quarter of a mile from our log-house.

The following is in my Diary:—

"*September* 19*th*.—Took the obstreperous chiefs before the commanding officer of the *Hecate*, who gave them clearly to understand, through an interpreter, that if they annoyed us again in any way whatsoever he would at once return and burn them out of home and hearth, and that they must deliver up all the articles they had stolen from us. This action on the part of the Governor will do an incalculable amount of good. It makes us feel a deeper pride in our country, and revives the patriotism which too long absence from home is apt to enfeeble. The officers very obliging, offering to supply anything we might require. I was glad of two dozen clay pipes, and a bundle of English newspapers."

Exactly at five o'clock that afternoon the *Hecate* got up her steam again and departed, after having fired a good many shells during the day from her largest gun, as a salutary warning to the natives.

For quite a week afterwards Indians of all tribes

continued to loaf about near our log-house, holding lively conversations with us in reference to the gun-boat. The general opinion amongst them was that it would be easy to destroy her by " setting fire to her powder-magazine;" but when pressed as to some practical plan for getting at the magazine, they were no more able to answer than were the respected nurses of our infant years when we used to question them as to the best method of putting salt on a bird's tail. What most of all puzzled the Indians was to understand how on earth " the same gun could fire two shots at once," by which they meant the report on the shell being discharged, and the bursting of the shell a few moments after on the ground.

Candour obliges me to state that, notwithstanding his friendliness in the main, Klue turned out more or less of a rascal in the petty larceny line. For this I had him up on board the *Hecate*, when he promised her commander to restore a lot of implements he had stolen, or had allowed to be stolen, from our stores. He never fulfilled his promise, which, judging by his subsequent manner in the *Hecate*, I expected would be the case.

Klue, I remember, came on deck in a nice stew; but as soon as he found that it was to be all talk, and no hanging or shooting, he plucked up courage and followed me about the ship wherever I went. Observing two young ladies aft, he inquired their names. Not knowing them myself at the time, I replied that they were the daughters of some English gentleman of rank, upon which he instantly proposed to purchase one, offering "two hundred blankets" down. I informed him that English ladies were not exchangeable for "goods." He was greatly surprised to hear it, and terribly vexed when, later, I explained our custom in this matter more fully. " Why, then, do your white men come and buy our daughters?" he indignantly exclaimed. And, it must be owned, I was as terribly at a loss how to answer him. The Indian custom is to take a woman to wife for a month on trial, the usual price asked for a chief's daughter being three blankets. In the event of the damsel not proving a desirable acquisition, she may be sent back within the month. Her relations then return the blankets. It is sad to know that this degrading traffic has been taken advantage of, to an unlimited extent, by the Californian traders who frequent the shores of the North Pacific. I did not wonder, therefore, at Klue's indignation on his discovering the true bearings of their practice. I never heard of his particular tribe having any such applications while I resided on Queen Charlotte Islands. But I strongly suspect that, should a Californian ever again seek a wife among them, Klue will insist on his price of two hundred blankets, if he does not give his unsuspecting applicant the length of his knife.

Although the *Hecate* stayed but one day, she left a most wholesome impression. For a long time after her visit, whenever the Indians showed a disposition to be saucy, we had only to glance with a smile towards the north-west (the direction in which the gunboat steamed off), and their bodies would quake from head to foot, whilst they rolled their eyeballs wildly.

On the Saturday following the *Hecate's* visit, the schooner *Rebecca* hove in sight. As the rain descended in torrents all that day and the next, I advised her lying-to in Harriet Harbour, which she did till Monday, the 29th of September, when, the weather having cleared, she unloaded our shipment of stores, and sailed the same evening for Stickeen River, with orders to call again on her return, in order to convey me down to Victoria.

I make note here of a melancholy accident which happened in the *Rebecca*, on her way up from the capital. On board of her was a certain Mr. Wigham, a native of London, and for years a speculator in Chilian and Peruvian mines. Our company had appointed him to come and assist me in working out my discoveries. The *Rebecca* having made the Inside Passage on this occasion, she was off the North Bentinck Arm, above Queen Charlotte Sound, when, one stormy night, Mr. Wigham tried to take an observation of the Polar Star. While engaged in doing this, the schooner's boom swung round heavily, and, striking him on the head, sent him overboard. In such weather, at night, his body could not of course be recovered. Now the schooner had left Victoria a week previous to the gunboat; and as the gunboat was ordered to call at our place before proceeding to Stickeen River, its commander had kindly given Mr. Wigham's daughters their passage. These were the young English ladies who had excited the Indian chief's curiosity in the gun-room of the *Hecate*. But the Misses Wigham, finding the *Rebecca* had not yet reached us, decided to go on to Stickeen in the gunboat trusting to return by the schooner, after she too should have reached Stickeen. The *Hecate* could not wait, however; and they were consequently forced to go back all the way to

Victoria, in ignorance of their poor father's death. Some few weeks later the duty devolved upon me of imparting to them the fatal news which made them orphans and absolutely penniless in a distant land.

I should now mention that, despite our migration to Burnaby Island in the foregoing Autumn, we had so far by no means forsaken Skincuttle. We paddled across continually; and a good relay of workmen having been sent up to me in the Spring from Victoria, I detached a party to Skincuttle, and kept them there all the summer. But that shaft did not repay the trouble and expense. I had been gradually determining to abandon it altogether, when an outbreak of the small-pox among the Indians brought things to a head. Several died, one of whom was a handy fellow, called " Indian George" by my men, and another, a pretty little Klootchman girl. Seeing these two were dying, the Indians strangled them, and immediately after struck their filthy camp on Skincuttle, making off in a body, and leaving us to bury their dead, if we chose to perform that office. This we did, to prevent the further spread of the small-pox. My foreman and I then set fire to the Indian huts and to the bushwood, and a fierce gale of wind beginning to blow at the same moment, the whole of Skincuttle Island was soon one sheet of flame. Not a stick would have been left on any part of it, if a dense cumulus of water, which we perceived to be gathering overhead, had not burst open of a sudden, and poured down such a flood as I never beheld, before or since, in my lifetime. The rain lasted without the slightest intermission or diminution for thirty-four hours, almost to a minute. Thus, by the action of two powerful elements, did poor Skincuttle receive its purification.

These incidents finally disgusted me with our pristine settlement, and calculating that there was nothing further of interest to detain us on the islet, I ordered its total evacuation.

I had lately been extensively engaged in prospecting Burnaby Island; and my researches having resulted in the discovery of what I believed to be the "lead" of the copper-ore, close down by the shore, I had set a number of men to work upon it. The storm interrupted their operations; but when, on the weather clearing, we arrived with our belongings from Skincuttle, the first sight which rewarded me for my venture was the "foot and hanging wall" of the vein splendidly defined. It had just been opened.

Early in the day of October 14th, the *Rebecca* once more made her expected appearance. As I had now important news for the shareholders of our Company, I resolved to return to Victoria in the schooner; and accordingly, putting my foreman in charge, I went on board in the afternoon, upon which Captain Macalmond weighed anchor at once. He agreed, very sensibly, to take the Outside Passage, hoping to get down with fair winds in about three days. In this, however, we were disappointed.

After clearing Cape St. James, a smart breeze sprung up. The *Rebecca* then crowded on all sail, which sent her cutting through the water at the rate of eleven knots an hour. But it seemed too good to last. By sunrise next morning she was scudding before the wind with bare poles, whilst the sea dashed incessantly over her bows. Towards evening another change came on. The wind fell, but not the sea, which continued to roll in huge volumes, pitching and tossing our dapper little schooner about like a shuttlecock, the " dead reckoning" showing that she made only half a knot to the hour. Who can describe the mortification which is the lot of the pioneer when, after a prolonged absence amongst savages, he approaches the haven and yet cannot feel sure of ever reaching it? As we lay tumbling in the trough of this wide sea, I could not but recall the fate of poor Mr. Wigham, hardly a month previous. What if our frail craft were to capsize, and to consign us all to make food for the fishes? Would anybody be one whit the wiser, until weeks, or almost months, after our friends began to miss us? To know this feeling fully, one must have found oneself within a day's steam of such a capital as Victoria, and yet have had to take one's chance of wind and waves, sometimes by the help of the tide making a few knots, but oftener losing sea-way to double the distance. The sole comfort derivable from our position was that, for two days, we could see no less than four other trading vessels labouring under the same difficulties as ourselves. Still not precisely the same; for, our craft being small and our Captain expert, we generally contrived to ground well in-shore, and hauling off with the returning tide, so gain a few miles in advance of the other ships.

At length, on Sunday morning, October the 19th, we sailed with a fair wind up the Straits of San

Juan de Fuca, and, rounding the Headland, dropped anchor in Victoria Harbour.

My arrival formed quite an event in the capital, not only because most of the leading merchants had now taken a pecuniary interest in my expedition, but because I was the first white man who had dared to go and live amongst the hostile Indians of Queen Charlotte Islands, or the Great Northern Indians, as some call them.

I need perhaps scarcely say that the primary consideration for me was a change of clothing, a civilized wash, and a " square meal." Nobody who has not experienced what it is to be deprived of the refinements of life can rightly conceive the joy of regaining them. When these invigorating tonics had been applied to my system I placed myself at the disposition of numerous old friends, and as many new ones, to answer their perplexing questions about the Indians, about the aspect and capabilities of Queen Charlotte Islands, and particularly about the promise of the country in mineral products. It required no little patience to satisfy such demands on my time and temper, to say nothing of the bodily constitution requisite to stand all the " brandy smashes " and bottles of champagne of which I had perforce to partake in my own honour.

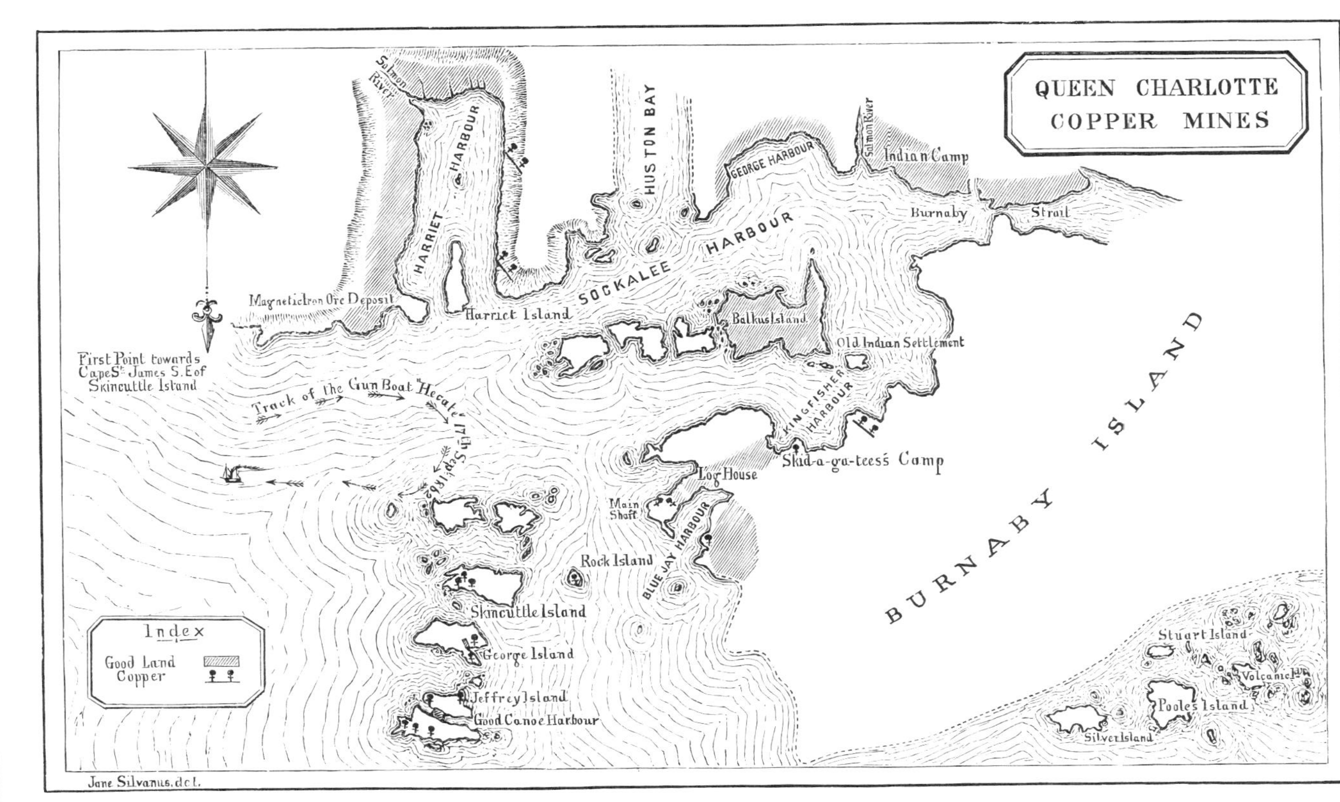

QUEEN CHARLOTTE COPPER MINES
Salmon River
HARRIET HARBOUR
HARRIET HARBOUR
HUSTON BAY
GEORGE HARBOUR
Salmon River
Indian Camp
SOCKALEE HARBOUR
Burnaby
Strait
Magnetic Iron Ore Deposit
Harriet Island
Balkus Island
Old Indian Settlement
First Point towards
Cape St James S.E of
Skincuttle Island
Track of the Gun Boat "Hecate"
17th Sep 1862
KINGFISHER HARBOUR
Skid-a-ga-tees's Camp
Log House
Main Shaft
BURNABY ISLAND
Rock Island
BLUE JAY HARBOUR
Skincuttle Island
George Island
Stuart Island
Volcanic
Jeffrey Island
Good Canoe Harbour
Poole's Island
Silver Island
Index
Good Land
Copper
Jane Silvanus, del.

By dint of a studied personal restraint, however, I got through my allotted task; so that, having devoted some few days to a most necessary rest, and employed the remainder in purchasing provisions, clothes, medicine, and ammunition, I was ready, before a week had elapsed, to charter another vessel to take me back to Burnaby Island.

Here I cannot do better than insert the official Report which, on occasion of this visit to the capital, I addressed to our Company :*—

"*To the Directors of the Queen Charlotte Mining Company.*

"Victoria, Vancouver Island, Oct. 22, 1863.

" GENTLEMEN,

"The copper-mines are situated on several islands, the approximate position being in about lat. 52° 18′ 00″ North, long. 131° 07′ 00″ West. Though the time occupied by me in prospecting these islands has been very limited, I have come to the conclusion that the copper on Burnaby Island is the most promising hitherto discovered. There is a bluff of rock rising to the height of about 150 feet on the eastern extremity of Burnaby Island. Com-

---

* The above Report is quoted by Mr. Macfie, in his work (p. 152).

M 2

mencing at the N.E. point of this bluff, at low-water mark, copper shows itself about one inch and a half in thickness. One half inch runs parallel with the level of the water for a distance of nine feet, mixed with a little spar, when it runs out. The remaining one inch then rises on an angle of 25° for the same distance, when it takes a horizontal course two feet above high-water mark towards the S.W., the strike being S. 35° W., with a dip W.N.W. 72°. Leaving these two threads and joining the main vein, as seen here, the copper gradually widens in the direction of the mainland. The length of this vein on the out-croppings is 200 feet, with an average thickness of sixteen inches on the surface or out-crop. The constituent (matrix or gangue) is composed of shorl, hornblend, garnets, and spar, presenting good gossan indications and two well-defined walls, the 'foot-walls' being slate overlaid with a very hard dark green rock, the 'hanging-walls' proving the existence of a regular and defined vein of copper-ore.

"The classes of ore to be looked for here are the yellow and grey sulphurates of copper, with the blue and green carbonates of copper, holding muriates and sulphurates of silver, with the purple and other classes of copper-ores.

"It is needless for me to enter into a long statement as to the probability of finding workable copper on Skincuttle Island. There are many serious objections to such a theory. The only use this island will be to us is to assist in determining the course of the 'Champion Lead,' which must be towards the mainland, as the latter island is too far north, which the formation plainly shows. For this reason I considered it a duty to the Company and myself to cease sinking the shaft on Skincuttle Island, for which I had bound myself by contract.

"I have directed a set of men to cut a drift in the most promising situation yet discovered, which is on Burnaby Island, and with a few more men I shall be in a position to extract copper for the market next Spring. I have no hesitation in recommending the working of this vein, believing, as I do, that, in a commercial point of view, the result will be most satisfactory to all parties interested therein. The regularity of the formation of this vein, its extent, and promising character, as well as its very convenient proximity to water (it lies within eighty feet of deep water, at a point suitable for landing a shipment or anything required), will satisfy the most anxious.

" From experience in mining for the last twelve

years, I am confident that success will attend the working of this mine, provided it is carried on with energy and prudence.   The mine so clearly possesses in itself all the elements of success, besides its convenience of situation, that no doubt can be entertained but that its working will prove a sound satisfaction to every one concerned.

"I have the honour to be, Gentlemen,

"Yours faithfully,

"FRANCIS POOLE,

"*Engineer to the Queen Charlotte Mining Company.*"

CHAPTER XII.

IT was not at all easy to procure a vessel for the
purpose of conveying myself and two of my men,
together with a suitable supply of provisions, back to
the copper-mines.

At length, however, a sloop named the *Leonide*,
which had been advertised to sail to the North Bentinck Arm on the mainland, failing to obtain more
than half her cargo, I chartered her to extend her
trip across to our islands.

The last moment had almost come, and the bargain
was struck in a hurry. When, then, I went down to
inspect the sloop, it rather staggered me to find her
only twenty tons burden, twelve tons of which were
already on board, whilst fifteen tons additional of
our Company's stores had yet to be shipped, con-

stituting a total of twenty-seven tons, to say nothing of the crew, passengers, and luggage. But we had to make the best of the bargain: for otherwise my men at the mines would have been wholly destitute of provisions.

On the 24th of October, therefore, about nine o'clock P.M., we left Victoria Harbour, with quite seven tons weight more in the *Leonide's* hold than she had any right to carry, and a very dangerous voyage before us. It was no wonder that, upon anchoring in Nanaimo Harbour, opposite the well-known coal-mines,* we found our sloop nearly waterlogged, showing fully a foot of water on her main-deck, even in smooth water—a fair sample of trading appliances in a new country.

The *Leonide* being bound in the first instance to the North Bentinck Arm, the Inside Passage was an imperative necessity. At the outset some idea may be formed of the vast difference between the two Passages, when I state that it took us three days and four nights to reach Nanaimo, whereas, in a good ship, the same period of time, by the Outside Passage, would have landed us at Queen Charlotte.

---

* The Nanaimo mines yielded 40,833 tons of coal in the year 1869.

In order to make clear how amply the facts bear out my comparison, I shall describe this voyage somewhat in detail.

Despite our extraordinary over-freight, I had really no cause to disparage the sailing capacities of the *Leonide*. What we wanted was wind to drive us ahead against the vexatious tides, currents, and eddies which so markedly characterize the Inside Passage.

Exactly at sunset of the 28th, a stiff but favourable breeze springing up, we weighed anchor and set sail from Nanaimo into the Gulf of Georgia. This gulf, owing to its strong currents and ever-varying winds, is the terror of all British Columbian naviga-tors.* By dint of good steering, however, we were fortunate enough to reach the head of the gulf by the evening of the 29th. Here a high promontory, known as Cape Mudge, juts out from the land on the

---

* The experience of Commander Mayne R.N., on the subject of the Inside Passage, is exactly mine. In his valuable work *Four Years in British Columbia*, he says (p. 176) that the Gulf of Georgia " forms a kind of playground for the waters, in which they frolic, utterly regardless of all tidal rules. This is caused by the collision of streams. The tide-rips are excessively dangerous to boats, and great care has to be exercised. A boat is almost certain to be swamped, and even a ship is so twisted and twirled about as to run considerable risk."

Vancouver side; and, observing a sheltered little harbour lying well under its lee, we decided to take shelter here for the night. The morning's dawn disclosed to us smoke in the bush, from which we inferred that an Indian *ranche* must exist in the neighbourhood, which, on examination, we found was the fact. We accordingly paid the natives a flying visit, purchasing from them five splendid salmon for the sum of two shillings sterling.

Johnstone Straits, which divide Vancouver from the largest-sized island in the Passage, was our next venture. It looks smooth work enough on the map. In reality, it is always the toughest tug of the voyage.

At daybreak on November the 1st we might have been seen, still in the trough of a rough sea, off Cape Mudge. We had then been beating about for two nights and a day, in a vain struggle to enter Johnstone Straits. Indeed, it was not till after three days, alternately advancing and retreating at the mercy of changing tides and coquetting winds, that, having taken to our oars as a last resource, we finally succeeded in clearing the long, ugly strait itself.

Some thirty miles distance beyond the north

entrance to the straits, a fine river discharges its waters with fearful velocity into this arm of the sea. It is called the Salmon River, from the multitude of fish of that species which swarm in it. We made several ineffectual efforts to cross the river's mouth. Our final attempt was not successful until the sloop had all but capsized, the sea making a clean sweep of the decks, and washing our live fowls and several casks of prime mess-pork overboard. Before we got completely across, a stiff breeze from the S.E., while working us up against a stubborn head-tide, swung the sloop's boom round from the port-side. Our cook, who chanced to be standing by the taffrail, was knocked into the water, but, catching fortunately at a sail which dragged along after us, he was hauled a-board again. I had the narrowest escape possible from a watery mishap of the same kind. Seeing the boom coming, I bent my head to avoid it, when the boom-sail lifted me neatly over to starboard. Scrambling into the rigging, I let myself down by a rope into the cabin, thankful to have come off without even a ducking.

This was a roughish introduction to the fair wind and comparatively smooth water which commenced immediately after we had passed the Salmon River, and held on till we entered the little bay where stands the fort erected by the Hudson's Bay Company. This is close to Queen Charlotte Sound, and at the extreme north-west end of the Inside Passage.

All along our route we could discern northwards the dim outline of a high mountain-range, as yet unnamed and unexplored by civilized man, but which is doubtless a spur of the Cascade Mountains. The Vancouver shore opposite lies low for a very considerable distance inland. It here consists of a rich loamy soil, likely to turn out extremely productive at some future period. For the present brushwood prevails exclusively. The high timberage of these regions begins again as one approaches Fort Rupert. In the low levels, the residents at the fort told us, the atmosphere is generally clear, dry, and genial; but we could distinctly see heavy snow falling on the mountain-tops far away. Until within a few miles of Fort Rupert this part of Vancouver presents an aspect of the dreariest monotony. Near that point, however, the wild and grand scenery of its other parts is resumed.

During the entire voyage up the Inside Passage, our best day's sail was twenty-five miles. Allowance should of course be made for our over-laden craft. But the *Leonide*, if fairly treated, almost rivalled the saucy *Rebecca*. Balancing computations, therefore, this sailing would not give more than an average of twenty miles a day at the highest; whereas the Inside Passage is quite two hundred and seventy miles long. In other words it seems clear that not less than fourteen days are required to accomplish it. Surely there cannot be stronger proof that the Outside Passage, which never takes above six days, is vastly more expeditious; not to mention its evident superiority in respect of sea-room and general safeness.

Only those who have navigated the tortuous seas between Vancouver and the mainland of British Columbia can conceive the freaks which wind and tide are capable of indulging in. It is a standing puzzle to the Indian. But the white man perfectly accounts for it on looking to the innumerable small islands with which nature has fringed the whole of the British Columbian coast. If ever these islets come to be named, I much doubt whether any nomenclature will be found sufficiently rich to include them all. The simplest plan would be to number them like the streets of New York. Commencing at San Juan de Fuca, and ending with Fort

Simpson, a distance of five hundred miles by an average of ten miles wide, the highest number, I feel sure, would then exceed 20,000. Such a quantity of islands, grouped together in so confined a space, does not exist in any other portion of the globe. Well, as the unsophisticated navigator pursues the tenor of his way along this little-known route, he is surprised by the wind suddenly describing a circle round one of these islets, then bowling down a funnel-like channel straight at him, and, after having literally turned a corner, sweeping madly up another gullet or ravine, from which again it descends upon him with quadruple force. The utmost care is consequently indispensably requisite in this navigation. Not unfrequently the morning dawn would reveal to us that, instead of having advanced, we had been drifting back all night. The contending winds seemed legionary. We usually managed, it is true, to have one or other of them in our favour; but the most powerful wind was invariably adverse to us. This shows, too, that the *up* passage is more tedious than the *down*. There were very few days, or nights either, on which we had not to use our long oars, passengers and all, like so many Thames bargemen, sometimes for hours together. In short, I can imagine no navigation attended with greater tedium, danger, and hardship. Steam alone is able to reduce it to submission.

It was now getting on in November. During the last week the cold had set in, and we had sleety rain and snow almost continuously. We sheered out of Queen Charlotte Sound, however, and, hugging the mainland, steered within a point or two of due north, towards Edmund Point and the Bentinck Arms.

Though now clear of the currents and peculiar winds of the Inside Passage, we had yet to experience another of the perils indigenous to this imperfectly known highway of the sea.

Whilst the slant sleet and borean blast were at their worst, the *Leonide* went a-ground on a sunken rock or reef. Our slow rate of progression necessarily weakened the sloop's impetus; else the danger, with such a cargo on board, off that wilderness of a coast, would have been extreme. As it was, a couple of hours' hard labour enabled us to haul the vessel back into deep water, and thus to save her not only from destruction, but from any serious damage.

This occurred early one morning. We had then arrived within a day's sail of our first destination. The captain now consenting, I took the sloop's canoe, and, with one of my own men to steer, paddled forward to the North Bentinck Arm, which I reached just three hours in advance of the *Leonide*.

Well do I recollect that 22nd of November, a dull, dreary, wintry day. It was a Saturday evening; but we had time to discharge a large portion of the freight, I acting as stevedore and supercargo.

It is strange what a man can do when he is put to it. I speak from personal observation and experience when I say that anybody, with ordinary intelligence and a fair amount of bodily health, may push himself along in a new country. At the date of my leaving England, what did I know of industrial work beyond the sphere of my peculiar profession? Yet I may point to my own case, and I trust without being suspected of vanity, as a practical instance. For there I was at the North Bentinck Arm, acting as ship's clerk and superintending the unloading of a vessel, having previously piloted it up the Inside Passage from Vancouver, in place of a " professed pilot," who, though purposely shipped at Victoria, had shown himself as incapable of managing a sloop on the high seas as any Highlander in his bonnet and breeks.

About latitude 52°, longitude 128°, and exactly

opposite Cape St. James of Queen Charlotte Islands, a large estuary occurs in the British Columbian mainland. This estuary is splendidly sheltered from the ocean by an island, measuring twenty miles in length, and called after its discoverer, one Captain Maclaughlin, a Scotchman. But the estuary itself leads up thirty miles into the interior by a broad and deep channel. It there divides into two channels, which have been named respectively the North and South Bentinck Arms, and which lead again, the one by a still scarcely explored route over the last range of the Rocky Mountains into Canada, the other into the heart of the Blue and Cascade Mountains.

A little above the conjunction of the two Arms, in the North Channel, a small colony had been formed, partly as a standpoint for barter with the Indians, partly with a view to the provisioning and accommodation of those who, like myself, were rash enough to probe the recesses of the famous Cascades, in search of gold or other minerals. I do not entertain the least doubt that, when capital is brought to bear upon this upper portion of British Columbia, the route thence into the interior, and so into Canada West, will be fully explored and speedily established. The scheme will meet with opposition; but, as it is sure to succeed eventually, all who know anything of our possessions in the North Pacific foresee an immense change in the mercantile state of this colony by the certain diversion of perhaps half its traffic from Victoria in Vancouver Island to the towns yet to be formed on the North Bentinck Arm.

Scotchmen have so far been the main projectors of this enterprise. Hence the aforesaid little settlement, for years known familiarly at Victoria as " The Arm," had assumed at last the style and title of New Aberdeen.

One Wallace it was who kept the *ranche* or hotel there, a thrifty and thriving speculator, well deserving of permanent success. I had twice previously spent some useful and jolly days under his roof, when engaged in my bootless Cascade expedition, and now it became my pleasing task to lend a helping hand in revictualling his store, and otherwise doing him a good turn. Those are the reciprocal services in which pioneers specially rejoice. In fact, with shame must it be acknowledged that, the more sparse the population in a given radius, the less selfish and the more genial, hearty, and obliging do we lords of the creation become in our dealings with our fellow-creatures. No tyro in colonization but will draw that inference.

While hob-nobbing with Pioneer Wallace, however, I had serious doubts of being able to cultivate friendly relations with the rest of mankind at New Aberdeen. I learnt that the small-pox had carried off hundreds of Indians since my first visit there; and as the party I then headed was the unfortunate means of introducing the fell disease amongst them, I began to fear lest the natives should oppose my landing. But I was soon undeceived.

Remarking a fine specimen of Young India (North Pacific section) gazing at me, not with eyes indicating intense hatred, as I had expected, but with an expression of sorrow, I sympathizingly inquired the cause. He was one of those whom the small-pox had spared, but had nevertheless so deeply marked that I did not recognise his face in the least. But the moment he spoke I knew him to be my old Indian friend Jim, our guide on the Bentinck Trail over the Blue Mountain. But for Jim none of that party of ours would be alive at this day. He answered my query by saying ruefully, but in very good English, "Do you not remember me, sir?" Of course I at once went and shook him warmly by the hand, which mark of my remembrance and sympathy so overcame the poor fellow that he had much to do to keep down his feeling; and yet the feat was indispensably necessary, if he would retain his character as an Indian *brave*. I never took so kindly to any Indian. Jim was in my opinion an excellent example of the real stuff that lies behind the dross and disfigurement with which Europeans are now only too familiarized in the Indian character. Had my position and circumstances allowed it, I should certainly have adopted him, as I felt sure he possessed a warm and generous disposition, besides great intelligence, which a few years of civilized life and training would have brought out in noble relief.

We made but a short stay on the North Bentinck, not longer in fact than was necessary to clear out the sloop and right her for the rest of the voyage. While this was being accomplished, I set off in company with Mr. Taylor, another courageous pioneer of these regions, on an excursion up the Bella Coola, or Belcoula River.

The country here may be described in a summary way as hilly, the hills sometimes rising to mountains with a rich loam for a soil, the river-banks, however, displaying a subsoil of gravel some twenty feet underneath the surface. Nothing appears wanting but the axe, the spade, and the plough to render such a land as productive as any in the British Empire. At the period of my visit it was one wild forest, save the wigwams of the Indians in the bush, and Mr. Taylor's ranche about three miles upward.

On our way thither we passed by two Indian settle-ments, or bivouacs rather. They were almost deserted, the small-pox having during the previous year reduced the tribes there from 4000 to a few dozens. I noticed that the river had an enormous stock of salmon. They tumbled over each other like sprats in the water, reminding one of some plant or vegetable run to seed.

Mr. Taylor's ranche presented nothing new. It was the same log-house-in-the-backwoods kind of scene to which British Columbia has a way of accustoming every emigrant. The spirit that could induce an educated man to brave the loneliness and discomforts of a quasi-permanent residence in such a desert calls for admiration. At the same time, when the tremendous risk of life and the distant hope of profit are considered, it seems hardly possible to look upon isolated undertakings of this description as other than foolhardy.

Mr. Taylor kindly gave me a fine buck-hound pup, which afterwards did me good service. I called him Cato. By-and-by he grew to be a very powerful animal, standing over two feet, and holding his own against any dozen of the curs with which the Indian wigwams on Queen Charlotte Islands are infested. Many a watch did my dog Cato keep for me. The Indians had a wholesome dread of him. He would think nothing of seizing them by the bare legs; and as, by some instinct or other, he used to pick out those whom we knew to be our worst enemies, the Indians often threatened to kill him. Whenever they said this in my presence, I always vowed to them, with both hands on my revolvers, that it would be the worse for them if they tried to execute their threats. Poor Cato, he had a hard time of it. By constant vigilance, however, and by making him stay indoors after dark, I kept him in safety the whole of my subsequent residence at the mines. On leaving, I gave the faithful animal away to a white-man friend.

Returning to New Aberdeen, I found the *Leonide* in nice trim for the second part of our voyage to Queen Charlotte Islands. We had just got the anchor on board, and were dropping down the Arm,

when an Indian of the Bella-Bella tribe came alongside in his canoe, and, speaking in very fair English,
informed us that Lieutenant Fisher of the Royal
Engineers had been barbarously murdered by the
Chilicooten Indians. He was engaged at the time in
surveying the route from the North Bentinck Arm to
Cariboo, which, in the previous year, I had roughly
mapped out for the information of the Colonial
Government. It seems he strayed away from his
camp. No sooner was he out of sight of his own
men than some Indians, who had been tracking his
party for several days before, pounced upon him,
stabbed him to death with their knives, and then
stripped the body naked. We hove-to, in order to
give me the opportunity of getting at all the facts
concerning poor Mr. Fisher's fate. These I collected
and despatched to Victoria, to the editor of the
Colonist newspaper, in the hope that, by this means,
whatever friends he had in England and his brother-
officers might hear of his untimely end.

On the whole, New Aberdeen left sad impressions.

For three irksome days we did our utmost to clear
the particular nest of islands which lie grouped
between the Bentinck Arms and the North Pacific
Ocean; but, owing to the usual cause, fickle winds

and vicious currents, we made but slow head-way.

As at length we began to steer to the southward, with a view of taking the sloop round the south of Maclaughlin Island, we were passed by the *Labouchere* steamer, belonging to the Hudson's Bay Company. We signalled in the customary manner, but she pre-ferred not to acknowledge our compliments. The reason of such exceptionally strange behaviour on the high seas we soon discovered. When failing to double Edmund Point, the *Leonide* had next day to put into the little harbour of a new Indian settlement about fifty miles further down the coast. The natives in the settlement were simply mad-drunk, the *Labouchere* having, on her way up, supplied them with an immense quantity of whisky, in barter for fur-skins.

This was the Bella-Bella tribe. We heard they had recently deserted their old camping-grounds up the Arm, and had come down here in consequence of the fearful gaps and ravages caused by the small-pox. Many mournful hours of reflection did it give me when I came face to face with the enormous sacrifice of life I had unwittingly brought about, through my unfortunate exploring party to the

Cascades introducing that pest in the neighbourhood of the Arm.

The Bella-Bella tribe, though not to be despised, were formerly by no means a match for their born foes the Bella-Coolas, who used always to cut off a great number of the Bella-Bellas whenever these ventured beyond their own territory. But now the Bella-Bellas, though deplorably reduced in their own tribe, found themselves in numbers and force far ahead of the Bella-Coolas, and were accordingly preparing, might and main, to administer condign punishment to their ancient enemies. Thus does one evil produce another. The few men at this settlement who had remained sober told us that the tribe intended to go off very soon on the war-trail, and kill every single man of the hostile tribe, out of revenge for the past. It is true they could not quite accomplish their sanguinary purpose. But there was terrible bloodshed none the less.

I prophesy that, before the year 1880, the Indians of British Columbia and Vancouver will be numbered by as many dozens as they counted thousands when I originally saw them. The cause of this is twofold: first, the natural antagonism existing between savage nations, resulting there in frightful internecine struggles; which spirit, secondly, has been lamentably increased by the intoxicating drinks the Indians have of late years so easily procured from the unprincipled traders who frequent the coast.

I tried to trade with the Bella-Bellas, but could not induce them to come to terms unless I consented to barter in whisky. This, neither I nor the skipper would do, under any circumstances. The surprise of the Indians at our refusal told its own tale. During the night numbers of them came alongside the sloop in a shocking state of intoxication, openly proclaiming that the Hudson's Bay Company regularly sent liquor round to the different tribes. The chief, who was sober, offered in barter a large ship's telescope, but would take nothing in exchange except *fire-water*. Within a week afterwards we discovered that the glass in question had been stolen, only a few days before, from our skipper's own brother. It was perhaps as well we did not know this at the time, or there might have been a fatal row with the Bella-Bellas, if indeed the temptation to redeem his brother's property by the sole means of a barter in fire-water, might not have proved too strong for our little captain.

Having filled our water-casks, and fearing

treachery from these besotted Indians, we stole away quietly at daybreak. But it was only to return with ignominy; for, although now in sight of the open sea, each time that we hauled clear of the shore, the wind perversely " died down," and we had actually to row the *Leonide* back to the Bella-Bella settlement. This went on for two whole days, amidst the derisive yells of groups of Indians on the beach. Tired at last, I succeeded in persuading the skipper and the ignorant pilot to risk it, by rowing out to sea, instead of running in for shelter every moment, as though we were a set of home-sick girls. " Nothing venture, nothing gain," I thought; and at this juncture I certainly did not err.

So we rowed out at 10 A.M. one sunny morning, and at sundown the same evening, Day Point, on Maclaughlin Island, was twenty miles astern, with a breeze nearly dead aft pushing us steadily through the water.

On the morning of the second day we dropped anchor *somewhere* off Queen Charlotte Islands, having taken just forty-eight hours to do our fifty miles across from Day Point—that is, about a mile an hour—and eight whole days to come the distance from New Aberdeen.

A steamer might readily have performed the service, there and back, four times over; whilst an Atlantic Cunard might have, meantime, accomplished its run from Liverpool to New York with ease.

And yet it was less than half our voyage from Victoria, Vancouver Island.

CHAPTER XIII.

Where are we?—Storms—Workmen in British Columbia—Powerlessness of a leader beyond the haunts of civilized life—Mutiny—To work again—Mining operations—Christmas Day at the log-house—Klue and his chiefs—How to civilize Indians.

Well, at last we had made Queen Charlotte. But whereabouts exactly were we in the Islands? That was the next question. And a very pretty puzzler it proved, too, with a lubberly pilot in charge of us, and not a single instrument on board to take the sun's altitude. Fancy what it would be to anchor off Start Point in South Devon, with a kind of misty doubt in one's mind that the land on the lee bow of the ship was possibly Flamborough Head.

Our guesses had hardly begun, however, when down came a squall upon us, sharper and much more sudden than any Mediterranean *burrasca*. Luckily we had reefed sails; for the squall did not give us five minutes' warning. With awful fury it uprooted trees in all directions, loosening huge boulders on the mountain-tops, and tumbling them into the sea like foot-balls, whilst the wind shrieked again through the sea-caverns, bounding up from rock to rock, and down again to the lower levels, till the islands seemed shaken to their very foundations. Presently, and with the same marvellous suddenness, the roar of the elements ceased, a death-like calm immediately supervening.

Upon this we examined our position, and congratulated one another heartily on having crossed Queen Charlotte Sound within a few minutes of the time required to save ourselves.

We lay there all night, thinking wisely that inaction was the best policy when a wrong movement might precipitate our ruin, particularly in the dark. Next morning our pilot declared his certain conviction that we were north of the Copper Islands. But as I knew every stone for sixty miles northward of that position, and yet did not recognise this coast, it followed, according to the pilot's " convictions," that we ought to sail south. We did so, and before noon a long string of rocky islets came in view, stretching right across our bows. Observing them with a glass, I pronounced them at once to be Cape St. James and its satellite rocks, which form the

most easterly point of the Queen Charlotte group of
islands.   Happily, we had already gone so far west.
If we had been only five miles more to the east, we
might easily have passed Cape St. James, and sailed
out, goodness knows whither, into the boundless
Pacific Ocean.

Without more ado, therefore, we bouted ship, and
shaped our course due north for the Copper Islands,
feeling sure by this time where we were going to.
Alas, we once more laid the flattering unction to
our souls too soon. Tacking against a dead head-
wind, we had barely gained ten miles on our right
course when another gale, a hundred times worse
than the one before, drove us like a piece of cork
into our last night's anchorage. Glad we were,
indeed, to get that much shelter.   But every instant
I expected we should be driven out to sea; and
then we should have turned a few marine somer-
saults, and have victualled the North Pacific fishes
for the whole Winter.   It was a little bay, and up and
down it we went, dragging our two anchors after
us as if they were two pins. Twice, another two
yards would have put us outside. On the last
occasion, thinking it was all over with us, I stripped
for a swim to the shore, two hundred yards distant.

I believe, too, I should have actually plunged into the angry flood, stemmed it with a heart of controversy, and have swum to yonder point, but that, seeing my mates so willing, I turned to lend them a last hand, as I imagined. Jumping into the boat, we hauled out the third anchor. Then, rowing like lunatics, we dropped it in the centre of the bay, just as the sloop was about to launch out wildly into the deep. It was a veritable snatch from the jaws of death. But it taught us a seaman's lesson likewise. We, therefore, continued buffeting the storm with lusty sinews for full six hours. As fast as our sloop dragged her two anchors, we carried a third further up the bay, and then half pulled and half rowed her in. Not a soul amongst us but contributed his quantum to this crucial test of manliness. We even forgave the pilot his lubberliness, in consideration of his expending himself at the helm and capstan. Every man on board fought for our joint-stock of life as for his own.

I may here state that my observations on Queen Charlotte Islands go to prove the duration of storm-weather in those latitudes to be almost invariably six hours. Thus, should the weather be calm, say from noon to six P.M., after six o'clock it will change to rough, at midnight it will double its force, at six A.M. it will begin to die off, until, by noon again, the wind and the water have become as still as a lakelet in England in Summer. Not that Queen Charlotte weather is always changeable, but that, when it does change, these are the rules of its changes. I see good reason for attributing this action to the tides, although the tiding there acts with no great regularity.

We had a quiet night's rest after the travail of that anxious day.

Early in the morning, a canoe full of Hydah Indians paddled into the bay. I engaged them to take me to the copper-mines, and to return with one of my workmen, who would pilot the sloop in.

It was three o'clock on that day when I reached the long-wished-for destination, and found my men all but out of provisions, and murmuring not a little. Of the murmurs I took no notice, beyond frankly explaining the cause of our detention. It is human nature, the world over, to feel disgusted at being kept waiting, no matter how right the reason. But when the rag-tag-and-bobtail of society vent their humour in irrational grumbling, wise men should remain silent.

Before night, the *Leonide* came to anchor within a couple of hundred yards of our old log-house on Burnaby Island.

The voyage from Victoria to the Copper Islands had thus consumed no less than thirty-six days. Now I did the same distance by the Outside Passage in four days, on board the *Rebecca*, and eventually, by the Inside Passage in twenty-one days, in an open canoe. Making, then, every allowance for our troublesome diversion to the Arm, this, I hold, constitutes irrefragable evidence that, from the Straits of San Juan de Fuca to Cape Scott of Vancouver Island, the inner British Columbian waters offer no facilities to sailing-vessels.

I have recounted above the shocking havoc of the small-pox amongst our Queen Charlotte Indians, likewise the summary measures I adopted to stamp it out of Skincuttle. Prior to that, it had been my already-mentioned misfortune to carry the plague to the tribes along the North and South Bentinck Arms of the mainland. And now a similar fatality seemed to be pursuing me.

At New Aberdeen we had compassionately taken a European on board as a passenger *viâ* Queen Charlotte to Victoria. As ill-luck would have it, what should he do but fall sick of small-pox, some days before we arrived at the copper-mines? I entered a vehement protest against his being put on shore, knowing only too well the certain consequences. The little skipper insisted, however, and then weighed anchor without him.

We whites, it is true, were not attacked; but scarce had the sick man landed when the Indians again caught it; and in a very short space of time some of our best friends of the Ninstence or Cape St. James tribe—to my sorrow, seeing how few genuine friends we counted in any of the tribes—had disappeared for ever from the scene. It was long before health could be restored to the surroundings of our little colony.

December the 1st was the day of my re-arrival. The Indian Summer had almost waned; and my first thoughts, therefore, were given to preparing for the approach of Winter, and for visits from some of our Indian friends, in reality our secret foes.

But neither of these preparations could now be satisfactorily made; for the mutinous disposition of my own working party became more apparent every hour. In fact, my forced absence of two months and upwards had quite demoralized them, which did not wholly surprise me, I must own, considering the riff-raff one so often has to engage with in colonies, the small personal interest these men could be expected to take in an enterprise of this nature, and my legal powerlessness to uphold the law.

It is extremely difficult to obtain the services of really good workmen towards any undertaking in British Columbia. The majority of the labourers for hire there are not English, but the scum of America. And as the scum of Europe rush to the United States, it may well be supposed what it is the United States send further west to us. On applying for an engagement, they say they can do anything. This cannot be disproved till they are actually seen at work. Wherefore, if workmen you want, take these random applicants you must. After you have defrayed their expenses to your field of labour—and that is always expensive in the North Pacific—they turn out, as often as not, to be completely worthless. Should a chance occur to send them back, even at the loss of paying the return-passage, their employer may think himself a lucky man. The ordinary mischance, however, is to have them hanging about one's premises, eating up provisions, drinking all they can grab, utterly idle themselves,

and interfering with the honest work of others. Now
a Captain on the deck of his ship possesses ample
legal authority to deal with such cases. But he
who heads a party of colonists on land, be his
location ever so far removed from the haunts of
civilization, is without a remedy, legally speaking.
No wonder that, in a former row, Chief Skid-a-ga-
tees could by no means understand the laws of the
white-men. For truly my position in that respect
was an anomaly. I cannot see, indeed, why the
leader of a residentiary enterprise like mine, encouraged and otherwise supported by Government,
should not be invested with plenary magisterial
jurisdiction within his circumscribed sphere of work.
It would be unusual, no doubt; but a two years'
residence in an almost unknown and totally uncolonized part of the world is not usual either. And
nevertheless, if our countries in the Far West are to
be peopled, those exceptional undertakings will grow
into a sort of rule, for which the Colonial Government ought to legislate. I do not shrink from saying that, had a magistrate's commission for Queen
Charlotte Islands been conferred upon me, our ex-
penditure would have been immeasurably less than it
was, inasmuch as I might have prevented or arrested

the demoralization of the men, whilst the beneficial results to civilized life of my residence there would have correspondingly increased.

The real cause for the men's discontent was their unwillingness to bend to my yoke, mild as I made it. They had been their own masters for two months—why should they knock under to me now? Their pretext was the food. Upon which I vainly reasoned " that luxuries could not be expected in the backwoods of America, but that, as for substantial food, they were better off than many a gang of labourers thrice their value, in civilized Europe." To show the incalculable difficulty of humouring a crew of this description, in a place where humouring only will do, I shall enumerate in the gross the stock of provisions which I had taken up with me in the *Leonide*: first, plenty of second-class bacon, a large supply of excellent prime beef and pork, countless ducks and geese; secondly, potatoes, beans, first-class tea, coffee, sugar, and butter, raisins, rice, golden syrup, and biscuits; thirdly, a fair relay of spirits for grog. All this abundant store I carefully looked after myself, always presiding at the daily distribution of rations. " What do you want more ?" I used to say to my eleven companions, " unless you wish to knock off altogether, and live like fine gentlemen?" But, though often silenced, they were never satisfied. "Why should you distribute the food? It is ours as much as yours," some grumbler would soon begin again; and so on indefinitely through the Winter. Once a drunken fellow, who had taken a double ration of rum, actually levelled a rifle at me outside our log-house door. The others thought this measure rather too violent, and disarmed him. In the state we were, however, it certainly did make me invoke lynch-law on the murderous villain's head; while the fear that I might really carry my menace into execution had the effect of damping the mutinous spirit of all the party for some time to come. It proved what might have been done had the law assisted me, instead of its abeyance impeding me at every step, during this second year of residence.

However, as soon as I could in any degree per-suade the men to work on with me, we set to at repairing our canoe, cleaning and "fixing" our fire-arms, erecting a regular blacksmith's forge, and enlarging our log-house, so as to make it hold our mining implements and stores more conveniently.

The alterations took long, owing to the want of

carpenters' tools. Our blacksmith, I remember, forged a large knife out of a spade. The knife was eighteen inches in length and six inches wide. With this I managed to split the shingles requisite for the roof, whilst another man did his best with a hatchet at carpentering some trees into logs for the walls. When the roof was on, we put up an empty powder-keg, to serve in the novel capacity of a chimney-pot, and a ticklish business we had of it, too. Before the keg got naturalized, it caught fire twice, and well-nigh put the house in a blaze. Fortunately our powder was all stacked at the other end of the log-house; but the twenty powder-kegs which we now had to keep in the proximity of possible fire, did not form the pleasantest reflection for the inhabitants of that log-house.

To anybody whose experience is bounded by Europe, exposing our lives thus wantonly must appear the height of suicidal folly. It was that, I do believe. In fact, on the other side of the Atlantic nothing is half so marvellous as the reckless familiarities with gunpowder, steam, or other explosives, in which every one indulges. But somehow, among Transatlantics you get used to it.

I next had both log-houses thoroughly cleansed,

and all the chinks in the walls filled up with oakum; and when the dangerous trees near had been cut down, in order not to afford them an opportunity of falling and crushing us outright in a January storm, as they nearly did the year before, I began to feel snug and comfortable, from a material point of view, for the approaching Winter.

Then came the mining operations.

I re-prospected all my old prospects, and reviewed the shaft-work, frequently going down our main-shaft at Burnaby, pushing onward into the lode, or instructing and stimulating the men. Much their laziness wanted it. Quite as I expected, next to nothing had been done. Whilst I was absent, spending myself and risking my life to forage for them, the good-for-nothing fellows had been playing and idling away their time, foreman included.

No resource remained to me, however, but to grin and bear the loss, and otherwise make the best of a bad job, by affecting to laugh it off, and trying to inspirit them to work. Had I not smothered my feelings, the scoundrels would have turned utterly rusty, left me in the lurch, seized the stores, and, fraternizing with the too-willing Indians, have perhaps ended by murdering me, and have afterwards escaped themselves to the mainland. Those are some of the chances a gentleman has to run when he stoops to associate with those beneath him, whatever be his ulterior object, in a land beyond the pale of civilization.

Except, then, that I kept a jealous guard over the stores and provisions, and that I continued, at least nominally, to direct everything, thus retaining my ascendancy, I pretended to take it all as a matter of course.

Such was the manner in which I tided over the Winter; although, by Christmas time, it had become pretty clear to me that, from these causes, our Company could never hope for success on the present system of operations.

As may be supposed, my Christmas was a dull one. The unsettled weather added to the discomfort. In that respect Queen Charlotte Islands, as well as the rest of British Columbia, seem closely to copy Old England. When the Indian Summer is over, you do not get your Winter at once. Quite a month ensues of muggy, sleety, and sloughy weather. You are often well into January before the real frost and snow arrive. Rain at Christmas-tide is unpleasant enough in all countries. What must it have been in that outlandish settlement, under a roof not rain-proof?

Despite all our efforts, the shingles with which the roof was covered would split open, sometimes quite suddenly, or the knot-holes would unaccountably grow larger. None of these defects could we remedy, for want of proper felting, then an unpurchasable article in the colony.

I think I never shall forget that unique roof of ours. My bunk was nearly under the barrel which did duty as chimney-top. Many a fine night have I lain there, prone on my back, intently watching the Plough as it curved beneath the Polar Star, or other of the sidereal groups as they appeared to career through the heavens, until hidden from my vision by the arc of our telescopic barrel chimney-top. But when it rained I had to manage as I could.

That Christmas-day our cook served us up roast goose, with a dish which he insisted on calling plum-pudding. Seated across the edge of my bunk, I was in the act of doing justice to the unwise but savoury bird, when a rising storm made the cranks of our log-house creak, and before we had time to take warning, a *douche* of rain-water came tumbling aslant from the chimney on to my plate. I confess I was very near profaning the sacredness of the day by a few hearty curses; until, chancing to remember a similar mishap in a civilized house near London, where the whole contents of a Christmas dinner-table were instantaneously destroyed through the ceiling falling upon it, I thought I might have fared worse; and so I bore with the loud guffaw of my men as they coarsely chaffed me over losing my Christmas dinner. This was the wisest policy — nay, the only one, with a set of men to whom I had in a measure committed myself for the time being.

All through those Winter evenings, mine and their principal resource lay in sitting round a good fire in our log-house, mending clothes, cleaning guns and tools, talking of homes and friends, and wondering what those friends were doing at that particular moment—not without a hope that they were thinking of us forerunners of civilization, inaccessible as a rule by any description of boat or small sailing-vessel during quite three months of the year.

The experience of the preceding twelve months made me very chary of admitting the Indians to our log-house at night. Before them I always took care to avoid any appearance of disunion amongst our-selves; and when they saw that we spent so much of our time shut up together it created a mysterious air of strength, which undoubtedly was of service.

Sometimes, however, I would allow Chief Klue and his compeers to pay us evening visits. Then, while my men worked and smoked, I have spent hours upon hours in explaining the phenomena of nature and the arts of civilized man to the chiefs.

I found them ever most attentive and interested, and, I must add in justice, far more intelligent than many illiterate white men in our own country. On the other hand, the Indians always believed me to be a great English chieftain—*Hyas-King-George-Tyhee**—by reason of the marvellous tales I used to tell them. The size and population of London and of Europe, the properties of gas and steam, the art of photography, but especially telegraphy, filled them with astonishment. When the chiefs heard how our countrymen could speak together at a distance, and that, ere the present race of Indians were very old, they at Burnaby would be able to converse with their stray friends at Victoria, or with other tribes on the mainland, and without either party moving from their respective positions, they held up their hands amazed. "Powerful is the white man, wise and powerful," exclaimed Klue frequently.

---

* Queen Charlotte Islands having been discovered in the reign of George the Third, the Indians associate with that king's name every Englishman they have seen since.

Yet for all our wisdom and power, or Klue's friendly reverence for those qualities of ours, I imagine, when the telegraph does come to Queen Charlotte, he will be the first to clip *just one little bit* of the wire, which crime, if not punished on the instant, will, I foresee, lead to a general robbery—*capswallo* — of the telegraphic apparatus.   The Indians will be sure to want to cut the wire all up, to make fish-hooks, fasteners, and rings for their own ears or their women's noses and under-lips.

That which astounded them most, however, was my account of the substance, movements, and relative positions of the sun, moon, and stars.   As the white man was so long mastering this branch of science, it is certainly no marvel that poor Blacky should manifest incredulity on having the planetary system first explained to him.   The Queen Charlotte Islanders, I perceived, did connect the sun and the moon, in some misty kind of way, with the Great Spirit.'   But they seemed not to possess the faintest notion of the earth being likewise a planet; whilst the stars, in their idea, consisted of mere sparks, which the sun had probably left behind him at bed-time. When I enlightened them on these points, and particularly when I declared that the planets were probably peopled worlds like ours, and that the earth went round the sun, instead of the sun round the earth, Chief Klue shook his head in a comically doleful manner, as much as to say "It is all gammon, Tyhee Poole; and I am only sorry you should turn out such a liar." But presently, after some moments' apparent reflection, he looked up again and asked eagerly, "How know? how know?" And as then, by means of homely proofs, I unfolded to him and his brother-chiefs the Copernican revelation, conviction appeared to strike upon their minds much more quickly than it did upon the minds of the Grand Inquisitors who imprisoned Galileo.

In order to effect a solid and permanent reform in these savages, it is absolutely necessary to enlist the sympathies of the heart as well as the head. I do not mean this as a truism. Heart and head must of course work in concert, wherever good is to be effected. But to reform the Queen Charlotte Indians, supposing they escape the portending fate of the other tribes in the North Pacific, will, it strikes me, be a work involving prolonged time, formidable labour, sound judgment, and tried patience. You can easily get them to imitate you: but that, I have seen, avails nothing, as it leaves them in the end worse than they were in the beginning. The ways and employments of civilized peoples should be very cautiously introduced, the temptations attendant on such novelties being anything but beneficial to certain weak places in the Indian character, namely, the tendency to theft and lying of every conceivable sort, the animal cunning which so soon shapes an Indian into an apt cheat, his total inappreciation of the virtue of forbearance; above all, his insatiable lust for drink, and the brutish violence he invariably gives himself up to when under its influence.

Only isolated settlements will serve the purpose. The Queen Charlotte Islander needs conversion, if ever savage needed it; but, to use a maxim of the great Lord Strafford, "less than thorough will not do it" for him. He must be continuously guided, watched, and controlled, that too by exceptional teaching and legislation; and, to our eternal disgrace, chiefest of all the requisite precautionary measures, is the necessity of keeping him from contamination with the average run of traders in the North Pacific, the majority of whom have a lower moral status than the veriest unconverted savage.

CHAPTER XIV.

SEABOARD OF QUEEN CHARLOTTE ISLANDS—STORM-TOSSED SEAS—ABOR-
TIVE BEAR-HUNT — INDIANS NEITHER BRAVE MEN NOR CRACK
SHOTS—HUNTING BEARS—STORMY PETRELS—TIDE-POLE—AN AQUATIC
SKEDADDLE—RIFLE-PRACTICE ON BURNABY ISLAND—TWO STUNNING
STORMS.

THE seaboard all round Queen Charlotte Islands, but especially its more southerly portion, is remarkable for the bold and rocky front it presents to the Pacific Ocean. As along the coast of British Columbia itself, so here, a cordon of black and beetling cliffs seems to forbid ocean aggression. The clusters of islets with which the larger islands are surrounded at intervals, give the notion of their being advanced out into the sea as scouts and vedettes. Those spots of insulated rock, even under the influence of Summer scenes smiling at them from the shore, offer to the passing mariner who chances to sight Queen Charlotte country a picture of absolute desolation. But when the Pacific rises in its rage, when its mountain billows, after having rolled unchecked over thousands of miles, meet here with a first obstruction, the mighty sea bursts in thunder upon the gloomy rocklets, which nevertheless emerge again from the foam like valiant warriors courting a contest.

Such was much the scene which, in Winter time, usually met our eyes whenever we stepped out of the shelter of our log-house. The sea did not appear to have time to freeze, as it does by the north-easterly coastway of America. The truth is that, in the North Pacific, the Winter ocean-roll comes nearly continuously from the southward. The water always retains a certain warmth, therefore, which its passionate tumbling and dancing only serves to increase.

But sometimes the stormy winds would retire; and then, though in the midst of Winter, the sea would soon smooth itself down till its surface became as gentle and unruffled as it looks on a lovely day in Summer from the south coast of Old England. The name *Pacific* seemed no longer a misnomer. And yet, strange to say, the very mildest and brightest days were those which invariably prognosticated frost and snow.

After Canada, or even England, the snow-fall we had was a mere trifle. I do not remember a single day on which the snow did not entirely disappear before sundown, whilst the frost never lasted above a few days together. The wind and rain storms proved to be our real enemies, for, when the sun and afterwards the frost returned, nothing could have been more beautiful than our winter weather.

I well remember, one bright and frosty night of that kind, a rough knock coming to our door. Happening to stand nearest, I answered the knock. Chief Klue and two of his councillors were outside, evidently feeling the unwonted cold keenly, for they had their blankets tight round them, while, for a wonder, he was enveloped in an antiquated great-coat I had given him, and which I appropriately named his wrap-rascal. They wanted to tell me that a bear had been seen in the neighbourhood, and, now pointing to the clear heavens, now clutching at the frozen air with their dingy hands, that there could not be a better time for a hunt.

I could not afford time to let the men go; but, never having seen what an Indian hunt was like, and thinking to vary our provender with a novel sort of steak, I consented myself to join Klue the next morning. Accordingly I promised to lend him an Enfield rifle, that being the arm he liked best, as

English make. Meanwhile I prepared a small-bore American rifle for my own use.

I can attest great objections to American rifles in general. They are too long and too weighty. For economy's sake the barrel ordinarily consists of one solid piece of steel, drilled while cold so as to take a half-ounce ball. This is all very well, if you can fire from a rest; but, with a rifle of that kind, prolonged and unceasing practice alone will enable you to fire steadily from the shoulder. Besides, the butts are carved. This forms a considerable obstruction in quick shooting, as you have not only to get your sight, but also to fit the carved butt into your shoulder: for otherwise, should the gun hang fire, you are certain to hurt yourself, American rifles out of order having a habit of kicking as well as their English fellows.

With the first streak of day, then, off we set—Klue, a small posse of his Indians, myself, and eight Indian dogs of the half-wolf breed, all together. As we entered the bush and began to crush down the brushwood, dry and crisp from the frost, the morning sun was tipping the heights of Burnaby Island.

We had not penetrated beyond half a mile before we came upon evident signs of our ursine enemy. At this the dogs commenced sniffing about in an animated manner, barking valorously, and throwing their long tails aloft. It was only, however, to drop them again the moment Master Bruin should choose to turn out and face them. I noticed a corresponding behaviour in the Indians, especially Klue. As if in expectation of a triumphant encounter with the "King of the Forest" on Queen Charlotte Islands, the chief took to handling his rifle in a fiercely determined manner, whilst his dark eyes rolled and glistened; but I knew that, like the dogs, he too would be sure to lose all his courage exactly at the time he required it most.

I cannot conceive how it is that Indians have the reputation of being so brave and reckless of danger. In all my travels I never met with a really brave man among them, unless it be Jim, my old Cascade guide. If Indians are palpably superior in number to their opponents, they will perhaps show fight, though by no means always even then. But if it should appear that they are only equal, their antagonists having the advantage of position, they will fly as fast as their legs can carry them. Their bravery generally lasts no more than a few minutes, during which time they will do any amount of talking and gesticulating; but in the event of an enemy surprising them, they will all fire at the same instant, and then run for their lives like deer, their shots whizzing harmlessly through the air. Indians are no marksmen, either. I once recollect seeing a rifle and twelve muskets discharged by as many Indians at an otter; and yet every man of them failed to hit the animal, though they were within ten feet of him. It was I who first observed the otter, and I of course wanted to pot him myself. But such was their intense anxiety to secure the prey for their own purposes, that I indulged one of the Indians with my Enfield. He fired ludicrously wide of his aim; and the ball, ricochetting from the rocks, took a piece clean out of the broad-brimmed hat of a Klootchman who chanced to be standing in a canoe down by the beach. The Indians are afraid to fire in fact, and generally shut their eyes for the operation. Yet I have also heard them described as crack shots, and their supposed exploits praised in just such terms as one might use in speaking of a Tyrolese chamois-hunter. Nobody, however, who has more than a mere casual acquaintance with the North Pacific tribes can seriously hold that opinion. I account for the illusion thus. When an Indian is hungry or in search of food, he husbands his powder to an extraordinary degree. Usually, he will crawl up on all fours, precisely as a tiger might, to within easy distance of his game; but he never fires till he feels certain of killing. From our log-house door, I have frequently seen sportsmen of this calibre out on the rocks to the right, patiently waiting and watching a whole day, and sometimes a night, in order to get a sure shot at a solitary seal which happened to be lurking near. At last the ambuscader would fire, and tremendous would be the excitement on shore. Other Indians, unseen before, but likewise ambuscaders, would rush from behind crags and trees, and in five seconds paddle off in canoes to where the poor seal had dived down, struggling for life among the kelp and sunken reefs. By-and-by the seal would rise, on which a general scramble would ensue, the canoes not unfrequently capsizing, to the disgust of the white-man eye-witness, whose common sense tells him that needless noise is ruination to hunting. And so the game escapes quite as often as not. All the same, the man who shot the seal obtains great credit for his shooting, the manner of it being nowise considered. None of the Indian tribes in the North Pacific display either real bravery or sporting qualities.

But where was the promised bear-hunt? In the

clouds, I may say. This was the first time, and like-wise the last, that I went on a hunting-expedition with Indians. I guessed how it would be; but Klue over-persuaded me, and right well was I served. The bear had left evident traces of his predatory descent from the mountains, but, with such a pack of dogs or curs as accompanied us, he would have been a flat indeed to have waited till our party came up to him. The dogs, despite the commands of their master, given in language full and loud, barked away at the top of their canine voices, the echo seeming to dance from ravine to ravine into the recesses of the furthermost hills. How the Indians imagined they were going to entice the bear down in that fashion, I could not understand. It was, for all the world, as though some gentlemen in the burglary line had sent a letter over-night to say they might be expected to tap at the kitchen-window early next morning. Master Bruin very sensibly kept to his private apartments, knowing well that, under the present uncontrollable circumstances, he could not be tracked there in a day, or in many days.

Consequently, after nine hours' laborious tramp through the dense underwood, including mazes and entanglements hardly to be believed, desperate fights to extricate oneself, and ruin to my habiliments, I regained the log-house, fagged beyond measure, laughably steak-less, but, on the whole, rather the better for the health-producing exercise.

Although my luck in bear-hunting on Queen Charlotte Islands stands below zero, I feel assured that bears must be very plentiful there. The Indians say they often see them, particularly when out with their canoes, and far away from their camps. The bear-lairs, however, are seldom disturbed; partly because of the natural density of the brushwood in the bush; partly because of the uneven ground created by much fallen timber, and also by the large rock-boulders which for ages have come tumbling down periodically from the mountains, but chiefly because of the cowardly and silly ways of the Indians when they try to hunt. Bears, I should say, abound on Queen Charlotte Islands as much as in any other part of North America. Yet on the mainland they are not by any means so numerous as one hears they used to be. This is specially the case with regard to the grizzly bear, which species lingers more in southern latitudes. Ere long it will become very rare. But the other species—the common black bear, *ursus americanus*—will die out too. In a journey through British Columbia extending over two hundred miles, I only saw three specimens, and that was on the higher grounds above the fifty-second parallel of north latitude.

No huntsman ought to go bear-killing without dogs, provided always that they can be made to hold their tongues while the game is being tracked. Odd as it may sound, those of the coward sort are the best. All animals, I believe, whether human or brute, dread an attack from behind. But bears have a specialty in that respect; and if the dogs are properly trained to worry Bruin's hams, his bearship is sure to turn round upon them, and thus afford facilities to the huntsman for dealing him a fatal blow. Then I know the opinion prevails in Canada that a bear does not die suddenly. Should a bullet, it is said, strike him in an apparently mortal spot, he will often be saved by the quantity of fat which envelops his flesh, and by cleverly stopping up the bullet-hole with grass—that is, if the dogs do not press him further; but well-trained dogs will leave a bear no time to stuff the grass into his wound, and so they literally do worry him to death. How far this theory is true I do not venture to determine, although I am disposed to credit it, because on more than one occasion, when out alone in the Canadian bush, I have given the contents of my rifle to bears that came across my path, and yet I did not find their bodies afterwards.*

I select the following from my Diary for the year :—

"*January* 11*th*.—Snow fell the first time this Winter last week. The fall continued during the greater part of the week, but was of so slight a character that no snow remained on the ground above three hours at a time.

---

* It may perhaps be allowed me to relate here a very narrow escape I had from a bear in Canada, the year before I went to British Columbia. It was the first of the genus I had seen in his wild state. The roads were very bad, just after the great springtide thaw, in fact axle-deep in mud. My journey was towards some mica-mines. About twelve miles from the town of Perth it occurred to me to make a short cut by taking a *corduroy* or side-line road, which divided a certain plantation in two. I had hardly entered the plantation, walking the horse all the time on account of the muddy ruts in the road, when a huge black bear jumped or rather clambered over the fence and coolly began shambling along by the side of my buggy or four-wheeled trap. This he continued with apparent unconcern for some two hundred yards. Arrived thus far, however, he seemed to think he might as well ride as walk ; for he growled, showed his grinders, and gave me significantly to understand that he intended possessing himself of both trap and driver. Fortunately at this point the road got much better. No sooner, then, did my uncanny fellow-traveller attempt to climb up into the trap than I brought down the butt-end of my whip with such a tremendous whack upon his snout that he let go the trap and reeled back on his haunches. The next moment I dropped the other end of the whip smartly over the sides of my trembling horse, and away the gallant animal flew at the top of his speed, never relaxing it until we had left Master Bruin a good mile behind, with his ugly nose out of joint, and doubtless considerably astonished at this unlooked-for result of his manœuvres.

"The stormy-petrels have been paying us a visit. They seldom appear in these parts. We must, therefore, keep a sharp look-out for storm-weather, see to our log-house trimmings, and cut down some other trees, which I perceive threaten to overwhelm us.

"My tide-pole has had a dirty time of it down among the wave-bedashed rocks. Certainly I might have pitched on a more sheltered position; but it is the most convenient one, especially as I wish to take observations three times a day. During the last fortnight I have found a marked difference between the rise and fall of the day and night tides. In the daytime the water rises exactly twelve feet; at night nine feet six inches only. While I was taking my observations this morning, I had an unexpected visit from Chief Skid-a-ga-tees, who has been lately rather fighting shy of us. The deep old rascal seemed very anxious to know what on earth I could be doing, and what my object was in watching and marking my tide-pole. However, as he had brought with him a basket of rock-bass fish and three fine geese (*bernaclæ canadienses*), I gave him some tobacco and biscuits in exchange: and so, with a shake of his paw, we have parted friends again till next time.

"*January* 18*th*.—The petrels are trustworthy, and no mistake. For this week past it has been storm-weather in earnest, the worst this season—so unbearably boisterous, in truth, as to have compelled all the Indians on Burnaby Island to quit their wigwam encampments, and to migrate, each tribe back to its own home, where, they tell me, the natural shelter and their housings are much more efficient.

" I have never visited Skid-a-ga-tees in his ancestral domain: but if, as he says, he is better housed there than Skiddan is in his frame-house up north (query), what does he and half the Skid-a-ga-tees tribe mean by coming down here and encamping in the Winter-time, unless it is with the hope of getting something in the general scramble for our goods and chattels? Perhaps they 'cutely foresee that crisis to be not so very distant.

" There is no doubt that, if they had not gone off quickly as the storm began to rise, their large canoes would have been dashed to pieces on the rocks round Burnaby and Skincuttle. It was as much as we could do yesterday to save our small canoe. I have yet to traverse the Bay of Biscay; but assuredly I never beheld a sea more truly mountainous than what our eye-range can now take in, from east to west, opposite our log-house door. The wind has been a Nor-wester throughout.

"To-day, the storm having somewhat abated, I killed a fine crow (*corvus caurinus*) with my Enfield rifle, as he was perched on the top of a tall pine-tree, at a distance of 750 yards."

This last Diary note reminds me to say that, weather permitting, we used to have splendid rifle-practice at Burnaby. We could sit outside the log-house, and pop away at whales, porpoises, seals, grelies, or divers, any of which were as plentiful as salmon in the river Tay. The loons I found the most difficult to kill, as, the very instant you drew the trigger, down went their heads into the water. Either they must see the shot, or else their coating of feathers must be so close that shot will not penetrate it. I should attribute it to a combination of both causes, for I have oftentimes hit a loon* when it was swimming from me, and yet not killed, or apparently even wounded, the creature. There was a long table

---

* It seems difficult to account for the term "loon" being used to express "a sorry fellow," as I see the dictionaries put it; unless, indeed, "loon" be a corruption from some other word. For my part, I cannot imagine a more wide-awake piece of goods than the loon of Queen Charlotte Islands. Its name may come from the noise it makes, yet hardly.

of rock which shelved at an angle of 45° nearly down to the water-side. This shelf, being breast-high, made such convenient cover that my rifle could barely be seen above it. I would frequently repair thither, to fire at the loons for an hour at a time, occasionally taking a companion to witness whether I really sent the shot home. But often, on his declaring that I did, the struck loon would just dip its head into the water, shake itself as though it had only been peppered with mud, and then quietly swim away out of gun-shot. Nevertheless, the shock, too, from the bullet must have been considerable. I remember also going out for a stroll along the shore, after that January storm, and firing at two large eagles— *haliaëti leucocephali*—with the same kind of shot. It had signally failed just before upon a tough little beggar of a loon; but one single shot sufficed to knock over both eagles. They were always a puzzle to us, were those loons.

I recur to my Diary:—

"*January 25th.*—Paddling yesterday afternoon to an islet a mile off, in a line towards Harriet Harbour, what should I come upon, inside a sheltered cove, but my tide-pole? It had been carried away two miles in the late storm, and landed high and dry by the tide on a pebbly beach. Much trouble I have had to-day in refixing it, the slippery rocks rendering a foothold hardly obtainable. But, as more trouble was required to make the pole, I am right glad to recover it.

" Also, near Harriet Harbour, I picked up a live oyster seven inches in diameter, besides several smaller ones, all excellent eating. This find is important, as it proves beyond doubt the existence of oyster-beds close at hand. They lie probably in deep water: for the oysters I found yesterday lay high on the rocks, having evidently been washed up by a recent tide."

" *January* 28*th*.—We have had another stunning storm. Happily it was short. It commenced with one terrible flash of lightning, after which followed a fearful peal of thunder, then a heavy fall of hail, accompanied by gusts of wind that shook our stout little log-house like a plaything. This is only the second flash of lightning we have had this Winter. Thunderstorms are usual hereabouts in the Summer season, but very rare indeed in Winter. The Indians, who have only just returned here after their aquatic stampede, testify to this storm having been the most violent of any ever witnessed by that ubiquitous personage 'the oldest inhabitant.' They are not averse, I think, to regarding it as a prognostic of evil; but whether their superstition points to themselves or to us, would seem, so far, an unsettled point. The storm lasted all yesternight, till the morning sun dispersed it.

"That first flash appears to have intimidated one of my men. I had just left him at the bottom of the shaft, trying to raise a large block of stone, when the flash came. The stone fell upon him, and his comrades had to convey the poor fellow in an insensible state to the log-house. He has regained his consciousness, but will be confined to bed for some weeks yet.

"One thing I am truly thankful for, namely, the safety of our gunpowder. I had not been able to make any provision against lightning, and was therefore on tenterhooks the whole of the past night, not knowing the moment we might all be blown into the sea."

This unfortunate accident added greatly to my troubles, for the men took advantage of it to become more mutinous than ever. I could scarce get them to put their hands to the work.

CHAPTER XV.

THE 1st of February was ushered in with summer-like weather.

My men, perhaps taking courage from it, began to work by *tribute and tut-work*,* a not unfavourable sign, as I then persuaded myself, that the hopes of our Company might, after all, prove less delusive than I had been recently anticipating.

At the same time two fresh hosts of Indians, deadly foes one tribe to the other, re-arrived at Burnaby together. The first belonged to a section of the Klue tribe, the others were Cape St. James

---

* This is the old Cornish term, now used in America, for working by contract and division of labour, according to the species of operations the miners are engaged in.

people, headed by their chief. These two tribes burned with jealous rivalry to secure the favour of the whites. The manner in which they set about it, however, was incomparably childish and ludicrous. Without meaning anything wrongful or offensive, at that time quite the opposite indeed, they would crowd round the shafts, or paddle after our canoe, each tribe elbowing its rival with such grotesque earnestness that often I had to hold my sides for laughter. Morning, noon, and night, they would beset our log-house, and our storehouse also, until I was forced to detail several men to stand sentry over us whilst we pursued our avocations. When, upon occasion, I allowed select parties of the rivals to come and sit with us in the log-house, it appears almost incredible how the great hulking fellows used to contend, like so many overgrown school-boys, for the best places near the fireplace, or the nearest to me on the benches, in order that the opposition should not be able to boast of having monopolized the *wah-wah* with the King-George-Tyhee Poole. Of course we took care to make no distinction; otherwise our position would have soon become untenable.

My men's ardour was not of long duration. And here, I must own, they had some cause of complaint.

The stock of provisions which I had last brought with me from Victoria was reckoned at four months. We were getting on towards the end of our tether, and yet no revictualling seemed at hand. It is easy to talk of over-anxiety; but imagine being on a semi-desert island, distant upwards of 200 miles from civilized beings, and possessing no possible means of communicating with them, save by the help of the savages who inhabit it. Nothing could compensate for such an isolation but thorough interest in the work before us, and as thorough confidence in our Company's solvency and foresight. I had both those moral aids at my command ; but the men's interest in the copper-find was merely accidental and mechanical, while the mere mention of possible short-commons sufficed to conjure up untold horrors in their crude minds. Naturally enough they looked to me who had taken them there, and upon me they vented their spleen when aught happened amiss.

Daily I felt the responsibility more and more. My feelings may well be fancied, therefore, when, early on Sunday morning, February the 8th, the man whom I had appointed as victualler came to me to say that he feared the four months was a mistake, and that we only had food for three months.

I immediately sallied forth to the storehouse, and finding after a careful inspection that what the man had suspected positively was the case, with a heavy heart I gave orders to weigh up the entire stock, preparatory to placing my party on reduced allowance.

This was a black look-out, indeed ; for, I said to myself, with such a grievance, the rest of the men will certainly throw up their work and mutiny the moment the news gets wind amongst them. I then fully believed that in October there really had been some serious mistake on the part of the Company's agent at Victoria. Only one hope remained. Might I not have mistaken the period originally assigned? If so, we ought shortly to be relieved. It had been snowing more or less for two days. Now it was clearing. I would go and scan the wide ocean, and see whether the horizon did not perchance hold out some forlorn hope to us.

In that desolate frame of mind I put down the weighing scales, and taking up my field-glass I prepared to mount the rocks which overhung our little settlement. No sooner had I begun the ascent, however, than a vociferous hullaballoo from some Indians in a canoe assured me that something out of the way had occurred. Hurrying down to the beach I beheld to my inexpressible surprise and joy a good-sized schooner in the very act of rounding the point from the direction of Harriet Harbour, and bearing in for our landing-place. Never did shipwrecked mariner hail his ship-ahoy with more heartfelt delight. It was like an instantaneous response from heaven direct.

The vessel proved to be the *Nanaimo Packet*, Captain T. Coffin, sent up by our Company with plenteous stores, and with four men to be employed at my discretion. It appeared the schooner had been lying-to in Harriet Harbour. She had got inside during a thick snowstorm; and fearing to face the high sea then on, there she had lain, unobserved by any of us, for forty-eight hours.

My four months' reckoning was a mistake, and it was not. We *had* been properly victualled for that period, but, whereas I erroneously counted it from the time of my departure from Victoria, the Company's agent had calculated from what he supposed would be the date of our arrival at Queen Charlotte. This explained both my miscount, and the vessel's coming to us about a fortnight before I should in all cases have looked for her. Happy mistake which served us no worse. However, it did help me to realize keenly what the straits of our situation might very easily have become; whilst I could not help sympathetically recurring to Wellington, when they sent a thousand left-footed boots for a regiment under his command in the Peninsula, and to our Commissary-General in the Crimea, when he received his ship-load of green coffee for the "immediate use of the army." My Queen Charlotte Mining Company treated me better.

I accepted three of the new-comers as miners at fifty-five dollars a month, and the fourth at fifty dollars as cook, besides board to all. Now fifty dollars being as nearly as possible ten pounds sterling, it follows that my cook's wages were at the rate of 120*l.* a year. In other words, to induce a man to cook "plainly" for us on Queen Charlotte Islands, we had actually to pay him higher wages than a "professed cook" would receive in a nobleman's family in London. That item will give no bad idea of the immense outlay required for an undertaking such as our Company had embarked in.

My little skit of a French cook I now discharged. And glad I was of the opportunity. Irrespective of his general good-for-nothingness, he had always been one of the worst of the grumblers, to say nothing of his having once, as already mentioned, seriously embroiled us with Chief Skid-a-ga-tees. I also dismissed another mutinous miner.

When the Indians had quite satisfied themselves that the *Nanaimo Packet* was not a " smoke-ship" with guns at long range, they flocked out to it by hundreds in their canoes, to see if they could not bag something. Great was the pleasure and pride of Klue, on detecting four of his own tribe, grinning at him over the schooner's taffrail. These fellows had been down at Victoria all the Winter. Klue knew by instinct that his tribe would have a " dram all round" of the infernal " fire-water," whilst the Cape St. James Indians would be condemned to look on with envious eyes and watering mouths, even Skid-a-ga-tees and his lot getting only a sop ; and so it eventuated. This quadruple piece of rascality had come back, sporting no superfluous luggage, but carrying between them, just as one might treasure ingots of gold, a large barrel of whisky, which pint by pint, I may say, they had earned and stored up at Victoria, with a view to a single day's gratification at home. What was the result? No advice, no entreaty, no menace, nothing availed from me. Swallow the " fire-water" they would and should. And hence within an hour's time after the first appearance of the schooner, Klue and all his tribe had drunk themselves mad.

As soon as our stores had been landed, Captain Coffin hauled his vessel off two miles to W.S.W., to a safer anchorage, there to await my letters and reports for the capital.

Concerning whisky-drinking among the natives, I cannot refrain from here putting forward a few reflections which I jotted down in my Diary, on the occasion of the debauch just mentioned:—

"The so-called whisky which is shamelessly sold to the Indians by traders along the coast, or even by certain unprincipled, merchants at Victoria, contains very little of what is wholesome or genuine liquor. What it really does contain is not generally known; but I hear on good authority that the bulk consists of water flavoured and coloured with grain-whisky in the smallest appreciable quantities. Its strength proceeds wholly from the blue-stone vitriol and nitric acid which the manufacturers largely infuse into it. The consequence is that, when the Indians imbibe this drink freely—and they always do so whenever they can get it—their naturally fiery temperaments are wrought up into a state of savagery so intense as to leave no white man's life safe in their presence while they remain under its influence. I take it that to deliberately supply the Indians with such body-and-soul-destroying stuff is not only glaring wickedness but shortsighted un-wisdom in the highest degree. The trader who acts thus may receive a few valuable skins each time as his bargain, but each time also he contributes materially to the demoralization and probable ex-tinction of the very races to whom he looks as his producers in the trade. In my opinion there ought to be a most stringent law on that head through the whole extent of the British Columbian colonies. Heavy penalties should be inflicted, and enforced too, in the case of any one, no matter who, infringing it. Moreover, better bargains, I quite think, could be made with the native tribes by means of the trinket traffic, provided it were thoroughly under-stood amongst them that, by no means, were they in future to obtain the 'fire-water' from one party more than another. I recollect seeing some tribes on the Fraser River pledging themselves to the missionaries who had gone to visit them. They promised never to taste spirituous liquors, and doubtless the pledge was meant to be kept. But an

Indian is the veriest of babies. However ardently he may have pledged his word, let his missionary leave the camp only for a few days, and he is a ready prey to the first pedlar who may chance to tramp in there. The pedlar perhaps has no evil intentions. Woe betide him, however, if he should betray that he possesses the merest flask of spirits. The whole tribe will cling to him like bits of steel to a magnet. Should he happen to take a taste himself, it is absolutely impossible for the Indians to resist. They will wrest the liquid fire from him, as many as can will gulp it, and then all is over with them. Again, permanent supervision alone reforms the Indian. Now, in a place such as Queen Charlotte Islands, where no tramps can pass through, an Indian mission might be most profitably established. But then, as an indispensable condition of success, every vessel, boat, or canoe coming to these islands, would have to be overhauled and well searched for spirits. More than this, every captain or trader wishing to land here should be legally compelled, before he puts his foot on shore, to bind himself by oath that he will not supply the natives with spirits. It would be despotism, no doubt. I hate despotic laws as a rule, yet betimes they become a rigorous necessity. And here is an evident case, in which the sole alternative between certain ruin and rescue lies in despotic legislation, be it as paternal as you will. Only, nothing but despotism, wisely forecasting and ever vigilant, can save the work of perhaps entire years being thus undone in one single day."

Some days subsequent to Klue's drunken debauch, an Indian of his tribe stole a pair of shoes belonging to one of my men, upon which I went down to both the rival camps and informed the chiefs severally that in future no Indian of either tribe should enter our log-house. This was to prevent one tribe from blaming the other for stealing. But, also, having in my possession a fur skin and a musket, the respective owners of which lived in different camps, I gave notice that I should retain both articles until the shoes were returned. It had the desired effect. Late in the evening I was pleased to see Klue himself coming up with the identical pair of shoes in his hand. It satisfied me that those whom we had long suspected were in reality the principal thieves round about us. Yet Klue's sorrow at one of his own subjects having committed the theft added still more to my satisfaction; inasmuch as true reformation need never be despaired of for any man who makes a frank acknowledgment, though his primary motive in doing so may not be of the very purest. I considered this a favourable trait of character in Klue. As far as disposition can indicate a character, he was the best of his race.

In Canada the coldest days of the year always come between the 20th and 25th of February. But though Queen Charlotte Islands lie very little higher up than the more inhabited parts of the Dominion, February the 25th had already seen us fairly into Spring.

Our two Winters were, both of them, wonderfully short and mild. In truth, if I except the turbulent storm-weather which now and then assailed us, and the frequent yet not continuous rain, which the immense timberage of the islands well accounts for, we had properly speaking no Winter. Judging from the climate only, one certainly could not have supposed that we lay as near the Arctic Ocean as Labrador. It never was so cold as when a week's frost occurs in London. In short, the most graphic comparison I can draw is with the Northern Island of New Zealand or our own South Devon.

The mining operations having much progressed during the past twelvemonth, the recurrence of fine weather produced a greater change in our regular business than it had done the year before. The rock down the shaft becoming every day softer, I was soon enabled to sink to an average depth of four feet six inches a week, instead of as many inches, which was what our weekly work about amounted to through the Winter season.

The weather on the 1st of March being all that could be desired, I took several of my men out with me, intending to continue my prospecting. Following up the course in a line nearly N.W. from our main shaft, I discerned strong cupriferous indications for a length of 400 yards. I likewise unearthed some singularly fine specimens of conglomerate. These I brought back to the log-house, and, on analysis, found the percentage of copper in them to be so very satisfactory as to lead me to conclude that I must have struck the vein itself.

That was a good day's work.

During the following week the nature of the rock altered too much to allow me to attribute it to the weather alone. The blasting-powder would only penetrate the seams, and even then did such poor execution that I had to order the pole-pick to be used, as the more serviceable power of the two.* We advanced rapidly, and as the copper indications improved both in quality and quantity at every step, the important fact was unquestionably settled that the true vein had indeed been struck.

The *matrix*, or mother-vein, now principally developed garnetiferous colours, namely, red, yellowish-red, brownish-red, and dark-brown. All the veins turned out to be both massive and crystallized, exhibiting the dodecahedron, with its modifications, opaque or feebly translucent struchore, lamellar, and granular. The lustre was glistening, the fracture uneven with marked brittleness, and the specific gravity 3·75. The three most common forms were :—

1st. The dodecahedron, with rhombic faces, primitive form.

2nd. A dark-green garnet, a solid, with twenty-four trapezoidal faces.

---

* The preceding week we sank down the shaft to an exact measurement of four feet four inches, consuming in the process twenty-five pounds of powder, 112 feet of fuse, four inches of steel, two bushels of charcoal, twenty-six candles, six boxes of matches, together with oil, soap, and grease—making a total in cost of materials of $19 73c. This well represents the large expenditure requisite in the beginning of mining transactions, especially when carried on in Winter time, and without the aid of elaborate machinery. I have no note of the next week's expenditure; but I remember it fell to quite one-third of the above.

3rd. A yellowish-red (much fractured), with rhombic faces, showing the course of the fractures, which was uneven, to be conchoidal.

The matrix measured rather more than two feet in thickness. But a distinct vein, two and three-quarter inches wide, soon showed itself; and I feel certain we should have eventually struck wider and thicker veins, if I had been able to develop in an oblique direction, as I hoped to do.

While this was going on at the shaft, the Indians seemed all at once to take a lively interest in my copper speculations. Klue had always given me great assistance. He generally used to accompany me in my prospecting explorations. I instructed him how to look for copper; and, there is no doubt about it, he displayed a degree of intelligence, when encouraged, far superior to any of the loutish white men with me. But now a daughter of George, one of the leading Cape St. James Indians, came and informed me of copper being down in her neighbourhood, at a spot which we called Antony Island. She produced specimens. I immediately detected the fraud, however, her specimens being merely picks from a ton's weight I had procured on Jeffrey Island, not long after my first landing. When found out, the wench only laughed impudently. Skid-a-ga-tees also sent me messengers who reported having discovered copper somewhere on the coast above Silver Island, but I had no time then to go and verify it. The most probable account was that of another tribe, with a slightly different name, from whom in fact the Skid-a-gate Channel to the north of Moresby Island derives its designation.* The Skid-a-gates said, and

---

* No intelligent white man, that I know of, has ever rightly explored the country of the Skid-a-gates, or, in this century, any portion of Queen Charlotte Islands higher than Skiddan and Cum-she-was Harbours, which I myself visited.

In 1852 the Hudson's Bay Company sent a small expedition under the command of a Captain Mitchell, to search for gold on the western coast of Moresby Island. In 1859, one Mr. Downie, an old Californian miner and explorer, led another party of twenty-seven men from Victoria to Gold Harbour, afterwards proceeding to Skid-a-gate Channel. A Captain Torrens followed in the same year. But all three parties were intent on the gold quest only, and almost immediately returned, Captain Torrens and his men having narrowly missed being murdered by the then hostile Skid-a-gates.

Captain Cook, R.N., in his *Voyage to the Pacific Ocean* (vol. ii.), gives a description of the appearance, which the northern coast of the islands presented from his ships; and an account of the western coast of Graham Island may be seen in Captain Dixon's *Voyage to the North-west Coast of America,* with views.

But the exploration of Skid-a-gate Channel and its surroundings is an undertaking yet to come. Captain Torrens, in his Report, says: "The country north of Skid-a-gate Channel is low, and thickly wooded, receding in one unbroken level towards a huge range of mountains about thirty miles off. Vegetation is there luxuriant, and at intervals patches of open land occur, in which the Indians have planted crops of turnips and potatoes." The Skid-a-gates unanimously described their country to me as flat, "good

I believed them, that a vein eight feet wide, and over two hundred yards in length, had been tracked in their country. They presented me with some splendid samples, which quite corroborated their statement. The chief earnestly pressing me to return with him and prospect the find, again I was obliged to reply that the time failed me. Here I should not omit to mention an extremely promising vein which I discovered in Sockalee Harbour, during the course of the foregoing Summer, as well as numbers of lesser veins, which I duly marked during a subsequent excursion, but never had opportunity to develop, around the shores of Harriet Harbour.*

To sum up on the subject of copper. The geological formation of the strata and my prospecting

---

for growing potatoes," that is, for agricultural purposes, and full of excellent harbours. It strikes me as the most likely locality for the capital when civilization shall have reached the islands.

* Mr. Downie, who, four years previous to the events here related, stopped a short time in Skid-a-gate Channel, reported that they found "trap and hornblende blocks, with a few poor seams of quartz" to the southward of the Channel. Northward, they found " coal, talcose slate, quartz, and red earth." All these were only in inappreciable quantities. From the samples of coal I saw at Victoria, however, I feel convinced that, for furnace purposes, the Queen Charlotte anthracite will eventually quite equal the famous Pennsylvanian. But, again, a paid-up capital of not less than 100,000*l.* would be required to put any coal-mine on the Islands into working order. As regards slate, the Skid-a-gate Indians brought me down a magnificent block of slate, as good as the finest Welsh slate. I secured a piece to carry home as a specimen.

combine to prove that Queen Charlotte Islands do contain immense mineral deposits. Gold is said to be there; but in regard to the existence of extensive copper-fields, no doubt whatever now remains. Only, in my judgment, although we struck a matrix on Burnaby, the islands possess in other parts more ample fields, where a much larger profit will one day reward some enterprising speculators.

I see every probability likewise of coal and slate being found on the islands in highly remunerative quantities.

CHAPTER XVI.

MY little colony on Burnaby Island now began to evince such signs of disorganization that the time of its dissolution, I plainly saw, must be fast approaching.

It became an absolute impossibility to control the men, and unfortunately they knew it. Talk and persuasion may do for a short time; but I can think of no state of society in which the power of enforcing the law is not the first of necessities. Except the isolation and our unsettled condition, my men had not a rational ground of complaint. They were fairly housed, sufficiently fed, and splendidly paid. Yet the mere fact of our Company's interests being placed so manifestly in their hands, instead of giving some zest to the work, seemed to suggest to the scoundrels to take every mean and dastardly advantage. It will doubtless excite surprise that men who had to earn their bread should misconduct themselves as these did, considering the assured means of subsistence they were thus dragging from under their own feet. The greater bait in the distance, however, nullified every present argument; for be it remembered that the only workmen then available at our copper mines, were those who wanted about as much as they could earn in a couple of months to enable them to go off on their own hook to the gold-fields of Cariboo.

Besides, frequent quarrels arose between our party and the various tribes of Indians. I do not mean to say that the Indians were not often in fault. I found those poor untutored savages, taken by themselves, to have good and trusting dispositions, if trusted in turn and judiciously treated. But the example they had continually before their eyes in those white savages of mine was execrable, whilst quite as often the Indians appeared to be either wholly in the right, or to have suffered gross provocation.

One day an Indian of the Klue tribe received unmentionable ill-usage from one of my latest comers. This so exasperated the injured individual that it cost

me a world of trouble to prevent a general *mêlée.*
As it was, the Indian, seeing my real want of power,
passionately declared he would shoot down the first
white man who should venture to pass the bounds of
the Klue encampment. To whom could I impute
blame? Added to this actively disorganizing source,
was its usual correlative, namely, too great a familiarity with the Indians. It sometimes worked in a
reactionary spirit after a quarrel, but more frequently
it provoked another. When the days had perceptibly
lengthened my men spent nearly the whole of their
off-time in the wigwams of the Indians, turning a
deaf ear to all my admonitions, remonstrances, or
entreaties. The consequences to be expected from
such a course were obvious to my mind, and I was
not deceived. It effectually emancipated the men
from everything save the merest semblance of control.
They worked when they liked, and left off when they
chose, the mass of the Indians correspondingly
losing the respect they used to have for my authority
or influence.

I will give one salient example of what we shortly
came to be reduced to. One evening I was employed
making entries in my Diary, just inside the door of
our log-house, when something darkened the thres-

hold. Looking up from my writing, I saw a surly Klue Indian, with a musket over his shoulder, and a Klootchman woman standing behind with a large box under her arm. At a sign from him of the musket the Klootchman advanced into the house, saying that one of my workmen had told her to come and take up her residence there, and that her box of things was to go underneath his bunk. I could not of course mistake the meaning of that. The proceeding was inadmissible for every moral and sanitary reason. But, besides, I might as well have relinquished the idea and object of my exploratory expedition altogether. If I was not to remain master, even in the log-house, there would be an end to all order and work in no time. I consequently made quick and fierce objection, upon which the Klootchman bride retired affrighted but not until her escort had fired off his gun in front of the log-house and then defiantly presented it at me, as much as to imply that I owed my life to his magnanimity. Possibly it was so, for the next day we were simply inundated with natives, who seemed not to have the slightest notion of leaving me sole master of our chosen premises. Never having seen any of their faces till then, I could not at first conceive where they had all come from. I soon learnt, however, that they formed a reinforcement of Cape St. James Indians, who had arrived in two large canoes during the night.   It was easy to see, by their abandoned manner and the tricks they commenced playing, that they had been well primed beforehand as to the state of the case in the white men's camp, and deliberately intended to be troublesome to me. I counted a hundred and twenty-two of them.   Not content with a mere visit, they encamped close to the log-house, regularly blockading it, threatening to burn it down, and then alternately singing, begging, dancing, stealing, so as to keep us idle for two or three days, and our minds, day and night, in such ferment and suspense that sleep was entirely out of the question.   It ought to have taught my men a good lesson, for, had a massacre ensued, they would certainly have been included.   But, instead of recognising in it the fruits of their stupid insubordination, hardly had this bullying ceased, or drawn off rather, than the fools went fraternizing again with the late arrivals as well as with the Klue Indians.

From this time forth, loose living on the part of the men, and thieving on the side of the Indians, was the order of the day.

I find these entries in my Diary :—

"*March* 14*th*.—Last night, while the day-shift men were asleep, with the door and window of the log-house left open for the sake of air, some Indians entered and took all the musket-powder we had left and all the bread we had baked. I happened to be down at the shaft myself, never conceiving it possible that my men would be such dolts as to allow themselves to be overreached in that manner. It was a sharp stroke of business for the Klue Indians. They were actually brazen and clever enough to abstract a powder flask and belt and a box of musket-caps from under the blacksmith's pillow without disturbing him or any one of the sleepers. At the moment that this crime was being perpetrated, a canoe belonging to Chief Skid-a-ga-tees, with two Indians half concealed in it, floated leisurely up and down in front of the shaft. This was a ruse to attract the attention of the shaftmen, and to make it appear afterwards as though old Skid-a-ga-tees himself had been implicated in the robbery. The Klue Indians had borrowed his canoe yesterday afternoon upon some pretence or other."

"15*th*.—A second glaring theft. As the shaft-men were away at dinner, a lot of Indians went down the shaft and walked off with all the candles.

I believe the principal thieves are still the Klue tribe; but they have accomplices, I fancy. I did hope my men would have profited by the raid of two nights ago. It is exactly the reverse—they do not seem to care one straw; for to-day the guard refused to stay at the shaft during dinner-time. Of course the ever wide-awake Indians seized their opportunity. It begins to look like collusion, though I am loth to think it.

"16th.—Last evening, again, I was myself going towards the shaft, while the night-shift had their supper, when I espied a certain Klue Indian whom we call Buckshot, darting away from near the works. I made after him, and found nothing; but for all that, on my examining the mining-munition, a dozen large candles, a can-full of blasting powder, and our best sledge-hammer were seen to be missing."

In consequence of these barefaced thefts, I held a long consultation with Klue and old Skid-a-ga-tees, as the only chiefs who, in our then position of affairs, would be likely to listen to reason. I told Skid-a-ga-tees that, on the whole, I had little or no cause to find fault with his tribe since their hostile demonstration soon after my first landing, and that, as far as I knew, they were guiltless in the recent robberies.

Klue candidly confessed the delinquencies of his tribe, but assured me he had done what he could to correct their thieving propensities, and so far without result; he would try to obtain the restoration of the stolen articles, and would continue to set his face against all thefts,* but I was not to suppose he had unlimited power. When I looked back to my own powerlessness, and also bore in mind Klue's persistent friendship, I could not refuse this explanation. I informed the chiefs, however, that, unless matters took some unexpected turn, it would not be possible for me to carry out my original intention of living long amongst them, and of establishing a white man's colony on Queen Charlotte Islands. Both chiefs seemed truly grieved to hear this decision. Yet as its wisdom could not be disputed, they said they feared we must part. The consultation ended amicably. And heartily did that rejoice me, for it testified to the "difficulty" having proceeded on either side from the subordinates, not from the leaders.

By this time, nevertheless, I had made up my

---

* When subsequently I got Klue down to Victoria, I had him up before the Governor, Mr. Douglas (now Sir James Douglas), who spoke like a father to him. Klue expressed such contrition for the errors of his subjects, that I trust he has of his own accord induced them to mend their ways.

mind that our exploration could not be pursued further on the present system.

I determined, therefore, to go back to Victoria, give a full report of my discoveries, and then resign my position as Engineer to the Queen Charlotte Mining Company.

However, the standing obstacle to every movement along the North Pacific coastways met me at once. Where was I to find a conveyance? One morning Skid-a-ga-tees came over to tell me that a fellow of his just arrived from Graham Island had seen a ship up north eight days before, making towards Stickeen River in the Russian settlements. When I state that I took seriously to calculating whether this vessel might not perchance call at our copper-mines on her return voyage to the capital, the anxious predicament in which real isolation sometimes places a man may be to some extent apprehended.

At length the splendid weather suggested to me to risk the voyage in a canoe. No such a venture had ever before been made in that part of the world. I sounded Klue on the subject, and he looked aghast. But Indians only want a proper lead to be venturesome themselves. On my arguing the point with him he finally yielded, and a bargain was then and

there concluded between us, he agreeing to take me
down to Victoria in his largest canoe, and I covenant-
ing to pay him at the same rate as if it were a
schooner without provisions.

The bargain had this limitation, that it was to be
void if, within another month's time, my workmen
should show satisfying symptoms of improvement.
I knew they would not. Meanwhile, Klue was to
make the necessary preparations, being careful to
keep it a solemn secret until I gave him the word to
speak. The poor savage kissed my hand in token of his
fidelity, and I am not ashamed to own I experienced
myself a kindred sensation about the region of the
heart.

We were in the first week of April.

The past month, as regards mining work, had been
an idle one; but the men, guessing probably what
I was cogitating, here threw off the mask. Forecasting that I should be obliged to pay them, work
or no work, they deliberately left the shaft to its fate
and made themselves comfortable. We had not
reached the middle of April before the whole eight
of them were to be seen lounging in and out of the
log-house at all hours, their hands stuck significantly
into their pockets, and their countenances thrusting

defiance at me.   When not engaged in this exemplary pursuit, they would go to sleep in the sun, like hogs, or, what was worse, saunter through any Indian camp that admitted them, till they got involved in a quarrel or other trouble.   Their sole plea was that the supplies of maple-sugar* and grog

---

* Sugar is as much a necessary as salt to the pioneer. Whether Queen Charlotte Islands will ever grow maple-sugar remains to be seen. But it is a staple with the Canadian farmers of the backwoods. What they will do there when all the maple-trees are cut down, it is hard to foresee. Even now, owing to the quantity of *sapping* trees which have of late years been felled, a sugar-famine would have already overtaken the country if it had not been for the prudent prevision of the Government of Canada, which opened a special commerce with the West Indies in 1866. Otherwise, the sugar would necessarily have had to come to Canada *viâ* England, and a requisite household article have been placed beyond the means of the poor settler.

As maple-sapping is likely soon to become extinct, it may not be uninteresting to note the present process of manufacture in Canada. At the first genuine touch of Spring, when the sun burns hotly during the day, but while the snow is still on the ground and the nights are cold and frosty, the " sap begins to rise freely." On some Spring day, in the first week of March generally, the tallest and straightest trees are singled out, all around, and marked as sound for operation. Each of these trees is then bored to the inner bark with a gimlet, a loose spile or chip being inserted, which leaves a few inches projecting outside, for the sap to drop clear of the trunk into troughs or hollowed logs. The trees are allowed to run thus until the third day, about a pail-full having by that time exuded from each tree. A stout plug is then inserted in place of the loose chip, while the farm-boys carry off the contents of the troughs to a large boiler, which they find suspended from a horizontal pole, and which, again, canny hands have propped up with five forked sticks. Under the boiler roars a fire, in a continual state of red heat, till the end of the operation. To purify the sap, and give the maple a crystalline appearance, the farmers add a little lime and charcoal. As soon as the whole has been boiled to a proper consistency, it

had failed. I felt extremely sorry for the sugar, but naturally enough not for the grog; and I said so openly. As neither defect could be then remedied, however, the revolt was not a simple strike. It was mutiny to all intents and purposes. Nothing indeed seemed wanted to complete the flagrant delict, unless, according to a hint I gave them, they liked to bind me hand and foot in the orthodox fashion. That experiment they declined, perhaps deeming it too dangerous.

It struck me that, my authority being entirely gone, there might yet be a chance of these misguided louts coming round, if I were to withdraw somewhat from their society. I therefore resolved to profit by the time which remained to me to make an excursion or two, and while still at Burnaby to take my meals alone, to sleep out of doors when practicable, and to keep to myself as much as possible. I only insisted on directing the distribution of the rations, which they did not oppose, partly

---

is ladled out into moulds, and left to cool and harden before being sent off to market, where it mostly fetches 4*d*. to 6*d*. the pound. The same maple-trees are sapped every year running, for seven years, more or less. At the end of that period, the farmers know they may as well cut them down for firewood, all the virtue having been extracted, and the trees having become quite hollow in the centre.

because it saved them the bother, partly through fear of my prosecuting them for stealing at some future day, in case they resisted.

I then went out in our canoe for a couple of days westward, taking with me two of Klue's best Indians as paddlers. We first landed on a small rock of an island reported by the Indians to have been at one time on fire. I made a hasty examination, my paddlers not relishing a long stay from superstitious motives. There were clear traces of a recently extinct volcano. I discovered a large bed of mundic, and also a boiling spring, in which I bathed. This was the islet I had visited in passing the year before, and named Volcanic Island. A high wind springing up, we made the best of our way to Silver Island, and, encamping there for the night, paddled back next day to Burnaby.

Klue telling me that the spring was considered a cure for all diseases, it occurred to me to return good for evil to one of my refractory comrades, and at the same time to test the curative qualities of the spring-water. Accordingly I advised our blacksmith, who had fallen very ill with rheumatic fever, to take a canoe and try Volcanic Island. The man took the canoe and my advice too; and in a few days he reappeared at Burnaby, not only fully restored in bodily health, but quite altered in a moral sense also. Devoutly did I wish to souse my other comrades in that miraculous spring. They chose, however, to go on riding the high donkey. So I left them to their asinine amusement.

Whilst the blacksmith was away, I one day had a formal *wah-wah* with the Skid-a-gate tribe. I found their camp clean and orderly beyond the others. In my opinion the Skid-a-gates are much the most intelligent race of any on Queen Charlotte Islands. I think great things might be done for them. But it would require a devoted man like Mr. Duncan, of the Metlakatlah mission, who has completely reformed the tribes in the Fort Simpson section on the main-land.* The Skid-a-gates impressed me so favourably in general that I regretted nothing so much as to have to quit Queen Charlotte Islands without visiting the

---

* Mr. Duncan's self-denying labours are referred to with just admiration by Mr. Macfie, F.R.G.S., in his *Vancouver Island and British Columbia* (pp. 476–86), and likewise by Commander Mayne, R.N., who in his *Four Years in British Columbia*, gives (pp. 279–95 and p. 305), interesting extracts from Mr. Duncan's own Journal. The most comprehensive account, however, of the work of reformation which has been accomplished among the Tsimsheean Indians, is to be found in a series of graphic papers, published in *Mission Life* magazine (vol. for 1871), and entitled *Stranger than Fiction*. Never was title truer.

tribe in their home. They showed me beautifully wrought articles of their own design and make, and amongst them some flutes manufactured from an unctuous blue slate. I bought one for five dollars. It was well worth the price. The two ends were inlaid with lead, giving the idea of a fine silver-mounting. Two of the keys perfectly represented frogs in a sitting posture, the eyes being picked out with burnished lead. A more admirable sample of native workmanship I never saw. It would have done credit to a European modeller.

I now turned to a short excursion which Klue had been planning for me. He said that, before I left, I ought to make a thorough inspection of the place, which already, at a distance, I had named Harriet Harbour; and from all accounts of it I agreed with him.

For this excursion I only took Klue himself and his little daughter, six years old ; and, in order to economize our forces, there being but three of us, I selected the chief's own private canoe, the very smallest on all the coast, and one easily managed along steep or shallow shores alike, up creeks or over rapids. It was scooped out of a solid cedar-trunk, and measured nine feet long, two feet four inches wide, and fifteen inches deep.

In this frail skiff we three put off together one morning from Skincuttle for the mainland of Queen Charlotte. Scarce had we cleared Skincuttle when up went the little canoe, head to the wind, her tiny bit of canvas flapping with a noise like distant thunder, and to an inexperienced eye seemingly in desperate disorder, until, paying off by degrees on the other tack, the sail filled out stiff; upon which the canoe heeled over to the other side and darted away as swiftly as a swallow, here leaping nimbly across the heavy seas, there staggering so uncomfortably under her canvas as to warrant the conjecture that we should speedily be consigned to a watery grave. But there was no fear of the contingency while I had two such good pilots in charge as Klue, who sat in the bow, and his daughter, who held the helm. Thus we tore along for about an hour through a thick mist which prevented our seeing ten yards fore or aft. At the end of that time the sun burst through the mist, and, rolling it up as if it were a yard or two of mere curtain, disclosed to my relieved eyes that Klue's instinct had guided our barque safely to the right spot, and within the right space of time.

For close in front of us lay stretched out a truly

splendid bay, more than a mile wide and fully two miles deep.

This was Harriet Harbour.

Having often viewed it from my canoe in paddling about, or from Burnaby Island with my glasses, I had long wished to be able to come and see it near. But nothing had prepared me for such a scene of beauty.

At the mouth of the bay is an islet some two acres in extent, which acts as a breakwater, and very effectively protects the harbour from the only wind (N.E.) that could assail it. The water inside consequently enjoys a perpetual calm. All round the other three sides are beautiful highlands, rocky and beachy towards the bottom, but otherwise densely wooded, and forming a superb panorama to our view as we leisurely paddled in.

We ran the canoe upon a rocky piece of shore two hundred yards beyond the N.E. point of entrance.

I had no sooner stepped out upon the land than my pocket-compass began ticking in a violent manner, by which I knew that the rocks must be one mass of iron; and so they proved. Purer crystallized magnetic iron ore I have never anywhere lighted on. My subsequent analysis of this ore gave—

Protoxide of iron . . . . . . 4·60
Peroxide of iron . . . . . . 82·30
Silica (and carbonate of lime 0·60) 11·60
Sulphur 85
Water and loss 65
                                ————
                                100·00

Before evening I had surveyed the whole surround-ings. I discovered two good veins of copper, plenty of limestone, and clear evidence of the vicinity of coal; but the iron ore predominated. Timber too was so extraordinarily abundant, even for Queen Charlotte, as to seem to promise to supply genera-tions of future settlers with fuel and charcoal. A broad and clear stream flows from the S.E. into the head of the bay. Klue assured me the stream was a famous place for salmon-catching. The hills rise up from high-water level, at an angle of 75°, to about 700 feet. Taken altogether, a more charming and more useful harbour of the same magnitude does not exist to my knowledge in the North Pacific. From want of a line I did not fathom the water; but a practised eye sees at a glance that the depths of the water will correspond to the steep heights above it. The bottom is evidently rock or gravel. Hence there never can be any danger of a filling-up, such as must always be the weak point at Victoria. Twenty ships of the line, I do not hesitate to say, could ride there at anchor together, with safety and convenience, to say nothing of other craft.

Darkness being near, and Klue not liking to return at that late hour in his frail canoe, we decided to rig a tent with the sail and a blanket, and to stay the night out.

Whilst he arranged the tent I rambled about the hills and beach for two hours, to probe the ground and scan the glowing landscape. Rich in quality and inexhaustible in quantity is the store there furnishing subsistence for living creatures. Every foot above and down the hill-sides is clad with shrubs, which bend to the earth with the weight of exquisite fruits, little mountain-springs meandering hither and thither through them. These springlets are a characteristic of Queen Charlotte Islands; but I had nowhere observed them in such marvellous abundance as round Harriet Harbour. Unless you watch very closely you are sure to pass them by, so completely does the vegetation bridge them over. As I descended to the grand sweep of gravelly beach which heads the harbour, the land became leveller at each step, but the timber and underwood thicker.

I stood by the beach for fully half an hour, thinking how difficult it would be to find a sweeter spot
in all the world, and how at no distant date that very
beach would assuredly give way to the wharves and
landing-places of a flourishing commercial town.
Harriet Harbour has only to be known in order to
be seized upon in the interests of trade and colonization.

Regaining the tent, I squatted down to a picnic
supper. Everything was laid out in true Indian
style, the two Indians standing up before me to see
that I enjoyed my repast. I might have done more
justice to their humble yet wholesome fare, if I had
not been previously indulging in the delicious
berries* which line the harbour-sides. However, my
bright-eyed little helmswoman was irresistible. So
I ate and relished the supper. Thereupon the
Klootchman girl (six years old, mind) proposed that
King-George-Tyhee-Poole should go to bed, so as to be
up betimes in the morning. Not to hurt their feelings,

* These berries, so far without any name that I know, grow in remarkable quantities all over Queen Charlotte Islands. The plant is a shrub,
generally four feet high. The leaves resemble those of our pear-tree, only
that they are much smaller. The fruit itself is about the size of a wild
gooseberry, and quite preservable by drying in the sun, after the manner
of Malaga raisins. It contains a good deal of nourishment, and forms the
principal food of the natives during the Winter season.

I submitted to their well-meant kindness, taking off my upper garments and laying myself down in the tent, *sub tegmine* of a wide-spreading cedar-tree, while six-year-old rolled a blanket round me, and with a winning grace tucked me in all right and tight for the night. I then perceived what they were after; for hardly did I appear to them to settle to sleep, when father and daughter made off in the canoe to catch a few fish for the morrow's breakfast. When they came back an hour later, it was with some fine salmon, which they quickly cut up to be ready for the morning's broil. Lastly, we all three huddled together under the same capacious blanket, the chief on my right and his Klootchie on my left, to court the favour of Morpheus.

Next morning I completed my survey of the beautiful harbour, and in the afternoon bagged several kinds of wild duck, as follows:—*anas boschas*, or mallard, *aythia vallisneria*, or canvas-backed duck, *bucephala albeola*, or buffer-headed duck, *melanetta velvetina*, or velvet duck; all which, being good eating, I kept to give to my recalcitrant crew at the log-house.

Chief Klue, Miss Klue, and myself then entrusted our lives once more to the miniature canoe, and by sundown we were on Burnaby Island.

CHAPTER XVII.

PARLEY WITH THE MEN—FAREWELL TO THE BEAUTIFUL ISLES—KLUE'S
GRAND CANOE—ACROSS TO THE MAINLAND—PARTING COMPANY—MISS-
ING THE WAY—SIX DAYS IN THE RAIN—THE SKID-A-GATES WELCOMED
BACK.

ANOTHER week at the log-house quite convinced me
that to wait any longer with the hope of working the
copper-mines would be only waste of time and money.
Those of the Indians who had annoyed me kept
aloof, it is true; but my own men continued as in-
tractable and dogged as ever.

It was plain they wished to tire me out.

I therefore summoned them all one day, and,
without stooping to bandy words, I told them of my
intention to proceed to Victoria forthwith, for the
purpose of resigning my post, and that I should be
under the necessity of reporting their insubordinate
conduct and breach of contract to our Company's
agent immediately on my reaching the capital.

At first some of the ringleaders, looking out into

the broad ocean, asked me jeeringly how I meant to go; whilst others affected to take it seriously, and begged me to intercede in their behalf with His Excellency, lest they should be sentenced and executed before they could make their wills. There was a total change of sentiment and tone, however, when, about noon that day, Klue's grand state-canoe, which my men had never seen and did not know of, came paddling and sailing like a huge swan round the headland. This proved to them that I both intended what I said, and was in a position to carry it out.

I then briefly explained my plan.

I should take back with me my account-books and all my personal effects. They should be left in responsible charge of the mine and implements, and have a supply of ammunition for their own firearms, as well as sufficient provisions to last them until a vessel could arrive with fresh orders or to convey them down. I should pay their wages up to the day of my departure: if they had further claims, they must look to our Company. I think I dealt more fairly and forbearingly with my foolish party of miners than many another leader would have done.

As soon as I had finished, one fellow pretended to feel for a small pistol he used to keep about him, whilst the others supported him in a low grumble. Upon that I simply glanced right and left, towards two crowds of Klue and Skid-a-gate Indians, who stood at a little distance ready to defend me. Deeply did I feel the humiliation of having to invoke the aid of an alien race against my fellow white men; but they had persistently brought it upon themselves. It produced the desired effect, too. The men saw that, if they touched me, they would be certainly overwhelmed. So in a few moments they sullenly acquiesced.

At last nothing remained but to get my things on board, which, by the help of my new travelling companions, was done during the afternoon.

The day was the 6th of April; and thus more than eighteen months had elapsed since I first landed from the *Rebecca* schooner on the adjacent island of Skin-cuttle.

I had meantime fulfilled my mission, amidst very great difficulties, but not without a success sufficient to compensate for the outlay, if it did not " lead on to fortune " absolutely.

The scene, as we pushed off from the beach below the log-house, is before me now.

The workmen, no longer mine, hung surlily back.

The rocks and woods, however, were filled with Indians, to see King-George-Tyhee-Poole sail away from amongst them. He was their good friend, they knew. They did not cheer, nor yet weep; but they moved their arms up and down, with a sort of moan or wail. It would have been strange indeed if I had not reciprocated their feeling.

At the same time the heavens were lit up in streaming splendour, while the sun began to sink low to the westward. But ere the red orb of day dipped behind its broken horizon, the eye of man caught a curved line running along the far east, from north to south. Although the distance to that darksome object exceeded a hundred and twenty miles, the curve was distinguishable as part of the mighty range of the Cascade Mountains. Heaving up their giant ridges into the very clouds, they looked like barriers fit to mark an empire, or as what they are, the boundaries of nature itself. Between us lay, calm and serene, the wide waters of Queen Charlotte Sound, reflecting gloriously the golden hues of the realms above.

With one steadfast gaze, then, upon the beautiful Isles of the Sea I was leaving, and one farewell wave of the hand towards Burnaby Island, I turned to commit myself to the most arduous voyage perhaps ever made in the North Pacific Ocean.

Our company consisted of two distinct parties.

The first was made up of one of the Skid-a-gate chiefs and six of his tribe, three males and three females. They were in a cedar canoe, fourteen feet in length. It carried those seven persons, with their goods, weighing about half a ton, well; but it appeared a mere cock-boat in face of yon out-spanning ocean.

Chief Klue, five young Klootchmen, and thirty men, together with myself, constituted the second or leading party. Besides our personal weight, we had shipped two tons of freight, namely, a bundle for each Indian, my goods and chattels, and the rest in copper or other ores. Our canoe was what is known in the Far West as a *dug-out*. Klue had cut and constructed it, foot by foot, with his own hands, out of cedar-wood (*thuja gigantea*). It carried three jury-masts and a considerable show of canvas, not to mention a main staysail. A proud and truly inspiriting sight was it to view all this canvas spread out to the breeze, and to see thirty-seven human beings all paddling together, with regularity, precision, and force.

The chief had carefully selected his crew. It was of course a pride to man his state-canoe with picked men; but at that time of the year it became a stringent necessity, April being always a severe season on the North Pacific coast, and its storm-weather lasting frequently many days together without intermission. I found them a lively and intelligent body of Indians, both willing to work and able to master the stoutest elements. Pleasant was it in good sooth, after the ungenial behaviour of my miners on Burnaby Island, to pass several weeks in the company of those poor savages, whilst they sang the songs of their country, and kept exact time as they sang, to the dip of their broad paddles. Yet, despite my knowledge of Indian character, their cheerfulness at the outset of so dangerous a voyage rather astonished me; for not only had we winds and rains above us, and waters beneath us, to contend with; but tribes of bloodthirsty Indians, more than one of which were personally hostile to Klue, would likewise have to be encountered all along the seaboard of British Columbia and the inner coastway of Vancouver, as we passed down them.

In our circumstances the Inside Passage to Victoria presented peculiar features of danger. Nevertheless,

I could not have counselled the Indians to adventure the Outside Passage in a simple canoe, albeit a first-class one. Either they would have been out of sight of land for many days, or they would have had to try the west coast of Vancouver, of which none of us knew anything.

The evening of our start, therefore, we hugged the shore to the southward for about two hours, and at 8 P.M. we drew up our canoes in the dark on a pebbly beach, fronting the broad strip of flattish land which stretches round from the mouth of Stewart's Channel near Cape St. James. This is the most southerly part of Queen Charlotte Islands, and our idea was to wait there for a fair wind, before attempting to cross the Sound. We hoped to make due east to the British Columbian mainland early next morning, so as to secure as much daylight as possible; but when morning came, seeing that a storm had partially arisen, the Indians unanimously voted against launching forth. The Klue Indians are reputed to be the most venturesome of all canoe-men in the North Pacific, and I do not wish to defame them, but the contrary. Still, it is always within sight of land. At the thought of trusting themselves to the high seas they quail. On this occasion they

would have shirked it altogether, only for their confidence in my guidance. There can be no doubt that
Indians look upon the white men as superior beings,
though they endeavour to conceal their conviction
till it comes to the test. They were afraid, and
manifestly regretted having set out on the expedition. When I praised their skill and judgment,
however, they would recover courage, until I
chanced every now and again to cast my eyes
towards the north-east. Then alarm would be de-
picted on each man's countenance, especially on those
of the chiefs, who would at once exclaim—*Itka mika
nanitch?*—what do you see?

Thus we waited forty-eight hours longer, encamped in an old Indian ranche, which Klue said
had been there time out of mind.

The third morning we knew was going to be fine,
for the storm had rolled off and the waves had
smoothed down again. At daybreak, then, we went
upon our way, pressing every stitch of canvas, with
a smart but not unpleasant S.W. breeze.

I cannot picture to myself anything more sublime
in nature than the retrospective view which I had
on bidding a last farewell to Queen Charlotte
Islands. It is a land of enchantment. One can

hardly feel melancholy living by those beauteous though uninhabited shores. Such varied and magnificent landscapes, such matchless timber, such a wealth of vegetation, such verdure and leafage up to the very crests of its highest hills. Its agricultural and mineral prospects are undeniable. Where does another climate exist like it, almost uniting the charms of the tropics to the healthiness of temperate zones, and yet remaining free from the evils of either? No rat or reptile has fixed its home on those islands, nor even a noxious insect. The sole annoyance is an occasional mosquito,* which will grow rarer as cultivation advances. Fogs rarely visit there. The storms, if sometimes severe, seem mostly sea-storms, invariably following a law, and never lasting long. The snows on the coldest day in winter dissolve soon after touching the ground; whilst the sun, during much the greater portion of the year, sheds its effulgence and its warmth, but not its glare, the whole of the live-long day, down upon that virgin country, as if to cheer its loneliness and to allure to it the colonists from afar.

---

* Although the mosquito, by some singular exemption, to a great extent keeps clear of Queen Charlotte Islands, that plaguing insect flourishes in full force on the coast of the mainland, and in the bush of British Columbia.

Just such a sunlit morn was it as we laid ourselves out for sea. I could not help sorrowing at the thought that I might never behold those Western Isles again; but I shipped my paddle in order to feast mine eyes once more upon their beauty. I watched their noble forms recede, I saw their peerless complexion fade, I inhaled the breath of their sweet-scented cedar-wood until I felt it evaporate like some ethereal spirit. At length the Eden of the North Pacific vanished from my sight, and sank down into the deep blue waters of the West.

The strength and skill of every man were now given to the arduous task before us. Onward we paddled, assisted by our sails, relays of the crew succeeding each other regularly, and sparing no effort, all day: not without reason either, for the sky lowered ominously, while the wind increased and the rain began to fall. It was getting on for six P.M., when a shout from an Indian in the bow told us that we had sighted the mainland on the other side of the Sound.

The news raised our spirits somewhat; but they were soon damped again, as almost immediately after it came on pitch dark, which caused us to lose the Skid-a-gate canoe out of hail, the wind changing and the rain descending at the same time in torrents. Nothing daunted, however, on we sped till about midnight, the wail of the land-fowl becoming more distinct with each mile we made. In a couple of hours Klue thought we should be close in-shore, and then we could heave-to and wait for the break of day. Away went the thirty-seven paddles; but upwards of two hours passed and brought no sound of rollers on the beach. Odder still, the cry of the land-fowl had entirely ceased. Suddenly it occurred to me that we were going backwards instead of forwards. On my hinting this to my fellow-paddlers, they only laughed at what they thought was very pardonable ignorance. However, first one man shipped his paddle, then another, and at last, suspecting something wrong, they all got thoroughly frightened. " *Closl nanitch, Tyhee Poole*," shouted Klue from the helm where he was, meaning, " Do you look after the canoe, Chief Poole." Fortunately I had my best pocket-compass stowed somewhere; so, striking a light with considerable difficulty, owing to the high wind and heavy sea, I found that we actually were going back, as straight as an arrow in its course. Putting a few facts together, I rapidly calculated our position to be some thirty miles from the shore.

The two hours had been consequently time and labour lost. Upon the word we put the canoe's head about, and having vainly hailed the Skid-a-gates, we gave our hearts to our paddles with a will, and towards five o'clock A.M. had the satisfaction to hear the breakers breaking on the rocks ahead.

Shortly afterwards day dawned.

The Skid-a-gates were nowhere visible; but our Indians recognised the land we had hit on as the south-east end of Banks's Island, and sure enough, close off the mainland.

Observing a small harbour we ran in. It proved to be Calamity Harbour, in lat. 53° 12″ N., long. 128° 43″ W. The distance from this spot to Victoria is perhaps 300 miles as the crow flies, but by the crooked course we intended to take, with a view of dodging the hostile tribes along the road downward, we reckoned on a distance of at least 750 miles.

Here we had the good luck to find the beach covered with cockles. We gathered a large quantity, and, stringing them on sticks, half toasted them before the fire, so as to preserve them for food in case our other provisions should fail. The island, too, was alive with a species of sea-fowl, the flesh of which tastes like goose. I shot some; but the Indians, being very fond of them, prepared torches for a great slaughter at night, in the event of the weather clearing. Unhappily the wet continued. It was as much as we could do to prevent our camp fire going out. I did dry my clothes, however; and eventually hauling the canoe to a safe place and covering it up with sails, we each contrived to secure a dry spot under some trees where to lay our wearied heads; for the night was again upon us, after thirty-six sleepless hours, during twenty-four of which we had continuously paddled no less than 120 miles.

Yet that now appears as nothing compared with our subsequent sufferings.

Next morning, seeing no improvement in the weather, we set off again in the midst of a most dismal drizzle, which in the course of the day developed into strong rain. At this distance of time it scarcely seems credible to say that, for six days and six nights, we kept on our voyage in that pitiable plight, battling against fearful head-storms, and making barely fifty miles. It is the fact, though. Sleep became impossible, the rain having soaked our clothes and skins through and through. As each morning broke, in vain we strained our aching eyes, to try to spy out something in the shape of a harbour. But it was not till the seventh day that one of our Klootchmen descried an object which on further observation we all pronounced to be a house. Surely a human habitation must bespeak the neighbourhood of a harbour of some sort? Without more parley, then, we steered in-shore, and in another hour we were entering a pretty little cove, headed by a beach which had shell-fish enough on it to supply a whole naval squadron for a week. Above, upon a conspicuous reach of ground, stood the large Indian ranche we had seen from the offing. It had not been recently occupied. Its dilapidated state proved that. But, after such misery as we had just undergone, we hailed it as one might a gorgeous palace, for the shelter, rest, and comfort it was about to afford us.

We stayed twenty-four hours at the ranche—not at all too long to recruit.

The following afternoon, feeling refreshed and hearty, I strolled by myself a short way into the bush. I was groping through the underwood, when a cry of distress from my party startled me. Making sure that they had been surprised by the Bella-Bella Indians, who claimed that part of the coast as their camping-ground, I hastened back to the rescue, and arrived just in time to see a canoe hurrying away from the shore. It was the Skid-a-gates. A turn of the coast had brought our encampment into view, as their party came along, upon which a panic had seized them, and all Klue and his people could do to assure the Skid-a-gates that we were friends only urged them to fly the faster. I ran at once to the harbour's head, and, perching myself on the highest rock, waved my cap at the poor fellows with my utmost energy. They were already a good mile out to sea; but noticing what I did, and knowing the waving of the hat to be the action of a white man they immediately turned back.

Warmly did we welcome our lost companions.

A sight to be remembered was it, to see how those savages greeted their old friends and neighbours. There was no kissing, nor embracing, nor shaking of hands, but a dance of the wildest description, that would have beaten the *cancan* all to fits, and have done one good to look at besides. Till then I had never remarked a genuine smile or tear on the face of a North Pacific Indian. The savages of both tribes danced in a circle together, the two chiefs capering more madly than any, whilst the air rang again with shouts, until I put a stop to it by reminding them of the probability of their enemies being near at hand; on which they instantly desisted.

The Skid-a-gate story was this.

It seemed our canoe had been kept in view much longer than we had been able to discern theirs, its inferior size quite explaining the difference. Like us, they had hardly noticed the change of wind; but, unlike us, when the critical moment came, instead of unwittingly turning back, they had gone northward, and had paddled away night and day out of sight of land, till at length they had accidentally sighted Fort Simpson, 200 miles above our landing-place on Banks's Island. At that point, after a needful rest and a solemn consultation, they had concluded that it must be right with the big canoe, since there was a white man in it. They had made all haste down the coast, in hopes of finding us waiting for them somewhere. And thus what we had been considering an awful hardship proved to be their deliverance; for without storm-weather in our part of the coast they would never have got over their part in time to overtake us.

Right well did our friends merit their welcome. The endurance of the women deserved special praise.

One and all had paddled for many consecutive days under the most hope-killing of circumstances, yet never losing either hope or courage. It was as desperate a life-struggle as ever I had heard of. Manfully they stood it too, and I told them so. Almost it persuaded me to retract my dictum regarding Indian bravery. I perhaps should have retracted if the Skid-a-gates had, in this instance, been embarking of themselves in an enterprise. Their feat partook of that kind of heroism which consists in heroically saving your own life and the lives of others.

If these poor Skid-a-gates had passed our encampment without observing us, they certainly could not have reached their destination, for their little store would soon have been consumed. On the other hand, we could have ill spared them; for though we alone formed a stout party, with the Skid-a-gate contingent we were strong enough to give a tough fight to any antagonist who should dare to attack us. No one could tell but what the very next moment we might have to face the redoubted Bella-Bella Indians. As yet we had not learnt that the small-pox had succeeded in depriving the Bella-Bellas for evermore of the power of mischief. But hearing from Klue how that hated tribe had often inflicted dire injury on the Queen Charlotte Indians when these tried to get down to Victoria, I thought it behoved us to hold ourselves in constant readiness.

The chiefs asked me to take the command in case of attack, to which I willingly acceded, and accordingly gave the two crews the necessary instructions beforehand. Having at that period mastered rifle-practice to the extent of being able to bring down an eagle on the wing at six hundred yards, I may humbly recount that the Indians considered me a host in myself. But besides my Enfield, we mustered thirty-two muskets, with ammunition to correspond, six revolvers, and any quantity of long knives. So that, unless the enemy were to take us one by one, I had no fear of a hostile encounter.

CHAPTER XVIII.

THE RUPERT INDIANS—FRAY WITH THE ACOLTAS—OVER THE TIDAL WAVE —NANAIMO COAL-MINES—THE COWITCHENS—A GENERAL BATHE AND DRESS-UP—ARRIVAL AT VICTORIA.

THE Skid-a-gates had rested before they overtook our party, and, as we all felt anxious to put the country of the bloodthirsty Bella-Bellas quickly behind us, we re-embarked the same night in our two canoes, to proceed to the entrance of the Inside Passage.

The wind was high and the tide was strong; but both worked in our favour, so that, by two hours after midnight, flaring lights ahead gave warning of our having at last crossed Queen Charlotte Sound.

Those lights were the hunting-fires of the Rupert Indians, within musket-range of whom we had now come.

At this season of the year bird-slaughtering is very extensively carried on by all the North Pacific Indians. The birds, which are small but plump, burrow their holes in the sand-banks on the shore. When the slaughter-season arrives, the Indians prepare torches composed of long sticks having the tips smeared with gum taken from the pine-tree. Armed with handy clubs, they then place these lighted torches at the mouths of the holes, and as soon as the birds, attracted by the glare, flutter forth, they fell them to the ground. The process is simple and easy, immense numbers of birds being thus obtained. Afterwards, without any previous plucking or cleaning, the birds are toasted before a slow fire. If the toasting has been properly done, the feathers and skin come off readily. The Indians say that, to clean the inside out, takes away from the flavour, which is perfectly true, as I have tasted the game both ways.

Well, my party swelled with jealousy to see the Rupert Indians enjoying themselves so thoroughly. Yet they dared not venture nearer, lest the noise of our paddles should attract attention. Luckily the night was as dark as if we had been crossing the Styx in Charon's boat. But unless we intended to provoke a fight it now became an absolute necessity to paddle hard out of danger, for the wind was dying away.

Very fierce feelings existed between the Queen Charlotte and the Fort Rupert Indians. Klue informed me that, some years previous, his brother-in-law, in those days the greatest chief on the coast, had been entrapped by the Rupert Indians on his way home from Victoria, and scalped and killed with all his males, his females being divided as slaves among the victors. It was Klue's intention, when he had been recognised as chief by the other chiefs on Queen Charlotte Islands, to collect an overwhelming force and abolish the Fort Rupert tribe altogether.* If he could accomplish this, but not otherwise, he would be considered a great chief by his compatriots, and qualified to take his brother's place as the leading man amongst the tribes.

Little did the Rupert Indians suspect that there was another grand prize ready-made for them, if, instead of indulging in the pleasures of bird-slaughtering, they had but kept a sharp look-out in the bay. They would have found us an expensive capture, notwithstanding.

Before morning we had cleared the territory of

---

* Chief Klue has never been able to conquer the Rupert Indians. His claim to the head-chieftainship is therefore still a moot point between him and the great chief of the Skiddans.

this section of our enemies; but, it was to jump from the frying-pan into the fire.

With the daylight the wind again rose, and by noon it had increased to a gale. Although the gale subsided, the weather continued so boisterous for the next few days that we had constantly to run in to the little coves which characterize the multitudinous island groups of the Inside Passage.

One of these was the scene of an exciting adventure.

I think we had paddled for a hundred hours well nigh continuously—in fact only stopping to hoist an occasional sail, or to take our food and an hour's rest in some sheltered spot. At last we thought of seeking some place where we might have a good meal and a regular lie-down. So, spying a likely-looking island in the centre of a large group, we made towards it and landed, fastening our canoes to the rocks. The men began at once to light a fire, and the women to get the shell-fish ready, whilst I, according to our established custom, trudged away into the bush in search of more substantial fare. I had not penetrated fifty yards when a clump of thick brushwood near me appeared to rustle. Was it only the wind? Or was it a deer perhaps?—deer being very numerous thereabouts. I stood still a moment, and then slowly went forward, fully expecting to bag my game. In place of the deer, however, a black object, with a brace of fiery eyeballs, lay crouching behind the clump and taking deliberate aim with a musket. I gave a yell, thinking to call my companions to the rescue; but it was too late. Having themselves observed several other Indians stealing down in my direction, they had already rushed to the canoes and were leaving me to be murdered. The strange savages, perceiving this, made a rapid dash. How I ever escaped the bullets from the dozen musket-shots simultaneously fired at me has always seemed to me a marvel; but I ran like lightning to the beach. On came my enemies, now certain of an easy capture; for by this time my friends had hauled off out of gun-range and sat poising their paddles and coolly looking to see the end. The situation I was in seemed desperate indeed; for what could one man do against two score of armed adversaries? Suddenly a bright thought occurred to me, and I as quickly resolved to act upon it. Knowing the superstitious nature of those Indians, I told them in their own language that I possessed the power to destroy all black men opposed to me, and that I could command the very author of their existence, the black crow. This announcement rather staggered the savages. But the petty chief who headed them said they would not kill me, but capture me. With that intent they commenced advancing in a half-circle, as cautiously as cats. I grasped a six-barrelled revolver in my right hand, and a long Spanish knife in my left, my Enfield being slung over my shoulder. When they were within a dozen yards of me, I again urged them to retire at the peril of their lives. They replied that what they wanted was simply a *wah-wáh*. I was not to be taken by duplicity, however. Seeing which, one hound partly raised his musket, and would have fired if I had not been too quick for him. With a deep groan he dropped to the earth. In an instant the whole pack were upon me; and another of the hounds having emptied his barrel without effect, I made him spring at least three feet into the air before sending him to the " happy hunting-grounds." I discharged the revolver once more; but, alas, it burst. Wherefore, thrusting that trusty old friend into my belt, I defended myself as best I could with the long knife, until, beginning to feel faint, I turned, dived into the sea, and swam to our canoe, into which I was dragged in a very exhausted condition.

The bloodhounds, from whose jaws I had thus been snatched, were the Acolta Indians, a tribe which has given more trouble to the Colonial Government than any other along the coast. The murders and outrages they have committed on inoffensive and defenceless white men and women are innumerable.

We did not land again for twenty-four hours. Even then we chose a very small islet, lying well apart, and which we first carefully examined in a prolonged paddle round it.

Thus ended my canoe-voyage down the Inside Passage.

We had to face many perils by land, and likewise many perils by sea, similar to those I had faced during my two up-voyages,* with the manifest inconveniences of canoe-travelling superadded. And yet it should not be supposed that a canoe, though in some respects greatly inferior to a decked and full-rigged vessel, is without its advantages. Canoes can go where schooners cannot, they run along more

---

* I made two distinct voyages up the Inside Passage, besides this voyage down it. The first was on board the sloop *Hamley*, almost immediately after my arrival in the colony, and when bound for the Cascade Mountains. The second was on board the sloop *Leonide*, as related heretofore in the text.

swiftly, and are much more easy to steer and manage; whilst, along a savage-beridden coast like that of British Columbia, their greater facility for conceal-ment was not to be disregarded.

As we sped onward the weather got gradually calmer. At length not a breath of wind stirred in the air, nor a ripple on the surface of the water. I would then frequently lie back across my broad seven-foot paddle, and enjoy that blessed institution, so conducive to the happiness of miners or travellers in uncouth countries, a pipe of good tobacco. My companions would always follow suit. Upon which our canoes would glide quietly down-channel, carried forward by the ebbing tide.

One forenoon we were all taking the benefit of this welcome relaxation, wholly thoughtless of any im-pending danger, when suddenly every Indian sprang to his feet in a paroxysm of terror. Had we been surrounded on the instant by a hundred canoes full of war-savages, my companions could not have shown greater alarm; and the moment my eye caught what was before us, I entirely shared their feelings. Right across our course, and not more than two hundred yards in our front, a long white line of foam seethed and boiled, and kept steadily advancing. It was the up-tide battling to predominate over the

OVER THE TIDAL WAVE.

down-tide, which again, burying itself beneath the crest of its more powerful opponent, formed an under-current, unimpeded, and yet, in conjunction with the stronger tide, indescribably dangerous. This is not a common occurrence in the Passage, but it does sometimes happen in its narrow parts. If we had met it at night, we should have failed to see the danger in time, and then nothing could have saved us. As things were, here we found ourselves locked into the narrowest reach of Johnstone Strait, with a line of angry surf running from shore to shore, and close ahead of the canoes. Should we survive? Two minutes more would decide. I do acknowledge, however, that my heart rose to my mouth, and that my blood seemed to freeze in my veins, as I looked death straight in the face: an ignoble death, and nobody left to tell the tale. Not a second was to be lost. Chief Klue roared to his men, *Hinda, kauit-law, mammock clue anta quita,* that is, " Be quick, sit down, and work the canoe with all your strength." Whereupon, dipping our paddles deep into the now rushing, now sinking tides, with four desperate strokes for life we lifted our noble canoe clean out of the water, and shot over the fearful surge. Nervous moments, never to be forgotten. But our difficulties had only commenced; for no sooner were we clear of this line of surf than one of the contending currents hurled us with electric velocity three-quarters of a mile nearer land. I thought we should have been dashed to bits against the rocks, and was making ready for a spring, when, lo and behold, another current spun our canoe round, and sent us, like a bolt from a bow, to the opposite shore. This was repeated several times in succession, not a soul on board uttering a sound. Each time, however, the canoe gained a little headway. On the last crossing we came to a sudden stop in mid-channel, and describing a circle thrice with most awful rapidity, we seemed to be on the very point of plunging headlong into the abyss. But the crisis had arrived. Up out of the united throats of the Indians such a yell was yelled as appeared to shake the very mountains to their foundations. Klue added the words, *Mannock whatluwan*, that is, " Paddle all together." We obeyed, and cleared the whirlpool at a bound. Thenceforward our task was confined to strong and steady paddling for about half an hour. When we shipped our paddles to rest once more, we looked back, horror-stricken, yet thankful, upon that terrible meeting of the waters.

I have here narrated the escape of Klue's canoe in particular. Naturally we had no eyes for aught but ourselves. None the less, our poor friends the Skid-a-gates must have incurred a far greater amount of danger. How indeed they got through, with their light craft, we never could comprehend.

Two or three days more saw us paddling proudly into Nanaimo Harbour.

We had a very cheering reception from the coal-mine people there, Klue's grand canoe and the recital of our adventures creating a special sensation; and further excitement was infused into it by the arrival, shortly after ourselves, of the schooner *Amelia*, the captain of which reported that a vessel named the *Thornton* lay at Fort Rupert with only one man on board, the remainder of the crew having been murdered. The Acolta Indians were the murderers.

That woful affair was briefly as follows. The *Thornton* chancing to be becalmed off the Acolta camping-grounds, a number of canoes manned from the tribe went out alongside and demanded whisky. The captain refused for the best of all reasons, because he had none of the noxious drug on board. The savages, not believing him, thereupon fired at the crew, who were engaged in rigging up sail. The volley was so tremendous that the captain and all the men save one fell dead on the deck. The survivor fled into the cabin, and, seizing a revolver, began discharging it through the port-holes, which effectually frightened off the Indians; for fancying from the rapid firing that there must be more white men concealed in the vessel, they skedaddled to the shore. The *Thornton* then fortunately drifted into a current, by means of which the saved man was enabled to steer his vessel to Fort Rupert.

Had not we of Queen Charlotte Islands good cause to congratulate one another on having come thus far in safety?

At that epoch the Nanaimo settlement was kept perpetually agitated in consequence of reports, which used to arrive nearly every day, of the revolting cruelties practised by the Acolta and Cowitchen Indians on the too confiding white population. I remember, as one dreadful instance, the case of the Marks family, who, lately from England, had gone to squat on a plot close to Nanaimo. They were cruelly murdered, every one, the body of Miss Marks being discovered shockingly mutilated on the beach, and the bodies of the others not long afterwards in the bush. The Governor sent down three gunboats to the Cowitchen camping grounds, but it only resulted in a waste of powder and shot, the bloodhounds hiding themselves in the dense shrubwood of the country, and yet lurking near enough to shoot two of our British tars dead. The very morning we left Nanaimo another ship arrived from Victoria with the news that the Cowitchen Indians had attempted to capture the vessel, but that the crew, having the luck to be well armed and headed by a plucky captain, had been able to repulse the piratical savages.

At Nanaimo our convoy was joined by a third canoe full of Indians, who, as friends of the Skid-a-gates, we allowed to accompany us. This raised our spirits; for, if the whole Cowitchen tribe had now molested us, we should doubtless have given them more than they bargained for. When we passed their encampment, however, we found the tribe otherwise employed. Their wigwams were undergoing a shell-ing process from two English gunboats, whilst they themselves were sneaking into the bush in all direc-tions, or jumping into canoes along the shore. Meeting one runaway canoe, we gave it instant chase. It was as pretty a sight as one would wish to see in a day's paddling. But, with us in pursuit, the Cowitchens had not a chance, so that we soon made them heave-to.

Nothing could well exceed the meanness and cowardice which the wretches then displayed. They threw away their paddles and muskets, and went down on their knees in the canoe, cringing, whining, and even shrieking. We might easily have shot or drowned every man of them. In the midst of it all, the grins, grimaces, and triumphant giggles of my own companions were highly amusing. They merely awaited a signal from me to fall to. I own I felt much inclined to give it; but after we had held our prisoners in suspense awhile, I said that Englishmen scorned to take advantage of the weaker party, and so we let them go. The mercy thus extended to those merciless bullies rather troubled my conscience afterwards; for during the following night we parted company with the friendly Indians who had joined us at Nanaimo. Their canoe was never heard of again, the general belief among the colonists seeming to be that it was cut off, under cover of the darkness, by the very Cowitchen canoe which we had spared the day before.

From this point we paddled away at our ease and pleasure, the glass-like waters reflecting the brilliancy of the sun above, whilst once more the Indians sang me their farewell songs, until, on the twenty-second morning after our leaving Queen Charlotte Islands, the two canoes turned into a little sheltered bay just below the old Spanish Cape Gonzalez, and within six miles overland of Victoria.

Stepping ashore on the diminutive beach of the place, we all bathed in the sea. My travelling companions then rummaged their bundles, and proceeded to don whatever pieces of clothing each man or woman possessed. This ceremony was preparatory to their presenting themselves at Victoria, where the law which compels blacks as well as whites to wear some sort of garment is rigidly enforced.

After the grotesque and laughable performance of people trying to dress who are not accustomed to it had been satisfactorily gone through, we breakfasted in the midst of a shade-giving pine-grove.

Finally I left Klue to "paddle his own canoe" round to Victoria Harbour, whilst I myself took the road by land.

It need scarce be added that my unexpected appearance in the capital, and my weather-worn looks, perfectly astonished the numerous friends who crowded round me.

What did they not say as soon as they heard my story?

" You seem to have dropped from the clouds," exclaimed Mr. R. George, our Company's trusty and indefatigable agent, expressing the legitimate astonishment of all the town.

For we had indeed accomplished what was undoubtingly acknowledged to be the greatest canoe voyage ever known in the North Pacific,* and that too along a coast full of dangers, in the short space of twenty-two days, and at a season of the year when all British Columbian vessels give the land a wide berth.

---

* Perhaps it would not be too much to add, " or in the entire Pacific Ocean." Really the only voyage to compare with ours is the celebrated one made by Captain Bligh, R.N., after the mutiny of the *Bounty*. He went in an open boat from off Otaheite to the island of Timor, a distance of nearly 1200 miles. But, then, he had a compass and sextant with him, and a good keel to his boat. Besides, his whole crew numbered no more than eighteen—just half ours ; whilst, during all his voyage, there was nothing to fear from tides and currents, and nothing worth mentioning from hostile natives.

CHAPTER XIX.

DURING my residence on Queen Charlotte Islands, I made many other observations, which, though they did not fall naturally into the course of the foregoing narrative, should not be omitted from these pages.

I shall treat the subjects* summarily and categorically.

Climate.—The average weather in British Columbia being acknowledged to resemble that of the north of

---

* The particular observations which I was enabled to make during my residence, will be found to agree substantially with the general description of Queen Charlotte Islands published in 1787 by Captain Dixon. (*Voyage to the North-West Passage of America.* Letter xxxviii.)

England, a good idea may be formed of the climate of Queen Charlotte Islands, when I report it as milder than that of any part of Scotland, or of Victoria, the capital of the colony. In Summer the heat averages less, while the Winter months are much warmer, the atmosphere at all times seeming clear, dry, and pure. The Autumn is decidedly the healthiest and pleasantest season there. The temperature, during my two Winters, was never lower than 8° below freezing point, and during my two Summers never higher than 80° in the shade. The mean temperature in the shade, throughout the year, was 68°. I calculated the rainfall in January and February at $21\frac{7}{10}$ inches. The regular and steady winds dried the ground up quickly. Snow fell rarely, and always in small quantities, soon disappearing. I saw only two electric discharges, and witnessed only one thunderstorm, although that was undoubtedly the most violent I ever remember out of Canada.

Also, as stated above, I kept a tide-pole in fair order for the months of January and February, marking the daily record accurately in my register. To be concise, I here give merely the sum-total of results, thus :—

METEOROLOGICAL REGISTER.

Burnaby Island, Queen Charlotte Islands.

Latitude 52° 19′ 30″ North, Longitude 131° 11′ 00″ West.

1863. Months.	Direction of Wind.				Total Quantity of Rain.	Total Quantity of Snow.	Clouds (a Cloudy day is represented by 10, a Cloudless day by 0).			Remarks.
	8 A.M.	2 P.M.	8 P.M.	Compass.			8 A.M.	2 P.M.	8 P.M.	
JANUARY.	1	...	...	N.	Inches.	Inches.	...	...	...	ft. in. Maximum rise of tide 14 10 Minimum „ „ 11 9
	...	...	1	N.N.E.	...	...	...	...	...	
	6	5	5	N.E.	...	...	...	...	...	High and low water, twice during the 24 hours.
	2	1	1	E.N.E.	...	...	...	...	...	
	...	2	2	E.	...	...	...	...	...	
	1	1	1	E.S.E.	...	...	...	...	...	
	...	...	1	S.E.	...	...	...	...	...	
	...	1	1	S.S.E.	...	...	...	...	...	At 5 P.M. on the 3rd one flash of lightning, at 7 P.M. on the 26th one flash of lightning and one of thunder.
	...	1	1	S.	...	...	...	...	...	
	...	...	1	S.S.W.	...	...	...	...	...	
	6	5	7	S.W.	...	...	...	...	...	
	7	5	5	W.S.W.	...	...	...	...	...	
	2	1	...	W.	...	...	...	...	...	
	1	2	...	W.N.W.	...	...	...	...	...	Tides stationary only about 30 minutes.
	3	4	3	N.W.	...	...	...	...	...	
	1	1	2	N.N.W.	...	...	...	...	...	
	...	...	...	...	$14\frac{2}{10}$	$3\frac{2}{10}$	130	145	160	
FEBRUARY.	...	...	1	N.	Inches.	Inches.	...	...	...	ft. in. Maximum rise of tide 15 3 Minimum „ „ 11 10
	...	...	...	N.N.E.	...	...	...	...	...	
	13	12	12	N.E.	...	...	...	...	...	High and low water, twice during the 24 hours.
	...	...	1	E.N.E.	...	...	...	...	...	
	...	...	...	E.	...	...	...	...	...	
	...	...	...	E.S.E.	...	...	...	...	...	6 inches of snow fell on the 7th, and 3 inches on the 10th, but melted off same day.
	3	4	3	S.E.	...	...	...	...	...	
	1	...	...	S.S.E.	...	...	...	...	...	
	1	1	...	S.	...	...	...	...	...	
	1	3	1	S.S.W.	...	...	...	...	...	
	2	2	3	S.W.	...	...	...	...	...	
	3	2	3	W.S.W.	...	...	...	...	...	
	1	1	1	W.	...	...	...	...	...	
	...	1	1	W.N.W.	...	...	...	...	...	
	2	2	2	N.W.	...	...	...	...	...	
	1	...	...	N.N.W.	...	...	...	...	...	
	...	...	...	...	$7\frac{5}{10}$	$13\frac{8}{10}$	100	100	120	

The tides vary from one to two knots an hour all round Burnaby Island. This, I take it, is probably true of the other islands as well.

Harbours and Inland Waters.—The inlets and arms

of the sea are countless. Spring-water of the very purest abounds in every part of the coast-land. As it mostly appears to flow from long distances inland, I am disposed to infer the existence of fresh-water lakes embosomed among the mountains of the interior, the labour and time required for a thorough exploration of the country having hitherto prevented either white men or black undertaking that duty.

I did not see or hear of any river worth the mention. But, with such coast-access, rivers would be of no significance.

The harbourage is simply magnificent. Stewart's Channel, which reminded me immensely of Spithead, can accommodate an untold number of ships of the heaviest tonnage, and securely shelter them against storms from whatever quarter. The same, relatively as to size, may be said of Sockalee, Harriet, Laskeek, and Cum-she-was Harbours, on the eastern coast, and no doubt of many another on the western.

Rocks.—To take Burnaby Island as an example, in the lower section of that islet considerable deposits of black slate mixed with limestone exist, the limestone being much disturbed by greenstone and granitic rockage, and its dense crystalline felspathic traps being grooved and furrowed by glacial action.

This semi-crystalline limestone is studded with small bunches of black scorial slate, furnishing strong evidence of its plutonic age. A system of metalliferous quartzose veins having parallel trappean dykes, also permeates that island. These veins consist of ragged masses of plutonic, metamorphic, and trappean rock. I prospected likewise a number of spurs and veins of yellow and white quartz, the general run of which lies north and south. Some of these veins are a few inches in width, others as much as six feet, all highly oreiferous.

Owing to the thick brushwood and the loose soil, composed of the *débris* of fallen timber and of vegetable matter lying undisturbed for centuries, I found it utterly impracticable to ascertain the extent or even the position of the rocks.

Occasionally the trees stand separate; but the weary explorer does not advance twenty paces before he is sure to tumble upon prostrate giants flung one over the other in every conceivable configuration, from the lowest to the highest angles. Sometimes, after having fought his way for hours through despairing entanglements, he emerges into an open space seemingly solid. He steps boldly across it towards the next thicket, but, on a sudden, the thin slippery crust gives way, and down he goes twenty or thirty feet amongst the rotten roots and the remains of eagles, crows, wild dogs, bears, and innumerable birds and beasts defunct ages ago. The bottom is usually dry; otherwise those frequent mishaps would often be fatal. As it is, such a combination of obstacles cannot fail to prevent the interior being explored, except in a very gradual manner, or unless the exploration should be undertaken on a colossal scale.

Land.—No one could pass a week among the islands without becoming convinced of their agricultural capacities. Vancouver Island has plenty of good arable land; but I saw nothing there, either in quality or in quantity, to equal what is to be seen on every side along the shores of Queen Charlotte Islands. The soil fit for farming purposes is not only extensive beyond all present calculation, but rich beyond description, and better still, wholly unappropriated. It seems to be ever crying out to the personifiers of civilization, " Come and farm me, and I will return you a hundredfold." In short, once colonize those islands with the English farmer-class, and, considering the richness of the soil, the excellent harbourage, the easy means of transport, and the markets that are certain to arise on the British Columbian mainland, one might safely predict for them an agricultural prosperity absolutely unrivalled on the face of the globe.

Trees, Fruits, and Vegetables.—The principal trees are the pine,* the spruce-pine, the alder, the crab, and the cedar, all in profusion and in first-class condition. I have made a calculation by which I am ready to prove that the cedars could be brought to the European market at a profit of eight per cent, which again might be increased to twenty per cent, if the other resources of the islands were included in the transit.

Potatoes have already taken kindly to the soil. The natives cultivate them in really large quantities, and convey them across the Sound to the nearest

---

* The largest pine-tree known to exist on Vancouver Island is one near Mr. Richardson's house, Chemainis prairie, and not far from Chemainis river. It measures fifty-one feet in circumference, which gives sixteen in diameter. Its height is one hundred and fifty feet. Originally it was about fifty feet higher; but the top has been broken off, either by lightning or by wind. Its name is " The Old Guardsman." And certainly it must have stood guard over the " forest primæval " for whole centuries before any of its giant neighbours were born.

It is common for people " on the trail" to turn aside to visit Mr. Richardson's famous pine.

What, then, will be thought when I say, that the Queen Charlotte pine-trees are, as a rule, taller than " The Old Guardsman," and not unfrequently quite double its height and circumference? I measured several which gave over three hundred feet high and sixty feet round.

white settlements for sale. So far, the potato is the only vegetable on the islands. There are no cereals, wild or cultivated, and none of the tropical fruits, not even wild grapes. But anybody acquainted with the soil, taken with the climate, will recognise in it a fertile field for much of that kind of produce over and above the products of our own farming and kitchen-gardening.

Crab-apples are plentiful, likewise strawberries, raspberries, cranberries, and the sweet-tasting berry which the Indians dry and preserve for winter use. Were all this raw material handled with skill, the country would soon be unsurpassed in ordinary fruit-gardening, to say nothing of the vines and wall-fruit of Europe that would be sure speedily to follow.

Fish, Game, and Fur.—Salmon of several different species, cod, halibut, sturgeon, haddock, trout, whiting, herring, smelt, rock-bass, and seals of two species, swarm either in the seas of the coastway, or in the creeks and fresh river streams running up from it.

As regards shell-fish, having myself eaten native oysters, I cannot question the fact of oyster-beds existing, although no actual beds have ever yet been seen there. The quantity and variety of the inferior sort of shell-fish are truly astonishing.*

The larger fish, such as the whale and porpoise, would appear to make Queen Charlotte Sound their playground. They doubtless prefer the warmer water. I have seen scores of them at a time amusing themselves within rifle-range of our log-house on Burnaby Island.

The game is snipe, duck, goose, ermine, marten,

---

* Subjoined is a descriptive list of the varieties of shell-fish found on the beach and rocks in front of our log-house :—

Diadema granulosum	Secondary	Cretaceous	Lower Green Sand
Pecten plebeius	Tertiary	Old Phoc	Red Crag
Bulla edwardsii	Cain	Eoc	Brack
Voluta luctatrix	ditto	ditto	Woll. Beds
Fusus regularis	ditto	ditto	Brack
Axinus angulatus	ditto	ditto	ditto
Mytilus antiquarium	ditto	Old Phoc	Red Crag
Voluta spinosa (6 varieties)	ditto	Eoc	Woll. Beds
Sanguinolaria hollowaysii	ditto	Eoc	London
Mactra arenata	Tertiary	Pleist	Norwich Crag
Pileopsis vetusta	Primary	Ceub	Ceub Strall
Pleurotomaria reticulata	Secondary	Vol.	Portland Sand
Murex sex-dentatus	Cain	Upper Eoc	Fluv. Marine
Voluta lamberta	ditto	Old Phoc	Coil Crag
Astarte elliptica	Tertiary	Pleist	Cavern Remains
Nautica pachylabrum	Cain	Eoc	Lond. Clay
Murex erinaceus	Tertiary	Pleist	F. and M. Deposits

I have verified the above list by Reynolds's British Chart; but I gathered many more varieties, which are not accounted for in Reynolds's work, or, to my knowledge, in any scientific book. Unluckily they were destroyed, together with all my valuable fossil and mineral specimens, in the great Canadian bush-fire of 1865.

common otter, sea-otter, and bears, besides numerous other birds* and animals. The stock of game seems a marvel in itself, until one remembers that there has never yet been any serious onslaught upon it. Colonization will, of course, cause a decrease; still for twenty years hence no colonist of the islands need starve, if he possesses a gun and can hit a hay-stack.

Fur will no doubt also die out, as a traffic; but, again, years must elapse before all the bears,

---

* The following is a list of the birds frequenting the neighbourhood of Burnaby Island :—

Night-hawk—*falco nocturnus*.
Sparrow-hawk—*falco sparverius*.
Gos-hawk—*astur atricapillus*.
White-headed eagle—*haliaëtus leucocephalus*.
Belted kingfisher—*alcedo accinctus*.
Western blue-bird—*cyanæus occidentalis*.
North Western fish-crow—*corvus caurinus*.
Wilson's snipe—*gallinago wilsonii*.
Canadian goose—*bernacla canadensis*.
White-cheeked goose—*bernacla leucoparsia*.
Mallard (stock duck)—*anas boschas*.
Canvas-back duck—*aythia vallisneria*.
Golden-eye (whistle-wing duck)—*bucephala americana*.
Buffle-head duck—*bucephala albeola*.
Harlequin duck—*histrionicus torquatus*.
Velvet duck—*malanetta velvetina*.
Glaucous-winged duck—*larus glaucescens*.
Suckley's gull—*larus suckleyii*.
Great Northern diver—*colymbus torquatus*.
Red-necked grepe—*podicetus grisergeria*.

seals, ermine, and marten are cleared out. The present breeds, in my opinion, would supply fur enough to make the fortunes of half-a-dozen fur companies.

Native Tribes.—Here are the tribal names of the principal tribes inhabiting the islands:—Klue, Skid-dan, Ninstence or Cape St. James, Skid-a-gate, Skid-a-ga-tees, Gold-Harbour, Cum-she-was, and four others, whose appellations I never could distinguish. Hydah is the generic name for the whole.

All these tribes together amount to a native population of about five thousand, rather less perhaps.

The Queen Charlotte Islanders are justly considered the finest sample of the Indian race in the North Pacific. They will stand comparison with any Indians in the world. Their faults are the usual Indian ones; but I did not find them to be naturally revengeful or bloodthirsty, except when smarting under the sense of a real and grave injury, or when seeking to avert an imaginary wrong.

If honestly and firmly treated, no natives could be better disposed towards the white men. Chief Klue, considering himself as a sort of suzerain to the other chiefs, and believing that he had a right to do what he liked with his own islands, made me a present, in the simplicity of his heart, of the whole of Queen Charlotte Islands, on condition that I lived amongst my Indian friends, and induced all my English friends to come and settle there too. No small gift, considering that the islands are nearly two hundred miles long, by an average of thirty wide.

The men are generally tall, and they would be handsome, or at least comely, if it were not for their atrocious custom of bedaubing themselves all over. Their real reason for using paint is that they fancy it improves personal beauty; and those poor savages of the islands are certainly not singular in hoping to be made " beautiful for ever " by means of paint. But they give as their excuse the necessity of having some protection against the weather. Until they consent to wear clothing, it must be owned, too, that there is something in the excuse. The majority of them, whether male or female, wear only a small-sized blanket, thrown loosely across the shoulders, like a Spanish hidalgo's cloak, and more with a view to warmth than from any sense of decency.

Some of the women have exceedingly handsome faces and very symmetrical figures. Their charms, however, are all but neutralized by the usage common amongst them of disfiguring their breasts, arms, ears, and under-lip. One particularly fine woman, a daughter of the petty chief Skilly-gutts, had half her body tattooed with representations of chiefs, fish, birds, and beasts. She told me that a halibut, laid open with the face of the chief of her tribe drawn on the tail, would protect her and her kin from drowning at sea. Most of the native females wear rings through their noses. The elder ones may frequently be seen with nose-rings large enough to serve as collars for cats in good condition. Every woman has three or four holes to each ear, one of the holes being generally of sufficient size to admit the little finger up to the second joint. The rings are bone, and their own manufacture ; but sometimes, rather than not decorate their ears, they will insert pieces of stick or strips of cloth into the ear-holes. Bracelets of the same material are not uncommon, likewise anklets, which, however, having usually been put on in youth and retained as fixtures, often cause lameness. My constant topic of conversation with the native women was the custom of our country in regard to females. The most frequent questions used to refer to *Tyhee Klootchman* and her *Papoose*, that is, Queen Victoria and her children ; for example, how they dressed, how much money they had, what price each of the children fetched in blankets, and their names. The names formed a never-failing source of amusement. I had to give each woman and papoose a name after some member of the Royal Family, past or present. When I had finished they would go away delighted; but the next morning they would be pretty sure to call upon me again, to beg to have their names told them once more, a function I was wholly unable to discharge, having meanwhile forgotten all about them.

Amongst these simple and primitive tribes the institution of marriage is altogether unknown. On the other hand, so is polygamy. They view a woman purely as a thing of purchase, to be had connubially for a month's trial, and then, if not satisfactory, to be returned to her parents, who are thereupon bound to give back whatever she fetched in blankets, trinkets, or the rest. The beautiful bond of attachment ending only in death, and the heroic constancy of affection often not ending then, which characterizes the lawful intercourse of the sexes in civilized countries has yet to be introduced into Queen Charlotte Islands. The females in fact cohabit almost promiscuously with their own tribe, though rarely with other tribes. Not only does no dishonour attach to that degrading practice, but, if successful in making money, it is highly honoured. I remember one singular case of this. Some Queen Charlotte women went to spend the Winter at Victoria, hoping to "earn blankets." They came back loaded with blankets, trinkets, tobacco, whisky. and other presents, which they proceeded to distribute among their people in the following manner. Perching themselves on a rocky platform near the beach, they tore the blankets into long strips of about eight inches wide, and threw them as far as possible into the midst of the crowd, who scrambled for them. When the crowd got tired and the fun flagged, the leader of the women produced a bundle of old revolvers and pitched them one after another into the shallow part of the sea, the men rushing in up to their arm-pits, mad with desire to possess a white man's " six-shooter." It certainly was very diverting, if one had not chanced to recollect whence and why the booty had come here. The really strange part of it all had to come, however; for, on my inquiring what the women meant by giving away their earnings in that way, 1 was told that they would all be rewarded. And so they were, Klue raising the " husband" of the principal woman to the rank of chief, and the tribe building her a house. Apart from the detestable traffic which enabled that woman to gain such a position in her tribe, I could not help seeing in the public wish to recognise her supposed merit a good forecast of what true civilization may one day do for those poor untaught islanders. She rose in the estimation of her *tillicums* (friends), because, having earned money— they cared not how—she had shown a good *tumtum* (heart), in assisting the needy. Not a bad criterion, surely; or, at least, a policy which not seldom is approved and acted upon amongst our home nations.

It is a common error, common throughout the American continent even, to imagine that the aborigines of Canada and British Columbia are *black*. We are called *whites* to make a distinction; but in reality, the natural skin which prevails in most of the tribes is nearly as white as ours. The " dusky " Indians of the Canadian prairies stain their skins with the bark of trees, and the " blacks," in our colonies along the North Pacific seaboard, paint themselves with wetted char-wood. Whenever this custom was temporarily relinquished, I was always impressed by the manly beauty and bodily proportions of my islanders. The Ninstence tribe, generally known as the Cape St. James Indians, appeared to me the handsomest, the Skid-a-gates the most intelligent, and Klue's personal tribe the most daring and trustworthy. Another error concerns the colour of the hair. No doubt it usually is dark; but the shade differs greatly. I saw a whole family or section of a tribe, on the British Columbian mainland, every one of whom had not only a clean white skin but light silky hair. On Queen Charlotte Islands there were numberless instances of auburn tresses, and a few positively of golden curls, amongst which Klue's little Klootchman daughter was conspicuous.

The chief food of the Queen Charlotte islanders is halibut. This fish amply suffices to support them during the fishing season, the flesh of it being substantial, satisfying, and well-flavoured. At the close of the fishing season they dry the fish. Before eating dried fish they break it into bits, and soak the bits in fish-oil, or rather in fish-grease having the consistency of uncooled jelly, and then devour them, just as boys amongst ourselves are wont to revel in bread and treacle.* Fish thus soaked is their Winter-food,

---

* This mode of eating dried fish curiously tallies with the manners of the Queen Charlotte Islanders in the last century, as described by Captain Cook, R.N., in his *Voyage to the Pacific Ocean.* (Vol. ii. p. 424).

their only additional relish being the preserved berry already alluded to. Quantities of berries are laid in stock; but, the eaters have such prodigious appetites that frequently whole tribes will be reduced to starvation before the Winter ends. Were it not for a few bulbs which they dig out of the soil in the early Spring-time, while awaiting the halibut-season, numbers of Indians really would starve to death. They use nets, baits, and a kind of club or flat mallet to fish with. Bears and other animals are caught by means of an ingenious method of trapping; for, odd as it may seem, the Queen Charlotte Islanders know nothing of spears, and, odder still, nothing of bows and arrows. Hence, until they got muskets from the white men, the game on the islands had a pleasant time of it. Even now the Indians are only able to shoot an occasional seal, or at most a duck or a goose.

Bark forms their grand medicinal specific. They have another curative remedy, however, which is apparently original and novel. For a long while I was at a loss to account for the large pools of water which, on returning after dinner, we often used to find lying round the shaft-head. I remember feeling somewhat anxious, as it occurred to me that possibly there might have been an overflow from the shaft itself, although I did not understand how such could have happened. But, then, the water never appeared in the night-time, and in the day-time only when the workmen were away. Concluding, therefore, that the Indians had to do with it, I watched behind a rock one day during dinner-time. Presently I saw a chief and two of his women come along. Taking a bucket apiece from the shaft-works, they went down to the sea, and having filled the buckets with sea-water they came quietly back to the works. What in the name of goodness were the perfidious wretches going to do? Perhaps inundate the shaft, and try to spoil our mining operations? Not so. Squatting down on their haunches, each Indian seized a bucket, and at one gulp swallowed every drop of its contents. This extraordinary performance puzzled me more than ever, particularly as the drinkers remained immovable in their squat position. I could perceive nothing to explain the pools of water. However, after I had waited patiently for fully twenty minutes, I was about to retire, when suddenly all three, rising a little, opened their mammoth jaws, and out rushed half a pail of water from each mouth. They then began twisting and rolling their bodies hither and thither, as one might shake up a bottle of physic, and immediately the rest of the water was ejected. The matter-of-fact ease with which they conducted the entire process made up not the least curious part of it. But the problem of the pools was solved. Going up to the Indians, therefore, and unable to smother my laughter, I asked them what they intended by the proceedings I had just witnessed. " They were washing themselves inside-out " was the answer, delivered in a very serious tone of voice, as much as to insinuate that they considered their water-cure to be no joke at all, in which sentiment I certainly, on reflection, coincided ; for to the indiscriminate adoption of this cure, it seems to me, is clearly traceable the fearful mortality among the natives when the small-pox visited them.

I never yet met with an Indian who was not a born gambler. On the British Columbian mainland, and on Vancouver Island, professionals travel about from tribe to tribe, trusting entirely to gambling for a livelihood. But the Queen Charlotte Islanders surpass any people that I ever saw in passionate addiction to the all-absorbing vice. I shall give one salient instance. I once stood by while a Queen Charlotte chief gambled away every article he possessed in the world. He continued playing for three days, without eating a mouthful of food, but perpetually losing. By the fourth day he had parted with the very blanket on his back. A woman of his tribe, however, having compassionately lent him her only blanket, he renewed the contest, and recovered not merely what he had previously lost, but all his opponent's property, which happened to be rather considerable in powder and shot, muskets, revolvers, blankets, skins, paints, tobacco, and fish. The game was *Odd or Even*,* which is played thus. The players spread a mat, made of the inner bark of the yellow cypress, upon the ground, each party being provided with from forty to fifty round pins or pieces of wood, five inches long by one-eighth of an inch thick, painted in black and blue rings, and beautifully polished. One of the players, selecting a number of these pins, covers them up in a heap of

---

* Mr. J. A. St. John, describing the sports and pastimes of the ancient Greeks, has the following:—"To play at *Odd or Even* was common; so that we find Plato describing a knot of boys engaged in this game. There was a kind of divination, the bones being hidden under the hand, and the one party guessing whether they were odd or even. The same game was occasionally played with beans, walnuts, or almonds, if we may credit Aristophanes, who describes certain serving-men playing at *Odd or Even* with golden staters." (Manners and Customs of Ancient Greece, Vol. I. p. 162.) The Roman game of *Morra*, still played in Italy by the peasants, is of a similar nature, although the hands only are used in it.

bark cut into fine fibre-like tow. Under cover of the bark he then divides the pins into two parcels, and, having taken them out, passes them several times from his right hand to his left, or the contrary. While the player shuffles, he repeats the words *I-E-Ly-Yah*, to a low monotonous chant or moan. The moment he finishes the incantation, his opponent, who has been silently watching him, chooses the parcel where he thinks the luck lies for *Odd or Even*. After which the second player takes his innings, with his own pins and the same ceremonies. This goes on till one or other loses all his pins. That decides the game.

The Queen Charlotte Islanders have a vague notion of a Great Spirit. They also share the belief, prevalent among all North American Indians, that, when they die, their spirits will pass to " the happy hunting-grounds," the chase being the type of happiness to the Indian mind. But I failed to trace the slightest connexion between these two semi-religious ideas and the current of their lives. They did not appear to look upon themselves as in the slightest degree responsible to a Supreme Being for their actions. In consequence they offered Him no worship. I observed that even their conception of duty towards their fellow-men was extremely limited, being in fact regulated solely by the supposed good that would accrue from any particular act to any individual person or tribe in whom or which they were interested. Unless when they followed the impulses of their hearts, gain seemed their sole motive, no inconvenient principles ever standing in the way. On the other hand, though prone to superstition, like all savage nations, they are far less grossly superstitious than other Indians in the North Pacific. Thus such horrible orgies as those enacted by the medicine-men among the Tsimshean Indians near Fort Simpson, one never sees or hears of among the Queen Charlotte Islanders.

They keep many feasts or festivals during the course of the year. These do not bear the least on religion, but are purely social gatherings. In preparation for a feast the Indians first wash the old black paint clean off their bodies. Then, after having besmeared their skins with fish-grease to cause the colours to stick well, they repaint their faces, chests, and arms red, with figures of men, birds, or fish. The black paint is their own preparation; the red is vermilion, which they purchase from the whites. When this repainting has been accomplished, it may be styled their full-dress. And yet they are not deemed presentable at the feast till they have furthermore besprinkled their painted bodies all over with the fine down of the duck or goose. Talk of tarring and feathering being mythical. It is pure and simple reality to them. As soon as the time comes for the feast to commence, the men squat down in large extended circles, and beat a sort of accompaniment by means of double sticks to the dancing of the women. That can scarcely be called a dance, either, which is but a contortion of the head and body into every imaginable shape and position, while the knee-joints, and often the entire legs, remain unmoved. Now and again a woman will throw in a new movement or figure, spicing it with a witty or slangy word, such as will highly amuse the outer crowd, and encourage them to redouble the excitement.

Here are two of their favourite songs. The first runs:—

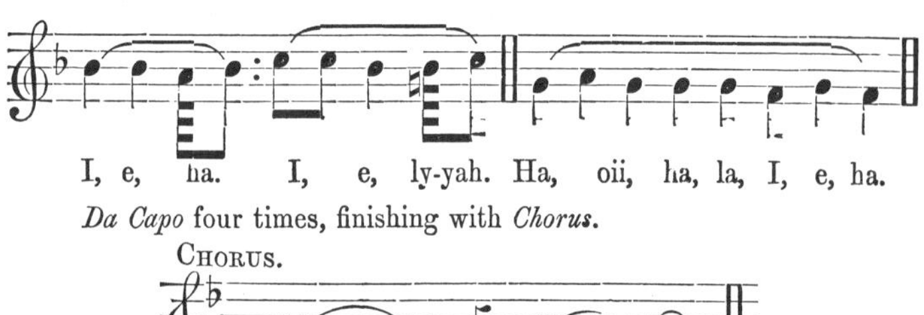

Da Capo four times, finishing with *Chorus.*

The second is nothing but a repetition of the note *B* in the key of *E*; and the words, like our *ri-fol-de-liddle-lol-ri-fol-lairy*, having no intrinsic signification, have no translation. They sing this song principally when out canoeing. The notes to the two upper lines are semibreves, those to the under-line crotchets, thus:—

Equàl—ah, ah, ah, ah, hè, hè, hè. *andante.*
Equàl—ah, ah, ah, ah, hè, hè, hè. *crescendo.*
Equàl—ah, equàl—ah, hè, hè, hè. *decrescendo.*

These specimens of native music were certainly composed before modern notation was introduced, and probably before the art of music was invented. I have tried to approximate the above rendering to our ideas. But the proper term for this kind of music would be *Plain Chant Run Mad*, if it were not for a peculiar plaintiveness of tone and a quaint hitch of the voice at the end of each line, which redeems the so-called singing from the charge of inflicting torture on human ears.

As I conclude this narrative of my discoveries and adventures along the North Pacific coast, my thought naturally reverts to the geographical position of the islands where, for the chief part of two years, I lived and worked.

Everybody who has personal cognizance of Canada and British Columbia feels assured of the day being near when the western boundary of the Canadian Dominion must comprise, not only the Red River and the Saskatchawn territories, but our outlying possessions in the North Pacific. The importance of so vast an agglomeration will explain itself to those who are strangers to America, by the reflection that the British Columbian colony alone contains 280,000 square miles, making no less than 179,200,000 acres. Let the political arrangements be once complete, and a Grand Northern Pacific Railway, opening up to colonization and culture immense tracts now waste and unknown, will inevitably follow. Great, however, as the acquisition appears at first glance, its primary value by no means comprehends all the advantages that are sure to accrue thence to the British Empire. For unbroken steam and rail communication, under our own control, with the North Pacific Ocean will also give both England and Canada a new outlet for the exports to the western seaboards of the two Americas, and, further on, to Japan, China, and Australasia.

But those isles of the Far West which I have been describing lie directly in the high-road of the anticipated commerce.

If, therefore, their beneficent climate, and the magnitude of their mineral and agricultural resources, be judiciously appraised beforehand, their prosperity is already secured.

I close with the earnest hope that such a colonizing scheme will ere long be devised as may, at one and the same time, utilize so favoured a country to us, and rescue from savagedom the poor benighted tribes who inhabit it.

Then I shall think that I have not laboured in vain on behalf of Queen Charlotte Islands.

CHAPTER XX.

THE Queen Charlotte Mining Company having approved my Report, provided for the removal of my late workmen, and handsomely acknowledged my services, I was free to return to England, or to resume the more regular professional work in Canada, from which I had temporarily severed myself.

Before briefly narrating my return-voyage, I shall say a word on the capital of British Columbia.

Outside Victoria, towards the north, is an excellent racecourse, with some high land in the centre of it called Beacon-hill. I took my stand there, to have a farewell look at the colony. In the North Pacific strangers are said to incline to the use of superlatives while surveying the scenery. Perhaps so; yet, "most magnificent, most glorious," are the expressions that do rise to one's mind in presence of the perfect natural beauty to be viewed on all sides.

The prospect for miles and miles round the capital could not but enlist enthusiastic admiration. What I saw included an interminable extent of bold sea-coast, cut up into lovely coves and future bathing-places, that forcibly recalled our Devon and Cornwall at home. Beyond these came, here the ocean in all its expanded beauty, there the straits and the inland seas I had learnt to know so well, and, beyond the straits again, the long mountain-chains of the Oregon Territory rearing their snow-clad crests in stern splendour. I sat for hours, hardly taking my eyes from off the landscape, rendered doubly beautiful by the clear atmosphere which allowed me to discern objects without a glass at wondrous distances.

It is grand that Englishmen should have such a land to colonize. Other nations, one felt, would spoil it.

Looking down, you see Victoria at your feet. It is laid out on rising ground, and promises from its plan to become a fine city. The streets are designedly wide; but it will be years yet before high houses can be built in sufficient numbers to make the width and height of the streets more proportionate. Every thoroughfare in the town stands at right angles with its neighbours, after the usual colonial fashion. If one adds that the whole place has a genuine colonial air about it, no dispraise is intended. Some day its streets will rival those of Melbourne.

I remember particularly, being in an observant and reflective mood on descending from my eminence, that I was struck by the neatness and comfort which seemed to predominate through the town; and that is more than can be said for Yankee beginnings in any given locality.

The immediate vicinity of Victoria looks bare. Amongst the few attractive spots near is Government House. The grounds which surround it are considerable and prettily laid out. Of the residence itself, I can only venture to say that it insensibly called to mind the house of an English farmer in easy circumstances.

After a pleasing interview with Governor Douglas, and an affectionate leave-taking with Chief Klue and his men, I at last made ready to quit British Columba.*

---

* By the official returns of the British Columbian Government in 1870, the white population in the colony was estimated at 10,496, inclusive of 1947 Chinese. But, of course, many roaming traders, miners, and fishermen are overlooked. The Indian population is variously estimated at from 30,000 to 50,000.

From this point my Diary will serve me to the end of the journey homeward:—

"*May* 15*th.*—Wishing many sincere friends good-bye, I mounted this morning into the stage, bag and baggage, and came quickly across from Victoria to Esquimalt Harbour. I am now on board the *Sierra Nevada* steamship, bound for San Francisco."

"18*th*, 8 A.M.—Just entering the " Golden Gate," within sight of Frisco, after a roughish but pleasant passage from Esquimalt.

" 2 P.M.—Have put up at the Tehaina House Hotel, and taken a berth in a small steamer to go and see the great copper-mines near Stockton."

" 19*th.*—Reached Stockton, by *Cornelia* steamer, at 3 A.M. to-day. Came along in the stage to Coppero-polis, distant thirty-nine miles, where I arrived at 3 P.M., having passed through enormous flats of the richest prairie land. About one hundred houses in Copperopolis (what a name to give a place, to be sure), nearly all hotels and stables. Went off at once to visit the works. Saw the famous Union mine, which, they say, has a vein sixteen feet thick, extending in one straight line for twenty miles. This mine is worked by three engines, one of six-horse power, and two others of fourteen-horse power each. I inspected also the Keystone mine, on the opposite side of the town. Smaller, but better ore. Obtained specimens* from both mines."

"20*th*, 2 P.M.—Arrived back at Stockton a while ago. Before leaving Copperopolis I hired a swift Mexican mustang (small mule), and rode out to see the "King of Trees," a few miles from the town, returning by another route over a spur of the Sierra Nevada mountains. Only a huge stump now remains of this once great tree. The top part† was cut off and conveyed to our Crystal Palace at Sydenham, some years back. There is a whole grove of gigantic trees, the one sent to England having been the largest. At first sight, these trees do not appear so very much larger-sized than those of the surrounding forest. It is only by measurement that one comes to apprehend their immensity. The largest tree now in the grove measures thirty-three feet in diameter, the same diameter, namely, as that of the Thames Tunnel. Another, called the "Grizzly Giant," fell down last year. As it lay on the ground, I took the diameter. It was exactly thirty-three feet. I also

---

* On my return to England I placed these particular specimens in the collection at Somerset House, London.

† This is the Californian trunk, which was afterwards burnt in the Crystal Palace fire in 1867.

measured the distance from the root to the first limb, and found it to be ninety feet, the diameter at the limb itself being over six feet."

"21st.—Got to my hotel at California at 2 A.M., after a disgusting passage of nine hours from Stockton. Steamer *Henry Hemsley* wretched, and full of drunken Yankee rowdies. Ran aground coming up, and had much difficulty in getting the vessel off, in consequence of the disorderly mob on board, republican institutions requiring that everybody, however ignorant, should have a voice in the matter. A never-too-highly-prized blessing is it, being born under the flag of Old England."

" 23rd., 8 A.M.—It warms one's heart to look out of the hotel window this morning. For what do I see, amidst all the rowdyism around me, but about forty English ships in the harbour, gaily decorated from stem to stern with flags and streamers? They are keeping the Queen's birthday. This cheery sight reminds me that in two hours I shall have embarked in the *Golden Age* steamer, on my way back to civilized life."

"28th.—We have now been five days at sea, having steamed some 1280 miles, or about 256 miles every twenty-four hours. The ship is nothing but an old punt, hastily refitted for this service.* She rolls like a wash-tub. The passengers, who hardly number two hundred, do not seem martyrs to sea-sickness, being for the most part old stagers on the briny deep. I am the only Englishman amongst them. They are principally Mexicans and South Americans, with a dozen successful miners from Cariboo and California."

"29*th*, 6 A.M.—Crossed the Gulf of California during the night, and, for the first time since leaving San Francisco, can see the land on our lee.

"7 A.M.—Off Corrientes, in the Republic of Halisco. Not three miles from the coast: but we are unable to make it out, in consequence of a cloud-like mist, drawn from the earth by the heat of the sun. The Captain tells me, that this mist will become more intense every day, according as we approach nearer to the Line.

"11 A.M.—Mist cleared. We can plainly discern the wreck of a large steamship in-shore. It was destroyed by fire when passing this way a few weeks ago. Ship's name, the *Golden Gate.* Cause of the accident, customary Yankee negligence. Many lives were lost, among which an old friend of my own.

---

* The same ship that had taken me, in 1862, to San Francisco. The vessel was very fair to look at, but completely worn out.

The wreck lies high and dry on the beach, exposed to the wild surf so common along the Mexican coast.

"2·30 P.M.—Dropped anchor at noon, in Manzanilla Harbour.

"Weather not so hot and sultry as when I came in here before. There seems much more liveliness about the place. The site for a city is well chosen, and the harbour capacities of Manzanilla are indubitably great. We have taken a large freight of silver on board, in coin and bars; also cotton in bales.

"Quite a crowd of Mexican ladies have come off in boats to inspect our ship: and they do look desperately handsome, with their lustrous eyes under the longest eyelashes in creation, and such tiny hands and feet. The length of the hand is the length of the foot; so, instead of getting measured for shoes, they merely hold out their hands. The female dress in Mexico is generally black, but I remark that some of these ladies have crimson or amber colours intermixed with it. They appear as though dressed for an evening party. None have head-dresses; but each one carries a coquettish little silk parasol, by way of protecting her head from the sun.

"4 P.M.—Steam up, and we are off again, with a fair wind.

"Goodness gracious! who would have thought that those lovely and apparently aristocratic ladies, whom I was admiring two hours ago, were sent down from the interior of Colima by their 'noble' husbands to steal—yes, actually to steal? It is true, I hear, that Mexicans as a rule consider it absolute folly to pay for anything, if they can possibly obtain it without. Numbers of articles are being missed by the passengers, and doubtless more will be. Three of the 'ladies' were seen handling some teaspoons in a very suspicious manner, whilst others engaged the attention of their admirers. One 'lady,' the most noble-looking of the party, was caught in the act. She had adroitly snatched up a shirt, and concealed it in the folds of her mantilla. But a vigilant Canadian, having observed the theft, informed the shirt's owner, who politely asked her ladyship whether she could not make it convenient to pay for the shirt to-day, as he did not contemplate returning by this steamer. With the utmost composure she immediately put her little hand into her pocket, and paid the price.

"We have some male Mexicans in the saloon, who endeavour to laugh all this off—vainly, however. They have let us into some entertaining facts as regards their fair countrywomen. No Mexican ladies are ever allowed to walk out alone. A duenna must always accompany them, even if it be to church; yet their morals stand very low. They are wonderfully captivating, on account of their light witty talk, their sweeping bright eyes, and their graceful persons. Reading is an institution almost unknown amongst them. They dally away most of their existence in listless idleness, varied occasionally by a ball, and of an evening by a walk in the *Ritretta* or an airing on the *Pasco*. They rise early, because matutinal attendance at church is an established custom. But after that the hours of the day are passed in lounging upon beautifully-worked hammocks, suspended under the verandahs, where they smoke their cigarettes, whilst little nigger-boys fan them off to sleep, or handmaidens come and coif their plenteous black hair. Alas, they know not the comforts of water: for, although a bath is now and then taken, they do not wash regularly, but in the morning merely moisten their faces with the corner of a towel dipped in rum. Can they be said to live?"

" 30*th*, 3 P.M.—Alarm of fire. Immense excitement amongst the passengers—small blame to them. But the stupe of a captain only wants to exercise the hands at the fire-engine. A nice sort of commander to be under, supposing a real crisis to occur.

"4 P.M.—Just spoke the *Constitution* steamer on her way to Frisco. She looked crowded with passengers, the majority, I hear, being an expected ship-load from New York, off in quest of gold to the Fraser river. Some will come back rich. But how many will die of starvation instead?

"7 P.M.—In the harbour of Acapulco, Republic of Guerrero, our vessel having fired a gun as she entered.

" This being the rainy season, we are fortunate in a deliciously fine evening, with a moonlight that makes one half think it is daytime.

"On my outward-bound voyage, as the English and French fleets were then blockading Acapulco, we could only ride at anchor a short while in the offing. I now got such a view of the town and harbour as the brightest imaginable moon could afford.

"The town is built on the shore of a landlocked basin. To the left, above a rocky point, was plainly visible a fort with ditches and strong embrasures, and the trees of the Alameda or Government House behind it.

"I believe the Mexicans made no stand whatever

in this fort during the late siege. It would have been impossible, indeed; for their shot could not carry above half-way to the French ships which were bombarding the fort; whereas the French easily sent both shot and shell into it, although firing from the mouth of the bay. The Mexican commander wisely spiked his guns, therefore, and withdrew his men to a mountain-fort higher up, where he knew the enemy's shot must be powerless to reach them.

" 10 P.M.—Steaming out of harbour again.

" For the last hour or so we have been having fun enough in the harbour itself. I had often heard it stated that a shark will never attack a black man. I long reserved my judgment on this head, until I could see a thoroughly satisfying proof of the statement; and I have seen one here with a vengeance. Soon after we had entered the harbour, I pointed out to a fellow-traveller a number of dark-looking units moving about on the water's surface between our ship and the out-shores of the bay. We took them for some kind of sea-fowl; but an officer of the ship told us that these were a set of professional swimmers, who, though not exactly negroes, belong to the lowest Mexican caste, their external casings and general characteristics smacking strongly of negroism.

Having learnt that the *Golden Age* was expected, they had taken the water at early dawn, and never put foot to ground all day. Soon they came in a shoal alongside the ship's paddle-box, wishing the passengers *buenas noches*, with a queer wave of the hand. And there, for more than two hours, they treated us to all kinds of antics and aquatics. We pitched them lots of five, ten, twenty-five, and fifty-cent pieces. It was wonderful, certainly, to see the fellows fight each other in the water, and then dive down ever so deep after the money, wholly regardless of hundreds of sharks darting about like tadpoles in all directions, but not once touching these black boys.

"I note a rise in the temperature. The ocean is tranquil, only a slight breeze rippling its waters. We have consequently no demon of sea-sickness to disturb our companionship. But the demon of heat takes his place. I do not feel it quite so much as I did when in these waters two years ago, probably because of the present season being rainy. Still the thermometer ranges from 75° to 84° at night, and from 86° to 90° by day. This I know is a lower temperature than we sometimes experience in the North: but here one has a muggy, debilitating atmosphere to contend with as well. Under its influence my energies flag, my active habits of mind and body are thrown aside, my very sensibilities seem weakened. Lying in my berth a while ago, I did long for the health-giving embraces of the northern winds. A borean blast is rude, but it tingles in your veins, and stiffens all your nerves, until it compels you to be up and doing."

"31*st*, 8 P.M.—Had a striking sunset this evening.

"The sunsets hereabouts are very peculiar. I have seen nothing like them, except in the Gulf of St. Lawrence. The sky, upon its ground-hue of rose westward, and of purple eastward, is mottled and freckled over with delicate clouds, the colours of which run through every shade of crimson, amber, violet, and russet-gold. No dead duskiness appears opposite the sinking sun. The entire expanse of the firmament glows with an equal radiance, reduplicating its glories on the glassy sea, so that we seem to be floating in a hollow spheroid of prismatic crystal. As the light diminishes, these radiant vapours gather together into flaming pyramids, between each pinnacle of which a depth of serene air reveals the same fathomless violet-green that one remembers in the skies of Titian.

"I had hardly noted down the above, when, going on deck, I found the ship's company and passengers gazing transfixed upon a dark black line which stretched across the whole length of the northern horizon. The sea had meantime changed its colour from indigo blue to a sheet of white phosphorescent light. While we gaze, nearer and nearer approaches the dark line. Not a soul speaks. We hold our breath, and almost cower; for instinct tells us one and all that it is a hurricane squall, so dreaded on this coast. Suddenly the passengers rush below, and the crew obey the order to " batten down the hatches." Preferring the deck, in the twinkling of an eye I had lashed myself to the capstan. The squall came along with giant steps. One fearful moment, it struck our veteran ship, shaking her as a cat would a mouse, and then all was instantly calm, as though nothing had happened. Again the silver moon illuminates the horizon and the intervening space of sea. The passengers crowd up the hatches, and the oldest sailors declare that it was the tail of a true hurricane, and the ' closest shave' they could recollect in their maritime experience."

" *June 6th,* 4 A.M.—Off the entrance to Panamà Harbour.

" The *Golden Age* has been firing rockets for the last hour, to wake up the sleepy-headed officials.

" 2.30 A.M.—At last she fires her biggest gun, which is answered presently by the waving of a lamp on shore. Soon a native pilot comes off to us, and we are made fast to a buoy just inside the harbour, but still at a distance of a mile and a half from the city, and of two miles from the railway-pier, to which we shall have to be conveyed in a lighter.

" 9 A.M.—I wish I could have seen more of Panamà City; but a few hurried rambles through its unused colleges, its ruined convents, its grass-grown plazas, and its massive fortifications, lumbered with idle cannon of the splendid old bronze of Barcelona, is all that our short allowance of three hours has enabled me to accomplish. As the train does not start for another half-hour, I shall jot down my information and impressions on the spot.

" The situation of the city at the base of a broad green mountain, three sides of which are washed by the sea, has a highly advantageous appearance. Yet other sites in the bay would have suited commercial purposes much better. Vessels of heavy draught cannot anchor within a mile of the nearest landing-place. Indeed but one point can be found where embarkation is practically safe, and that only after *dug-outs* made roughly by the natives. The bottom of the bay is a bed of rock, which at low tide lies quite bare, far out beyond the ramparts. It would cost enormous sums to blast and clear this away. The eastern shores of the bay form a portion of the South American continent; and the lofty mountain range inland is for ever wreathed with airy clouds, or shrouded from view by the storms it attracts. Thence westward are the verdure-covered isles of Taboga, and others not known to fame, but which serve beauteously to break the blue curve of the watery horizon. Panamà is considered one of the most picturesque of the many picturesque cities of South America. Though small in extent, and as antiquated as a city of some past age, it reveals ravishing points of interest, both externally and internally. I looked out of the angle of a venerable watch-tower in the ramparts, down upon the sparkling swells of the Pacific Ocean—it was my last view of the Pacific —and there before me at one glance lay presented to my vision the stupendous sweep of a hundred curvilinear miles, which the gulf takes on either side.

"The principal plaza in the city is fronted by a splendid college, left incomplete nearly a century back. It has a portico of red sandstone pillars, once proud and imposing. They are now broken and crumbling, whilst from the crevices of the pediments spring luxuriant bañana creepers, shooting their large leaves through the classic windows, or folding them round the columns of the gateway. *Sic transit gloria mundi.* I thought the remains of the Jesuit church of San Felipe a grand old ruin. Majestic arches, betraying the mosarabic traditions of the architect, still intersect its long-drawn nave and aisles; but here again an overgrowth of wild vines festoons the spandrils of the arches and falls like fringe to the floor. The building has been roofless from time immemorial, yet daylight can scarce steal through the embowering foliage. And as though in silent mockery of the works of man, several bells with a silvery ring may be seen propped up by tottering beams, and stowed away in a dark corner. How many score of years is it since the crafty but devoted brotherhood rang those dulcet bells to call the faithful to the *Oraçion?*

"Thus Panamà.

" 11 A.M.—I am writing in the train.

" Passing with the same slowness through the same gorgeous isthmus-land as two years back, every mile of the road exhibits well-remembered, yet ever new beauties. One misses the sharp-marked hills of the north, all outline of landscape being lost under this deluge of vegetation. Not a trace of soil can be discerned. Lowland and highland seem merged into one mass. A mountain is but a higher swell of the mass of leafy verdure. What shape the country would assume if cleared, who can tell? Meanwhile, your eye wanders over the scene with never-sated pleasure, until your brain aches again. And yet, as when contemplating the ocean, you have an indefinable sense rather than a direct perception of its beauty.

" Isthmus railway-guards are either venal rascals or extremely accommodating to sight-seers—perhaps something of both. We have stopped at two or three villages for no ostensible purpose but to let the villagers squeeze money out of the travellers. Boys and girls brought us fruits, offering them with pretty Mexican-Indian words, which signify *bite, sir*. These natives are a mixture of the Indian and

Spanish races. Their skin is black. The boys, however, took care to tell us that, although niggers, they
were *muchos caballeros*—very much gentlemen.

" 2 P.M.—We are driving on from a town where the
Alcalde's daughters gave us a fandango. Fancy a
whole train full dropping down at a station on the
London and North Western, to take part in a ball,
and then off again.

" The ladies were dressed in pink and white, with
flowers in their hair, and danced upon a green sward
to the music of violins and guitars. Señora Cata-
lina, a rich widow of pure Andalusian blood, danced
charmingly, holding a crimson scarf up over her
shoulders, and tossing her little head from side to
side in the most inebriating manner.

"Travelling across the Isthmus is certainly delightful."

" 7*th*, 10 A.M.—At sea, on board the *Ocean Queen*,
for New York. Only about a hundred passengers.
Great difference between a homeward and outward
voyage in that respect.

" Our ship appears seaworthy. I recognise an
improvement in the accommodation since my voyage
out, if the other vessels of the line are to be judged from

this one. But can an Englishman ever find himself at home amongst citizens of the United States?"

" 8*th*, 4 P.M.—I did not think I should so soon have an apt illustration of the foregoing sentiment to enter in my Diary.

" News of a desperate row in the forecastle. A smart-looking young Englishman, who was unfortunate at the gold-mines, and who joined the ship to work his way home, got into a quarrel with the boatswain, which has ended in the poor lad having to be put to bed in consequence of a zigzag cut from the right eye down to the neck, and another deep cut eight inches long up his left thigh, just above the knee. I hear the affair was duly reported to the Captain, who talked it over with his friend the chief mate, who laughed it over with his friend the second mate, who slurred it over with his friend the boatswain. And there it will end, doubtless.

" An Englishman deserves to be pitied, indeed, whose necessities oblige him to entrust either life or property to a country where everybody lives so freely that nobody has any rights, except through the intervention of a knife or a revolver.

" 14*th*.—Rounded Sandy Point, in the State of New

Jersey, at nine o'clock this morning, after a quick but totally dull voyage of eight days from Aspinwall. Now at my hotel in New York, Broadway."

Let it suffice to add that another week found me back at my Canadian head-quarters, in the city of Montreal, and on my way to dear Old England.

THE END.

The Northwest Library

Written history of the Pacific Northwest began only in the last years of the eighteenth century, but there is a rich variety of books covering the area's early exploration, settlement and cultural development. Very few of these were originally published in Canada, and fewer still have been available to the public except through libraries. It is with this in mind that J. J. Douglas Ltd., in co-operation with the Vancouver Public Library, is happy to announce a program to bring back into print many of the most outstanding of these books. The hope is to make available to many more people the best of Northwest sources, and each volume will be a facsimile of the original edition produced in a handsome, uniform, clothbound format. The titles available are:

NWL 1
British Columbia Coast Names 1592-1906
Captain John T. Walbran

NWL 2
Queen Charlotte Islands
Francis Poole

NWL 3
Overland to Cariboo
Margaret McNaughton

Volume 2 of the Northwest Library
J. J. Douglas Ltd., Vancouver